Psychopharmacology Handbook for the Non-medically Trained

Psychopharmacology Handbook for the Non-medically Trained

Sophia F. Dziegielewski

W. W. Norton & Company
New York • London

For information about permission to reproduce selections from this book, write to
Permissions, W. W. Norton & Company, Inc., 500 Fifth Avenue, New York, NY 10110

Manufacturing by Haddon Craftsmen
Book design by Paradigm Graphics
Production manager: Leeann Graham

Library of Congress Cataloging-in-Publication Data

Dziegielewski, Sophia F.
    Psychopharmacology handbook for the non-medically trained / Sophia F.
Dziegielewski.
        p. cm.
    Includes bibliographical references and index.
    ISBN 0-393-70459-9
    1. Psychopharmacology—Handbooks, manuals, etc. I. Title.

RM315.D956 2005
615'.78—dc22

                                                                2005047289

W. W. Norton & Company, Inc., 500 Fifth Avenue, New York, N.Y. 10110
www.wwnorton.com
W. W. Norton & Company Ltd., Castle House, 75/76 Wells St., London W1T 3QT
0 9 8 7 6 5 4 3 2 1

NOTICE

The author has made every attempt to summarize accurately and concisely a multitude of references. However, the reader is reminded that times and medical knowledge change, transcription or understanding error is always possible, and crucial details are omitted whenever such a comprehensive distillation as this is attempted in limited space. We cannot, therefore, guarantee that every bit of information is absolutely accurate or complete. The reader should affirm that cited recommendations are still appropriate by reading the original articles and checking other sources including local consultants and recent literature.

DRUG DOSAGE

The author and publisher have exerted every effort to ensure that drug selection and dosage set forth in this text are in accord with current recommendations and practice at the time of publication. However, in view of ongoing research, changes in government regulations, and the constant flow of information relating to drug therapy and drug reactions, the reader is urged to check the package insert for each drug for any change in indications and dosage and for added warnings and precautions. This is particularly important when the recommended agent is a new and/or infrequently used drug.

This book is dedicated to all family members who have a loved one who suffers from mental illness. No one knows better than family members how difficult it can be to watch a loved one's torment. As family members we all share a very special bond because we know how difficult this life path can be and how important it is to be understanding, flexible, and supportive during the turbulent times.

CONTENTS

ACKNOWLEDGMENTS

I am very grateful for all the insights I have received from consumers and their family members. Having worked closely with these individuals and listened to what they think and feel has in many ways provided more valuable information than one could ever gain from a textbook, research study data, or a clinical trail.

I am also forever indebted to the incredible medically trained providers who took the time to share their experiences and expertise with me. Throughout my career, these MTPs taught me so much about what is needed beyond simply prescribing the medications. MTPs such as Rochelle Wasserman, Nathan Stinson, Kathryn Goldin, Eugene Farley, Rupert Francis, Harold Navels, Leslie Scott, James Moore, Lane Johnson, Richard Leedy, Steven Reissman, Linda Walker, and Gabriel Mayer are just a few who have touched my life.

Furthermore, I want to thank all the non-medically trained practitioners I have met across the country. Most of these NMTPs are social workers who clearly know the importance of individualized treatment regimes, recognizing the "person-in-environment" stance that constitutes the cornerstone of our profession. Utilizing a team approach, these social workers have worked to provide the best comprehensive care possible for the consumer, forever advocating for the recognition of the "individualized" situation.

In closing, I would like to thank Deborah Malmud at W. W. Norton & Company for believing in me and asking me to write this book for non-medically trained professionals. She, along with Andrea Costella, have remained tireless in their support and editing efforts.

Finally, I want to thank my family members, colleagues, and friends who supported me and understood when I said "I can't" because I had to work on this book. With the encouragement and support from all those mentioned above—all things really are possible.

Psychopharmacology Handbook for the Non-medically Trained

Introduction

Psychotropic Drugs and the Culture of Mental Health Treatments

I dentifying and understanding the effects medication can have on the human body is an evolving process. Among the numerous pressures for accountable, efficient, and effective service, the advancement of medication use stands at the forefront. According to Walter (2000), science and technology have created many changes in the environment that, coupled with advances in the area of medicine-based research, have pushed medication use as a means of addressing daily problems.

Some professionals argue strongly that the desire to address some mental health problems too quickly may actually disrupt normal life processes. For example, feelings of depression are quite normal when a person loses a loved one and has difficulty adjusting to the life changes that must be incorporated. The *quick-fix* or *magic bullet* mentality so predominant in the U.S. culture may lead the person to ask for a medication to alleviate the symptoms presented by the crisis. In bereavement and crisis, however, grief is a normal part of the experience. Yet, if a person is medicated and not allowed to experience this pain, will his or her eventual adjustment be hampered by this limited treatment strategy? When the psychosocial component is overlooked, the opportunity for growth, whereby the consumer learns new problem-solving and coping skills that may be of benefit in other similar situations, is missed. Furthermore, immediately placing a consumer on a medication can change his or her energy level and desire to make informed, action-oriented changes.

This mentality has led to the view that medication is either an adjunct or sole remedy for treatment in mental health. From this perspective, the simple act of taking a pill, by itself, is considered curative. Many people believe a pill will help relieve the symptoms that they are feeling. Today, so many consumers who visit a prescriber's office not only believe they will be given some type of medication for what ails them, they expect it (Dziegielewski & Leon, 2001). This misconception permeates our society and is extremely hard to dispel because, at times, these medications can quickly alleviate signs and symptoms of discomfort. Feeling better with so little effort is often equated with being cured. Taking an aspirin for a headache may relieve the headache pain, but is the person cured? Whatever condition that caused the headache probably still exists; the person simply feels better because the pain is gone.

Dealing with the societal expectation that a pill alone can cure requires that all helping providers, including non-medically trained providers (NMTPs), become knowledgeable about the most common medications that are being prescribed, the specific uses of medications, and their side-effect profiles. Medically trained providers (MTPs) and NMTPs must spend time educating consumers, their family members, and other members of the health care team on the benefits of combining medication regimens with effective psychosocial strategies—in short, a multidimensional approach.

The days of authority-based practice, where clinical decisions were based on consensus, anecdotal experience, and tradition have ended (Gambrill, 2004; Thyer, 2004). Internet-educated consumers may resent being told what to do and question what their physician or primary medical provider is telling them. Regardless of the intervention regimen to be followed, consumers expect that the effectiveness of the intervention is clearly established. (Corcoran & Vandiver, 2004; Dziegielewski, 1996, 1997, 2002a, 2004; Roberts & Yeager, 2004).

According to the Food and Drug Administration (FDA), 50% of all consumers of drugs may not take their medicines as prescribed. This means that many individuals are taking medicines incorrectly and without proper professional supervision. All supportive helping providers (also referred to as *practitioners*) must help consumers understand the treatment regimen recommended, because this will help to ensure compliance.

CREATING A PARTNERSHIP

As discussed throughout this text, a partnership must be created between the consumer, his or her family and support system, the prescriber or MTP, and the NMTP.

The Consumer

Throughout this text the word *consumer* is used to refer to the person who is taking the mental health preparation being described. In the past this individual has been referred to as the patient, client, or the covered person (Dziegielewski, 2004). Using the term *consumer* conveys the point that medications are considered part of a service that is being provided. Consumers of a service are expected to be an empowered and active component in this process. The more educated and supported consumers (often traditionally referred to as patients) are in this process, the safer the service becomes. The more aware consumers are of what to expect, the better their compliance with the medication regimens prescribed. This connection is critical in the intervention partnership. In this partnership, wherein the consumer is capable of making informed decisions, the seat at the head of this alliance is theirs and theirs alone. The needs of the consumer should always be considered paramount in guiding any and all intervention efforts to follow.

The Prescriber or Medically Trained Providers

Next in the partnership is the role of the prescriber. In the United States few professionals would debate that, next to the consumer, the most important member of the health care team is the physician. Most times this team member is a physician trained in mental health. Other times, the physician may not be trained specifically in mental health, but should be familiar with the medications he or she is prescribing. Traditionally, it is the physician who is considered responsible for providing, prescribing, authorizing, and coordinating all medical care and treatment. However, increasingly prescriptions are being written by physician's assistants, nurse practitioners, pharmacists, and others who are granted *limited* prescription-prescribing provider status (Dziegielewski & Leon, 2001). Consumers need to be alerted to the fact that physicians are no longer the only prescribers. Regardless of whether the prescriber is a physician or a related provider, when serving as part of a team or as the physician in solo practice, these prescribers often spend the least amount of time with the consumer. This restricted contact often means that consumers will need to get essential information from outside sources (both professional and nonprofessional) to maximize the monitoring of, and adjustment to, medication side effects.

Other essential MTPs include nurses, nurses' aides, physical therapists, and medical technicians. For the most part, although medically trained, these providers may not be particularly well versed in the specific medications an individual is taking or the side-effect profiles that could result.

Non-medically Trained Providers

Another important ingredient in this partnership and the primary focus of this book is the NMTP. This provider can come from a variety of professional disciplines, including social work, psychology, the mental health profession and counseling, marriage and family therapy, and other subfields in the area of supportive counseling. The NMTP is the practitioner responsible for the supportive interventions described in this book.

There are two primary roles the NMTP plays in this partnership. In the first role as a clinician serving as an integral part of the intervention team, he or she is often called upon for a variety of supportive tasks. Although the NMTP does not prescribe medications, his or her role in supporting this activity cannot be overestimated. At times NMTPs work closely with the physician, making recommendations and helping to monitor the consumer's use of medications. NMTPs can increase consumer medication compliance by identifying reasons for noncompliance as well as by helping to identify side effects and signs of addiction and withdrawal.

In addition to serving in a clinical capacity, the NMTP may also be called upon for supportive interventions (e.g., providing follow-up information needed for case management purposes) and to act as the conduit to the family system, facilitating home-based support, or, in the case of inpatient treatment, successful discharge back into the community.

Family and Support Systems

Lastly, this section would not be complete if, in describing the partnership, no mention were made of the family or individuals who constitute the consumer's support system. These individuals are often called on not only to support the consumer in the environment, but also to provide supportive information that can best enable continued care. For example, if a consumer is given a medication regimen and the family system is not aware of, or does not understand, what is needed, noncompliance could be the outcome because a nonsupportive environment does not engender compliance. Family members can create a supportive bridge between the consumer and his or her environment. Creating this linkage, however, requires not only understanding what the consumer is experiencing but how to help the family or other members of the support system handle this relationship in the least disruptive way possible.

To create a supportive environment family members need to be aware of the consumer's medical condition, including signs, symptoms, and how to deal with emergency situations. Education about the consumer's condition needs to be presented in easy and understandable language. If support for the family is not provided, consumers may not be able to access community support systems, the absence of which might place them at enormous risk for admission or readmission to inpatient facilities. Furthermore, although the consumer is considered the primary patient, important factors can impact caregiving. For example, what are the number and level of consumer demands that will need to be addressed? Will taking medications in the home setting place additional responsibilities on the caregiver? What is the physical condition of the caregiver? For example, what if others in the family are also frail or sick and unable to provide this level of care?

Assessing this family system can be a crucial component of intervention success. What degree of social support is available (e.g., respite for the caregiver)? Do family conflicts surround the caregiving situation?

Clearly, if the family and other support system members are not included in the partnership to help the consumer, they can quickly become over-burdened and withdraw their support. This is such an important area for collaboration that each section of this text addresses the role of these significant individuals in the therapeutic partnership.

FORMING THE PROFESSIONAL TEAM

Many helping providers working in the area of health and mental health frequently serve and participate in team intervention efforts (Dziegielewski, 2004). The role of the NMTP remains clear as part of a collaborative effort or *team approach*, often referred to as either a *multidisciplinary* or an *interdisciplinary* team. For the most part the multidisciplinary team is composed of both MTPs and NMTPs (e.g., physicians, psychiatrists, nurses, social workers, physical therapists) who direct their efforts toward a common problem (Dziegielewski, 2004). Each of these providers generally works independently to solve the problems of the individual. Afterward, these separate approaches are brought together to provide a comprehensive method of service delivery for the consumer. The role of each MTP and NMTP on the team is usually clearly defined, and each team member knows the role and duties that he or she is expected to contribute. Communication among professionals is generally stressed, and goals are expected to be consistent across the disciplines, with each contributing to the overall welfare of the consumer.

Although the term is still often used, the multidisciplinary team approach seems to be losing its appeal in today's health care environment. This team approach is being replaced by a more collaborative and integrative approach (Dziegielewski, 2004) involving the *interdisciplinary* team (IT). The major difference between the multidisciplinary team approach and the interdisciplinary one is that the latter takes on a much more holistic and collaborative approach to health care practice. Interdisciplinary providers, both MTPs and NMTPs, work together throughout the process of service provision and develop a plan of action *collectively*, rather than separately. Collaboration replaces independent (albeit multimodal) assessment and intervention. Indeed, interdependence throughout the referral, planning, assessment, and treatment process is stressed. In the interdisciplinary team process, each professional team member is encouraged to contribute, design, and implement the group goals for the health care service to be provided.

If the team approach is utilized, the role of the prescriber is pivotal in starting the process. During the intervention process, however, the prescriber is not the one who spends the most quality time with the consumer. There is a high probability that NMTPs will be expected to be familiar with, and knowledgeable about, the medications individuals are taking and to assist them with compliance issues, pharmacy shopping, side-effect monitoring, and medication insurance coverage. Increasingly, NMTPs are expected to perform this supportive role (Bradley, 2003; Dziegielewski & Leon, 2001). In addition, they must provide advocacy and brokerage services related to the identification, implementation, and monitoring of medication regimens.

> **QUICK TIPS:**
> **Serving on an**
> **Interdisciplinary Team**
>
> When working with several different professionals as part of a team, remember to . . .
>
> 1. Recognize the values and ethics of the different professionals and how they can contribute to the processing and assessing of consumer information.
>
> 2. Recognize and acknowledge the interdependency of team functioning and the contributions and expertise of each team member to the helping process.
>
> 3. Take into account the consumer and his or her family or key support members who will play a supportive role in the planning and implementation of the intervention regimen.

ABOUT THIS BOOK

Depression, anxiety, schizophrenia and the psychotic disorders, dementia in older adults, and attention-deficit/hyperactivity disorder in children are the main focus of this book; supportive information that surrounds these conditions is given high importance. The most common time-limited supportive interventions are highlighted and encouraged as a necessary part of the intervention strategy.

Part I provides the framework for how medications can facilitate practice interventions, and Part II examines an expansive array of the most popular mental health medications and herbal preparations in use. This text also addresses issues and answers questions that NMTPs may have wondered about. For example:

- How do mental health medications affect behavior?
- What is the difference between a prescription medication and a nonprescription one?
- Is there really a difference between a brand name and its generic counterpart?
- What may result when a pill is split (i.e., dosage is reduced) or a dose is missed?
- When should cost be a major consideration for switching a medication?
- When does dependence on a medication impair a consumer's functioning?
- Are medications alone sufficient to address the problem or situation being experienced? If not, what other options or supplemental treatments are available?

Finally, as practitioners who hold the best interests of the consumer in mind, it is equally important that medication not be prescribed to the exclusion of other psychosocial counseling strategies. Throughout this text these psychosocial methods, in addition to the medications, are highlighted.

In this era of managed health care, where intervention success is often measured by the specific outcome or behavior change that results, many of the counseling disciplines have been forced to examine treatment methods and modalities with a new vigor. To survive in the health and mental health care arena, practitioners must provide effective and *accountable* practice. Although medication prescription is not an exact science, it is perceived as such, for the most part. NMTPs are expected to provide support by incorporating knowledge of medications into diagnostic and intervention efforts. Practitioners must know how to complete a medication history and be willing to support efforts toward compliance. Because adverse medication effects are most likely to occur early in the intervention process, and because the non-medically trained professional may be the first to see these effects, he or she will assist all medically trained professionals by recognizing and reporting what the consumer is experiencing. This fact has never been more prominent than with the 2004 MedWatch reports of suicide attempts related to the use of newer antidepressants (see Chapter 4). An individual may be more likely to harm him- or herself not when he or she is in the throes of depression, but rather when these feelings start to subside and energy returns. Medications can quickly increase energy levels but may not address problematic life circumstances when used as a sole modality. When energy returns, unaddressed life problems, often dealt with through counseling, could leave the consumer vulnerable to impulsive actions and self-harm. Because NMTPs take a supportive role in medication treatment or can recommend what medications would best serve as an adjunct to the current therapy being provided, they can assume a role as consumer advocates, watchdogs, of sorts, who are knowledgeable and ever-vigilant in seeking ways to best help consumers. Providing these professionals with effective tools for participating in all courses of mental health treatment is the purpose of this book.

This book is designed as a resource that can serve as a reference guide or a primary textbook in both beginning and advanced practice areas. In addition to covering prescription medications (see Table I.1 for a complete list), this book also provides summary information about herbal preparations, essential oils, and flower essences (see Table I.2), reflecting the increased use of these alternative substances as part of mental health interventions.

This book encourages assessment of medication use in relation to the personal circumstances of the consumer. The importance of this type of combined knowledge—that is, medications used in conjunction with the most effective psychosocial interventions—cannot be overemphasized, especially in this era of increased litigation, limited service delivery access, and controlled health care costs.

TABLE I.1
Medications Discussed in this Book

Brand Name	Trade or Generic Name	Primary Purpose or Most Common, Labeled Use
Abilify	aripiprazole	Psychotic disorders
Adderall	dextroamphetamine and amphetamine	Attention-deficit/ hyperactivity disorder
Akineton	biperiden	Antiparkinsonian
Aricept	donepezil	Enhance cognitive functioning
Artane	trihexyphenidyl	Antiparkinsonian
Asendin	amoxapin	Depressive disorders
Ativan	lorazepam	Anxiety disorders
Benadryl	diphenhydramine	Antiparkinsonian
BuSpar	buspirone	Anxiety disorders
Catapres	clonidine	Anxiety disorders
Celexa	citalopram	Depressive disorders
Clozaril	clozapine	Psychotic disorders
Cogentin	benztropine	Antiparkinsonian
Cognex	tacrine	Enhance cognitive functioning
Cylert	pemoline	Attention-deficit/hyperactivity disorder
Dalmane	flurazepam	Anxiety disorders
Depakene	valproate or valproic acid	Bipolar mood disorders
Depakote and Depakote ER	divalproex	Bipolar mood disorders
Desoxyn	methamphetamine	Attention-deficit/hyperactivity disorder
Desyrel	trazodone	Depressive disorders
Dexedrine	dextroamphetamine sulfate	Attention-deficit/hyperactivity disorder
Doral	quazepam	Anxiety disorders
Edronax, Vestra	reboxetine	Depressive disorders
Elavil	amitriptyline	Depressive disorders
Eldepryl	selegiline	Depressive disorders
Effexor	venlafaxine	Depressive disorders
Eskalith and Eskalith CR	lithium carbonate	Bipolar mood disorders

continued

TABLE I.1 (*continued*)

Exelon	rivastigime	Enhance cognitive functioning
Geodon	ziprasidone	Psychotic disorders
Halcion	triazolam	Anxiety disorders
Haldol	haloperidol	Psychotic disorders
Klonopin	clonazepam	Bipolar mood disorders and anxiety disorders
Lexapro	escitalopram oxalate	Depressive disorders
Librium	chlordiazepoxide	Anxiety disorders
Lithane, Lithobid, Cibalith-S	lithium citrate	Bipolar mood disorders
Loxitane	loxapine	Psychotic disorders
Ludiomil	maprotiline	Depressive disorders
Luvox	fluvoxamine	Depressive disorders
Marplan	isocarboxazid	Depressive disorders
Mellaril	thioridazine	Psychotic disorders
Moban	molindone	Psychotic disorders
Mondafanil	provigil	Attention-deficit/hyperactivity disorder
Nardil	phenelzine	Depressive disorders
Navane	thiothixene	Psychotic disorders
Neurontin	gabapentin	Bipolar mood disorders
Norpramin/ Pertofrane	desipramine	Depressive disorders
Pamelor/ Aventyl	nortriptyline	Depressive disorders
Parnate	tranylcypromine	Depressive disorders
Paxil	paroxetine hydrochloride	Depressive disorders
Paxipam	halazepam	Anxiety disorders
Prolixin	phenazine	Psychotic disorders
ProSom	estazolam	Anxiety disorders
Provigil	modafinil	Attention-deficit/hyperactivity disorder
Prozac	fluoxetine	Depressive disorders
Razadyne	galantamine	Enhance cognitive functioning
Remeron	mirtazapine	Depressive disorders
Restoril	temazepam	Anxiety disorders
Risperdal	risperidone	Psychotic disorders

continued

TABLE I.1 (*continued*)

Ritalin, Ritalin-SR	methylphenidate	Attention-deficit/hyperactivity disorder
Serax	oxazepam	Anxiety disorders
Seroquel	quetiapine	Psychotic disorders
Serzone	nefazodone	Depressive disorders
Stelazine	trifluoperazine	Psychotic disorders
Strattera	atomoxetine	Attention-deficit/hyperactivity disorder
Surmontil	trimipramine	Depressive disorders
Tegretol	carbamazepine	Bipolar mood disorders
Tenex	guanfacine	Anxiety disorders
Thorazine	chlorpromazine	Psychotic disorders
Tofranil	imipramine	Depressive disorders
Tranxene	clorazepate	Anxiety disorders
Valium	diazepam	Anxiety disorders
Wellbutrin	bupropion	Depressive disorders
Xanax	alprazolam	Anxiety disorders
Zoloft	sertraline	Depressive and anxiety disorders
Zyprexa	olanzapine	Psychotic disorders

Note: Many of these medications have multiple purposes and/or medicinal uses. This table lists the primary purpose and general usage so that the reader can easily find the medication in this book.

TABLE I.2
Herbal Preparations, Essential Oils, and Flower Essences

Name	Type	Supportive Purpose
Bleeding heart	Flower essence	Depression (grief and loss)
Capsicum (Cayenne)	Herbal preparation	Pain relief and relief from gastrointestinal disorders
Cascara, casara, sagrada	Herbal preparation	Relief from gastrointestinal disorders, digestion aid
Chamomile	Essential oil/flower essence	Anxiety (relaxation)
Chasteberry	Herbal preparation	PMS relief, decreased libido
Cohosh (black)	Herbal preparation	Menopause relief
Cypress	Essential oil	Diuretic

continued

TABLE I.2 *(continued)*

Echinacea	Herbal preparation	Immuno-stimulant
Elm	Flower essence	Anxiety (stress)
Eucalyptus	Essential oil	Germicidal, diuretic, analgesic
Evening primrose	Herbal preparation	Anti-inflammatory
Feverfew	Herbal preparation	Migraine relief
Frankincense	Essential oil	Depression (stimulant)
Garlic	Herbal preparation	Cholesterol reducer
Geranium	Essential oil	Appetite stimulant
Ginger	Herbal preparation/ essential oil	Relief from gastrointestinal disorders, appetite stimulant
Ginkgo	Herbal preparation	Dementia (memory/ concentration booster)
Ginseng	Herbal preparation	Anxiety, fatigue
Goldenseal	Herbal preparation	Immuno-stimulant
Gotu kola	Herbal preparation	Dementia and depression
Grape or grape seed	Herbal preparation	Headache relief
Green tea	Herbal preparation	Dental cavity prevention
Guarana, guarana seed	Herbal preparation	Headache, cerebral stimulant
Hornbeam	Flower essence	Energy booster
Impatiens	Flower essence	Anxiety
Jasmine	Essential oil	Depression
Juniper	Essential oil	Depression
Kava-kava	Herbal preparation	Anxiety
Lavender	Essential oil	Depression and anxiety
Mimulus	Flower essence	Anxiety
Morning glory	Flower essence	Depression
Peppermint	Essential oil	Depression
Sandlewood	Essential oil	Anxiety
Saw palmetto	Herbal preparation	Irritable bladder relief, prostate complaints
Shasta daisy	Flower essence	Anxiety
St. John's wort	Herbal preparation	Depression
Star of Bethlehem	Flower essence	Depression
White chestnut	Flower essence	Anxiety
Wild oat	Flower essence	Anxiety
Zinnia	Flower essence	Depression

Note: Many herbal preparations, flower essences, and essential oils are used to address the related signs and symptoms of mental health disorders, not the disorders themselves.

Note: Herbal preparations, essential oils, and flower essences are not regulated by the FDA and the supportive purposes listed are generally not supported by research or controlled studies.

Part I

MEDICATIONS IN THE BODY AND IN CLINICAL PRACTICE

1

How Medications Work

The science of psychopharmacology, when used as an evidence-based medical intervention, is considered new, although its roots go back at least 40–45 years. From a scientific perspective, the 1990s were called "the decade of the brain"—a label that was extended past the year 2000. Over this time period, scientists have learned more about the brain and the role of medications in treatment than ever before. What has become increasingly evident is that the brain is a complex laboratory of chemicals whose workings and interactions can determine the state of a person's mental health, including the most extreme forms (Kotulak, 1997). The application of this knowledge to evidence-based medicine, however, remains in its infancy. Until all extraneous variables can be controlled, and all consumer variability can be minimized, evidence-based methodology in the field of psychopharmacology will remain an evolving process. Therefore, we must remember that the scientific methodology used in establishing the precise role of medications in the healing process is not an exact science.

There is still no single theory in psychopharmacology that explains how psychotropic drugs produce *therapeutic* effects (Cohen, 2003). The biggest wild card is individual response: We simply do not know exactly why one person responds in one way, whereas others do not. Variables that affect individual response include age, body size, body chemistry, habits, and diet. For example, a 200-pound person has a lot more weight and body mass when compared to a 100-pound person. It makes sense that this difference would need to be taken into account when dosing. Yet, it is much harder to ascertain how other factors such as body chemistry, habits, and diet affect an individual's response. Consequently, although general guidelines for prescribing medications exist, prescribers must also remain flexible in individualizing dosing regimes for each consumer, taking into account these unique variables and how they can affect medication absorption and potency.

FEELINGS, EMOTIONS, AND THE BRAIN: THE MIND-BODY CONNECTION

The brain is the most intricate organ of the human body. As a "black box" of secrets, the brain mediates mood and conscious thought processes, controls most voluntary movements, and directly regulates unconscious body processes such as breathing and digestion (Centers for Disease Control, 2004). The virtual maze of interconnected activity within brain tissue involves utilizing information from the environment to shape how it functions. This feedback process has serious consequences in the first few years of life, during which crucial periods require certain types and levels of stimulation in order for abilities such as language, smell, vision, muscle control, and reasoning to develop (Kotulak, 1997; Brain–Body Connection, 2000). Therefore, it is not surprising that our personality traits, thought processes, and behaviors are linked to, and greatly influenced by, the way our brain functions. The brain can be visualized as an orchestra, with the cerebellum serving primarily as the conductor. This conductor orchestrates all the essential life functions and keeps everything responding in perfect tune. The best way to keep this orchestra performing at its best can be summed up with one intervention: exercise. Like the muscles, the parts of the brain best keep their strength and agility through regular, strenuous use; and physical exercise, in turn, helps the brain stay active. Indeed, exercise is the greatest predictor of maintaining cognitive excellence. Exactly what type of exercise is needed, however, remains unclear (Brain–Body Connection, 2000).

Exercise can influence key body processes such as sleep, mood, appetite, and strength. Therefore, it makes sense that an intervention that can affect so many diverse systems in the body would clearly be related to mental health. Of all the interventions available, the importance of exercise in every area of a person's life should never be underestimated. For example, elderly consumers who suffer from brain deterioration may feel helpless and hopeless, perhaps influenced by the belief of family and friends that little can be done to help them to recover. Helping professionals often share this belief, which in turn produces a disincentive for engaging in the helping process.

What has led to this belief? Earlier studies of the neuron (the basic building block of the brain) suggested that this highly specialized cell does not undergo cell replacement by cellular division. Therefore, when the neuron was damaged, clinical improvement was impossible. However, research has revealed that the brain does appear to have the power to heal itself (Brain–Body Connection, 2000). Brain deterioration can be altered by creating a type of "fountain of youth" that prevents the cells within the brain from drying up and becoming nonproductive. Although much of the research remains experimental, scientists are now convinced that there are many hormones and other chemicals that can enhance cells' self-renewal activities (Baizabal, Furlan-Magaril, Santa-Olalla, et. al., 2003; Cao, Benton, Whittemore, 2002; Kuhn & Sevendsen, 1999). New findings supporting the capacity for repair and renewal of the brain offer the following possibilities.

First, researchers are striving to achieve a better understanding of hormones such as estrogen, progesterone, testosterone, and other growth-related hormones. These hormones may become the most powerful forms of treatment to prevent debilitating conditions such as Alzheimer's, Parkinson's, and other degenerative diseases.

Second, certain brain chemicals, called neurotrophic factors, can help keep brain cells healthy and open to communications signals and patterns. When these factors diminish and dry up, so do the brain cells that they nourish. Studies are now being conducted to see if new brain cells can be grown to replenish those that are no longer functioning (Coyle & Enna, 1998).

Lastly, brain cells, just like muscles, need exercise (i.e., stimulation) to maintain healthy functioning. Brain growth is not limited to childhood; experience-based learning can excel throughout the entire human life cycle. Education is now being considered a powerful deterrent to brain degeneration, because it excites the construction of connections between the brain cells. These connections make it easier to withstand the destructive forces that accompany a debilitating disease.

Most researchers agree that mental health conditions are closely related to physical conditions, and that in addressing mental health the link between mental health and physical health should never be underestimated (American Psychiatric Association, 2000). For example, the person who suffers from depression may also experience physical symptoms that can affect many other areas of the body and influence conditions such as cancer, Alzheimer's disease, stroke, and heart disease (Brain–Body Connection, 2000). Another example of this mind–body connection involves *cortisol*, which is a normally occurring hormone in the body that is released during periods of stress. When stress reactions are coupled with depression, this hormonal release of cortisol becomes prolonged, and with time, increases the risk of developing heart disease, problems with bone density, and other medical conditions (Brain–Body Connection, 2000). This mind–body connection can help to explain why taking antidepressant medications for the mental health problem of depression might also help to address what might appear on the surface to be an unrelated medical condition.

Considerable debate among scientific professionals as to whether mental illness is biological or organic in nature (Kotulak, 1997) has characterized the history of psychiatry. Although this debate is by no means settled, it does appear that aspects of both are involved. Areas of the brain can now be identified that are directly related to the production of certain feelings or emotions. Brain mapping and biochemistry can identify and directly link the occurrence of these feelings to specific areas of the brain (Kotulak, 1997). This procedure allows us to image the activity of the living human brain. Two technologies that make this possible are positron emission tomography (PET) and magnetic resonance imaging (MRI). Both show neuronal firing, blood flow, and blood oxygenation in the brain, allowing maps of activity to be formulated (Surgeon General, 2001).

Using this technology, certain mental health conditions and the dysfunctional behaviors that result can be directly linked to chemical activity

within certain areas of the brain. Although not often trained in the biomedical aspects of the brain, helping practitioners must acquire a general
working knowledge of the brain and how this organ affects the consumer's physical and mental states. For this purpose, a simplified review
of the brain was presented; now attention will be given to the specific role
and function of the neuron.

THE BASIC BUILDING BLOCKS: NEURONS AND NEUROCHEMICALS

To better understand the connections among brain activity, emotions,
behaviors and feelings, we need to learn about the *neuron*, which is the
basic functional unit of the nervous system. The neuron is a highly specialized cell responsible for signal transduction and information processing (Coyle & Enna, 1998). The brain contains approximately 100 billion
nerve cells, or neurons, and it is estimated that over 100 trillion different
types of interconnections are possible. The responses that result from
these connections are too numerous to count, although each is finely
tuned and results in a large repertoire of cognitive, affective, and behavioral capacities. (Surgeon General, 2001). Basically, the neuron serves one
primary purpose: to receive, conduct, and transmit signals to the other
cells. Neuronal signals are transmitted from cell to cell at specialized sites
for contact, called *synapses*, which bridge the physical gap between neurons. The number of potential connections and interconnections is almost
beyond comprehension.

Superimposed on these vast structural connections in the brain is the
chemical component. Coyle and Enna (1998) contended that knowledge
of basic neurochemical transmissions can provide the context for understanding how and why brain activity is influenced. Within the brain, messages can be transmitted in two ways: electrically and chemically. Electrical
impulses cannot bridge the synapse, so completion of the transmission is
dependent on *neurotransmitters*, the chemical messengers. A neurotransmitter is synthesized within the neuron out of precursors that are brought
into the neuron by outside cells. Enzymes within the neuron break down
the precursor and ultimately form the neurotransmitter. (Another name
for this newly formed neurotransmitter is *neurochemical*.) The role of the

neurotransmitter is essential in either exciting or inhibiting a response. Understanding the role of the brain, the neuron, the neurotransmitter, and what happens at the receptor sites can help us delineate how specific responses are generated or inhibited through the use of medications. Exactly how medications affect this process is not known. What is known, however, is that they can affect the neurotransmitter process and the way the body interprets what is happening.

Identifying the role of each neurotransmitter in addressing mood is complicated because there are numerous chemical messengers at work within the human brain. Over 100 different neurotransmitters related directly to health and mental health emotions have been identified so far (Surgeon General, 2001). Newly discovered neurotransmitters that can influence feelings, thoughts, emotions, and behaviors are being identified all the time (see Table 1.1), a process that is complicated further by the different types of receptor sites for each neurotransmitter. For example, serotonin has at least 16 different serotonin receptor sites in various parts of the brain, all modulating different drives and emotions (Kotulak, 1997).

TABLE 1.1
Neurotransmitters and Selected Applications

Neurotransmitter	Selected Applications
Dopamine	Psychosis
Norepinephrine	Depression
Serotonin	Depression
Acetylcholine	Dementia (Alzheimer's disease, Parkinson's disease)
GABA	Anxiety
Glutamate	Dementia (Alzheimer's disease, central nervous system disorders [epilepsy])
Glycine	Depression, dementia, schizophrenia
Enkephalin	Addictive disorders, depression
Beta-endorphin	Addictive disorders
Dynorphin	Depression, addictive disorders

Note: Summarized from Surgeon General's Report, 2001.

In this text the intricacies of the human brain are discussed primarily as they relate to mental health. Keep in mind, however, that these mental-health-related neurotransmitters actually make up only a small portion of the neurotransmitters in the brain. Examples of general neurotransmitters found in 75–90% of all neurotransmissions are glutamate, gamma-aminobutyric acid (GABA), and glycine. Of all of the general neurotransmitters, many professionals would agree that GABA plays a large part in mental health reactions; indeed, GABA has been identified as essential in exciting reactions and initiating many of the brain's chemical transmissions (Coyle & Enna, 1998). The neurotransmitters that are involved in mental health responses are less common, found in only 2% (approximately) of the synapses in the brain (Kotulak, 1997). Three common neurotransmitters involved in mental-health-related behaviors and actions are norepinephrine, serotonin, and dopamine.

Chemical messengers that regulate basic feelings and emotions are designed to work together with other neurotransmitters. Researchers no longer assume that only one neurotransmitter is needed to perform a neurotransmission. They now believe that more than one neurotransmitter is involved in the creation of the response–action pattern. When more than one neurotransmitter is needed to initiate a particular process, it is referred to as *colocalization* (Lehne & Scott, 1996). Participating neurotransmitters work together to excite the same receptor site, helping to fine-tune the neurotransmission process.

Newer medications incorporate certain aspects of the colocalization process to restore normal brain chemistry. When a neurotransmitter's level in the brain is either too high or too low (by a margin of as little as 5 or 10%), it can affect the way other neurotransmitters function (Kotulak, 1997). A minor disturbance in levels can trigger a major chain reaction that results in chemical errors that affect or contribute to a range of mental-health-related behaviors.

Understanding the role of these neurotransmitters is critical, whether they work alone or in concert with others, because they provide the communication connections for all the activity that takes place in the brain. It is the electrical impulse (triggered by hearing a sound, for example) that makes the neuron start the process, followed by the release of the neurotransmitter (or chemical messenger) that creates the connections that complete the unification process. It is the presence of the chemical in the receptor that sparks the electrical impulse in the next neuron (see Table 1.2), and the sequence continues until a thought, feeling, or behavior is initiated (Coyle & Enna, 1998).

For example, a relationship exists between serotonin and depressive symptoms. This relatively simple neurotransmitter appears vital to the brain's regulation of many bodily functions, such as sleep, appetite, muscular activity, breathing, and blood circulation. Abnormal secretion levels of serotonin have been associated with a large number of mental-health-related problems, including depression, obsessive–compulsive disorder, and panic disorder (Hickling, 2000). When serotonin levels are low, depressed mood and suicidal thoughts and feelings may develop. The depressed consumer is left desperately trying to control these feelings that may be the result of factors related to internal causes (often referred to as *endogenous* factors) rather than environmental causes (often referred to as *exogenous* or reactive factors).

Following the steps within the synaptic process, serotonin is *synthesized* by the precursors in the transmitter sites and *stored*. When *released*, it flows into the synaptic junction and fits into a specifically shaped receptor, where *receptor binding* takes place. Medications can influence the release of serotonin from storage and its "fate" in the synaptic junction. Many scientists liken receptors to a door waiting to be opened. The availability of the neurotransmitter to the receptor site brings the key, and the binding is where the door opens. Once opened, the developments that occur can be studied and observed. For example, one such receptor door that has been identified is the 5HT1 serotonin receptor; it is the workings at this juncture that affect aggression, mood and appetite. In addition, serotonin receptor 5HT3 plays a role in learning and memory as well as nausea and vomiting (Kotulak, 1997). Other identified serotonin receptors are 5HT2 and 5HT1C, which, we now know, relate directly to psychosis, depression, alcohol abuse, and mood fluctuations.

Once the binding occurs, termination results. For the most part, the most desirable of the termination routes is reuptake because the neurochemical returns to the receptor site and is available again, if needed. By

TABLE 1.2
Steps in the Synaptic Transmission: The Role of Medications

Synaptic Transmission	Role of Medication
Step 1: *Synthesis*. Precursors present in the transmitter site are activated by an enzyme and become a neurotransmitter.	Medications can affect transmitter synthesis by either increasing this action.
Step 2: *Storage*. Once created, neurotransmitters are stored in vesicles, to be released when signaled.	Medications can influence transmitter storage, leading to reduction of transmitters and, in turn, reducing the number of synaptic transmissions capable of being stored. When the process of transmitter storage is disrupted by medication, transmitter storage is depleted.
Step 3: *Release*. Neurotransmitters are released into the synaptic gap.	Medications can either promote or inhibit transmitter releases. If a drug promotes release, it will intensify transmissions; if it inhibits release, it will suppress transmissions.
Step 4: *Receptor binding*. Neurochemicals bind at designated receptor sites.	Medication can function as an *agonist* by directly activating the receptor, or as an *antagonist* by preventing receptor activation.
Step 5: *Termination*. Transmitters are cleared from synaptic gaps in three ways:	
(1) *reuptake*—once the action is completed by the neurotransmitter, a little "pump" pushes it back to where it originated so it is available to be used again;	Reuptake medications enhance the environment where neurotransmitters flood the gap, causing an intensification of the action.
(2) *enzymatic degradation*—the synapse contains large quantities of transmitter-interacting enzymes that terminate the potential for reresponse;	Medication can influence enzymatic action and break down and terminate the potential for a response.
(3) *diffusion*—the neurotransmitter is taken away from the gap and dissolved (this process is very slow and not often considered a realistic therapeutic option).	In diffusion, medications can stimulate the occurrence of this slow process whereby the neurochemical is no longer available to assist with the transmission.

understanding the reuptake process, we can understand the action–reaction that results. Marano (1999) warned, however, that this understanding exactly how medications influence this process might not be as simple as it seems because evidence exists that, in cases of recurrent depression, neurodegenerative processes can occur in which the structure and function of brain cells are affected, even destroyed, thereby precipitating future cognitive decline. This finding indicates that when a person is depressed, it is important to address possible environmental factors that might contribute to the depression, rather than ignoring them. By addressing the internal and external factors, mental as well as physical symptoms can be avoided.

It is especially important that non-medically trained practitioners (NMTP) have some working knowledge of how medications work, especially important when serving as a part of an interdisciplinary team where discussions to facilitate consumer care involve the usage and application of these terms. Understanding the basics of how pharmacological interventions may affect the consumer can help the NMTP to gain credibility as a contributing member of the team who is aware of the purpose, use, benefit, and side-effect profiles of medications.

THE FEAR OF ADDICTION: MEDICATION DEPENDENCE VERSUS CHOICE

It is an accepted fact that biological and biochemical processes can increase the possibility of medication dependence. Due to the fear of potential addiction many consumers avoid using medications. Others, in contrast, crave the medication and despair over addressing their addiction. When taking prescription and nonprescription medications, many individuals may not immediately think of addiction, or at least not in the same way as they would realize the addictive potential of illegal substances such as heroin, cocaine, or methamphetamines. Some of the most common drug addictions to legal substances relate to substances such as alcohol, nicotine in the form of tobacco, and caffeine in the form of tea, coffee, and caffeinated sodas. Yet many prescription and over-the-counter drugs can become addictive, especially if they are abused. Drugs addressed in this book that can be considered addictive include the barbiturates, the benzodiazipines such as Xanax, pain killers such as hydrocodone and oxycodone, and over-the-counter medications that contain dextromethorphan (found in many cold preparations). Regardless of the legality of the substance, addiction is best understood as a process that evolves over time as the person becomes gradually more dependent upon the use of the substance. The substance gains in importance and can become so influential that the consumer is unable to escape the desire to experience it. This desire can become so strong that it affects all areas of a person's daily functioning. Some mental health medications that could fall into this category that will be discussed later in this book are the general antidepressant and antianxiety medications, particularly the benzodiazepines. The benzodiazepines work by mimicking endorphins, the chemicals produced naturally by the body that have effects similar to dopamine, or by disabling the neurons that normally inhibit the release of dopamine. The benzodiazepines can be very helpful in addressing the symptoms of panic and anxiety that often inhibit an individual's performance of daily activities.

QUICK TIPS:
Assessing for Signs of Addiction

- Assess the person for co-occurring mental health conditions or problems, especially those involving anxiety and depression. Identify any comorbid symptoms that may be related to "self-medication": that is, attempting to control these mental health problems using alcohol or sedatives to relax.

- Assess whether the person is able to complete activities of daily living (ADLs). Two major areas to immediately screen are sleeping and eating: Is the person eating regular meals, and is he or she sleeping adequately (6–8 hours a night)?

- Assess the person's family history for the presence of substance abuse. If substance abuse was present, who was involved and how did it affect the client's earlier life experiences and life patterns?

- Assess current family factors for any recent changes in structure or expectations (e.g., divorce, separations, death).

- Assess for personal or situational factors that directly affect potential use or abuse of substances. For example, did the person recently lose a job?

- Assess for recent activity involving criminal behavior or incarceration related to substance-seeking behaviors.

Addictive behavior has a strong physiological component (the "high" feeling) because it directly affects neurotransmitter activity at specific receptor sites. Mood-altering substances fill the receptor sites with endorphins, which make the user feel good. Because the neurotransmitters are not needed, the receptor sites may dry up. Therefore, when the medication or substance related to addiction is stopped, the consumer is left in a state of receptor site depletion (Substance Abuse: Risks and Responsibilities, 2001).

The potential for addiction is present with any substance that influences neurotransmitter activity. By affecting neurotransmitter activity, and responses, these substances have the potential to affect mood, actions, or behaviors. Substances that fall into this category include everything from chocolate to caffeine, nicotine, and some prescription drugs, nonprescription drugs, herbal preparations, and illicit drugs.

Some drugs present unique properties that determine how often they are used. For example, to stay awake to complete a specific task, caffeine or a stronger stimulant might be the drug of choice. This functional use makes a substance reinforcing and contributes to the pleasure gained from taking it. The more reinforcing or pleasurable a substance such as caffeine becomes, the more consumers are inclined to continue taking it. It is this type of reinforcement that is most likely to create a physical dependence in the user. Many supportive care professionals claim that oftentimes this sense of rapid relief provided by a substance such as caffeine, in which the consumer reports feeling better quickly, can actually undermine the willingness to deal with issues that may have caused or contributed to the condition in the first place. When the body is satisfied, little effort will be exerted toward changing and controlling behavior to prevent future problems from occurring. After all, it is easier (and sometimes even perceived as more cost-effective) to have the quick fix than to struggle with uncomfortable issues that will need to be identified and discussed in the therapeutic relationship. Therefore, using a legal and often assumed-to-be safe substance such as caffeine can clearly affect the body's response to pain as well as to conditions such as diabetes (Diamond, Balm, & Freitag, 2000; Salazar-Martinez, Willet, Ascherio, et al., 2004). There is also some evidence that caffeine can impair the catalyzing of certain antidepressant medications, such as Luvox (fluvoxamine) (Jeppesen, Loft, Poulsen, et al., 1996).

When a medication is used for a purpose it was not intended to be used for, it is called *substance misuse*. When a substance is used excessively, it is considered *substance abuse*. Increased dependence and addiction can develop with any substance that has the ability to change neurotransmitter activity. Addiction can even occur purely by accident, when consumers take substances regularly, perhaps even daily, without thinking about the relationship these substances may have with other health factors. For example, there is a misconception that over-the-counter (OTC) or nonprescription drugs are safe because they are easy to purchase and available on demand. Some of the most frequently used OTC counter drugs—NSAIDs (nonsteroidal anti-inflammatory drugs) such as aspirin or ibuprofen—are generally viewed as harmless. Yet use of these medications can cause stomach bleeding or ulcers and abnormal kidney functioning (Arthritics, Rejoice, 1999; Stack, Atherton, Hawkey, et al., 2002).

Addiction does not always have to do with reactions of pleasure, and many addictive responses are not related to attempts at getting high from the medication. Rather, addiction can stem from taking the medication longer than expected, which can then develop into the need to continue taking it. Addiction is easily revealed by the emergence of an "abstinence syndrome." That is, upon discontinuance, a consumer experiences physical or psychological withdrawal symptoms, then addiction has occurred. If a person cannot have his or her morning coffee or tea and is forced to start the day off without it, what happens? If a headache soon develops, the chances are high that the person is addicted. If the person drinks a beverage with caffeine, rather than taking aspirin, the pain will subside quickly. The caffeine-rich beverage will elicit a quicker response, thereby reducing the headache more quickly. Simply stated, the body was craving the drug of caffeine, and by taking it, the body becomes satisfied.

In further understanding the term *addiction*, special attention needs to be given to the relationship between addiction and tolerance. *Tolerance*, as defined in the *Diagnostic and Statistical Manual of Mental Disorders—Fourth Edition—Text Revised (DSM-IV-TR)* (American Psychiatric Association, 2000) is characterized by the need for increased amounts of a substance to achieve intoxication (or the desired effect) due to a markedly diminished effect that occurs with the continued use of the same amount of the substance. A person is found to be experiencing substance dependence when he or she becomes physically "normal" only with the frequent ingestion of increasingly larger amounts of the substance creating the dependence (Miller, 1997). For example, the hypnotics and sedatives work to inhibit the actions of endogenous inhibitory neurotransmitters. When tolerance develops, changes in brain receptors result in the consumer's experience of withdrawal. Anxiety, restlessness, excitability, and in some cases, even seizures, may follow. Therefore, while the body is superficially benefiting from the effects of the medication, the body is likewise organizing metabolic enzymes and neurological changes that tend to counteract the desired effect. Thus the person needs an increased amount of the drug to achieve the preferred state. When tolerance is exhibited, the person must use the substance regularly to avoid withdrawal symptoms (Dziegielewski, 2005).

Regardless of the type of medication a consumer is taking, noting the tolerance level is important because once this stage of tolerance has been reached, the consumer can be considered physically "hooked." When the consumer is addicted to the medicine and is tolerant to its effects, the *opposite* of the drug's favorable result may be experienced.

Clarification and understanding of the powerful relationship between addiction and tolerance is essential. Levels of tolerance can be experienced in relation to use of a medication. *Initial tolerance* is the degree of bodily reaction, or lack thereof, that is displayed during the first experience with the drug. This level is dependent on the particular dose; thus the less intense the effect created by the substance, the larger the tolerance. Initial tolerance levels can vary due to genetics, physiological factors, or environmental circumstances. For the NMTP, it is important to assess whether the medication in this initial stage interferes with the person's ability to determine whether the substance is affecting or impairing his or her usual level of activity.

In *acquired tolerance* the consumer's ability to experience the effects of a medication is related directly to a lowered sensitivity to the substance as a result of the body's adaptation to the drug. The experience of acquired tolerance can be attributed to two types of processes: metabolic and functional. "*Metabolic tolerance* is created by an adaptive upsurge in the degree at which the substance is inactivated by metabolism in the liver and other tissues" (*Encyclopedia of Drugs, Alcohol, and Addictive Behavior*, 2001, p. 25). This response results in lower concentrations of the drug in the body after the same dose, so that the effect is less intense and shorter in duration. "*Functional tolerance* is formed by a diminution in the sensitivity of the tissues on which the drug acts, primarily the central nervous system, so that the same concentration of drug produces less effect than it originally did" (p. 25).

Acquired functional tolerance can develop in three time frames: acute, rapid, and chronic. In *acute tolerance* symptoms are displayed each time the substance is taken and may start with the initial exposure to the substance. Upon ingestion of the substance, changes in psychological or physiological response occur that may become more definitive with time. When the effect created in the consumer by the identical concentration of the substance is stronger at first than later, it is referred to as the *Mellanby effect. Rapid tolerance* refers to an increased susceptibility when the consumer is exposed to the drug a second time. This effect should occur shortly after the intake of the substance. In the third type, *chronic tolerance*, a consumer constantly desires the effects and uses the substance regularly. Regardless of the type of tolerance that the consumer develops, addiction to a substance will always involve significant physical changes in the central nervous system.

When an NMTP suspects medication addiction, he or should make every effort to anticipate or rule out the subsequent occurrence of withdrawal symptoms in the consumer as the body desperately attempts to achieve balance or homeostasis. According to the *DSM-IV-TR, substance withdrawal* occurs when a substance is terminated or reduced and results in negative physical and psychological consequences (American Psychiatric Association, 2000). The symptoms of withdrawal experienced, also referred to as the *withdrawal syndrome*, must cause a marked impairment in the social, occupational, or other significant areas of functioning. Often the state of withdrawal can create a situation for the addicted consumer that is highly uncomfortable or, at times, unbearable. A variety of

**QUICK TIPS:
Assessing and Addressing
Tolerance and Addiction**

- Clearly identify any substances a consumer is taking that could lead to tolerance and addiction.

- Assess the degree to which these substances impair personal, occupational, and social functioning.

- Gather a comprehensive history that includes medical factors, risk behaviors, and peer, family, and social supports.

- Identify problems or factors that will need to be addressed to ensure consumer safety.

- Formulate a plan of action to address the problem areas.

- Establish a means of monitoring and follow-up for all intervention strategies.

- Help the consumer develop a support system that will assist him or her in addressing problem behaviors.

symptoms can be attributed to withdrawal—for example, nervous system rebound from overstimulation, anxiety, diaphoresis, elevations of pulse and blood pressure, and a sense of acute physiological distress. Extreme physical and psychological suffering due to substance withdrawal can place consumer at risk for serious permanent physical damage or even death.

2

The Basics of Medication Prescription and Use

The effects of medications should be taken seriously, whether prescribed directly by a helping practitioner or taken as an OTC remedy (including herbal or other "natural" remedies). Mental health medications are prescribed for a multiplicity of health and mental health problems. The 53rd edition of the *Physicians' Desk Reference* (*PDR*) in 1999, and the 54th edition in 2000, have over 3,000 pages of text and describe over 4,000 drugs by product and generic name. The 58th edition in 2004 describes over 4,000 medications, with drugs cross-referenced to the label information.

In addition, over 100,000 OTC and herbal products are currently available without a prescription (Food and Drug Administration, 2003). These remedies have become so popular that the *PDR* has developed two volumes on herbal and OTC medicines: *Physicians' Desk Reference for Herbal Medicines*, 2000; *Physicians' Desk Reference for Nonprescription Drugs and Dietary Supplements*, 2004; *Physicians' Desk Reference for Nutritional Supplements*, 2001. The latest 2004 version of the *PDR* for Nonprescription Drugs and Dietary Supplements lists over 1,000 substances that fall under this classification. Just the sheer number of medications presented in these reference books should make us all aware that medications, whether by prescription or not, are clearly being used more and more in the therapeutic environment. This increased availability has

17

made the supportive role of the NMTP all the more crucial. All helping providers must not only be aware of the sheer number of medication choices available, they must also assist in monitoring the consumers using these products, when prescribed or self-prescribed.

Given that writing a prescription is so simple and quick to do, it is no accident that prescribing practitioners have been accused of simply writing medication prescriptions without thoroughly examining other possibilities or recommending additional complementary interventions. The Centers for Disease Control and Prevention and the Federal Food and Drug Administration (FDA), have estimated that, among antibiotic prescriptions alone, there are approximately 50 million prescriptions that are unnecessarily written each year (Food and Drug Administration, 2003). This practice can be of particular concern for mental health disorders because it could lead to consumers being placed on medications for problems that could be addressed by counseling strategy—if not totally, at least in part. Yet many times, in the haste of the prescriber's office visit, it remains a concern that referrals of this nature may not occur.

UNDERSTANDING PRESCRIPTION MEDICATIONS

For the non-medically trained, the use of two names for the same medication can be confusing. Common questions are, which name is correct to use, and what is the purpose of the second name? Consider, for example, two commonly prescribed SSRI antidepressants:

- Sertaline (Zoloft)
- Fluoxetine (Prozac)

In these cases, the second names listed (Zoloft, Prozac) are the *brand names* of the medications. The companies that created them, Pfizer Incorporated for Zoloft and Lilly Research Laboratories for Prozac, chose these brand names. These are the companies that first produced the medications and originally petitioned the FDA for the patents. In this example, the first name is the chemical name of the product (i.e., sertraline, fluoxetine). In most cases, if a generic medication is available, it is referred to by the chemical name and often listed first—though it may initially seem confusing to all, because prescribers and other NMTPs could use either name when referring to the medication being used. For example, if a prescriber ordered the brand-name medication Prozac, and now the generic equivalent is available, the generic would most likely be substituted (it costs less), and a prescription for fluoxetine (short for *fluoxetine hydrochloride*) would be filled. Therefore, on most prescription medicines, either one name or both the brand name and the generic/trade name could be listed. When a prescriber does not want the consumer to take a chemical equivalent, generally he or she will specify that no substitutions should be permitted.

It is also critical to know the differences between whether a medication is *biomedically equivalent* or *therapeutically equivalent.* Drugs are deemed biomedically equivalent by the FDA if they are considered chemically equivalent and deliver the same dose level to the system (Haynes, Patterson, & Wade, 1992). Equivalency evaluations do not include coating, coloring, or other additives, because they are not strictly part of the chemical composition of the medication. That is why consumers will state that the biomedically equivalent version of a brand-name medication (i.e., the generic) does not taste the same or is a different color when dissolved. Think about taking an aspirin that is coated and one that is not. The pain relief of both tablets is said to be equivalent; however, if it sits in the mouth too long before swallowing, the uncoated pill will taste bitter, whereas the coated one will slide down the throat without much notice. The pills may be considered biomedically equivalent, but the fillers and by-products used within the medication can taste different. When drugs are considered biomedically equivalent by the FDA, they are considered chemically equivalent, and deliver the same level of administered dose to the system.

As an NMTP it helps to know the differences between whether a medication is biomedically equivalent and therapeutically equivalent. Medications are considered therapeutically equivalent when they provide the same efficacy and controls for toxicity (Haynes et al., 1992). Can the medication help the consumer achieve the same results, even if it is not a chemical match with another similar medication? This consideration is particularly important when money is allocated to purchase medications in bulk. Bulk purchasing requires that certain therapeutically equivalent medications be purchased and used based on their cost-savings features (Haynes et al., 1992). So-called cost-effective measures often result in the changing of medications by managed care companies that deem a specific drug too costly. When medications are switched for the benefit of the agency and not the consumer, the NMTP can monitor the change and empower the consumer to advocate (with their physicians and insurance companies) on his or her own behalf that effective medications not be changed for purely economic reasons.

Reports indicate that consumers who suffer from mental health problems, whether they are being treated on an inpatient or outpatient basis, may have limited access to certain groups of medications, such as the newer antipsychotics, due to the cost factors involved (Mental Health Report, 1999a). The NMTP can serve as an advocate to assist the consumer in exploring the best way to get the intended medication. In addition, keeping abreast of the newest brand-name medications to hit the market is important because (even though they are more expensive) they may have fewer side effects. NMTPs need to recognize the factors related to efficient service provision (i.e., insurance reimbursement requirements, cost and insurance coverage) in helping to get the *best choice* for the consumer.

The fact that each consumer is different and may require a slightly different compound of a medication to get relief has led some prescribers to customize prescription medications by compounding (Nordenberg, 2000). *Compounding* may involve nothing more than crushing medications into a powder with a mortar bowl and pestle (a crushing tool) and then turning the powder into a liquid. This practice has become more common since the 1997 FDA Modernization Act, which defines the limits of compounding. The practice of compounding prescription medications can be very helpful for consumers who have allergies to certain substances, such as product fillers or dyes and for those who cannot swallow tablets or capsules and need a liquid form (Nordenberg, 2000). When compounding is used, the pharmacist should always combine the ingredients, not the consumer. However, since the compound itself has not been subject to the testing required of all approved drugs by the FDA, it should be used with caution. According to Nordenberg (2000), the FDA recommends that, whenever possible, an approved drug be utilized before a compound is attempted. For more information on pharmacy compounding, try the FDA's Website at *www.fda.gov/cder/pharmcomp/*.

MEDICATION ERRORS

When addressing the topic of prescription medications, the possibility of a *medication error* must be considered. There is considerable room for errors of all types in the prescription process (Zellmer, 1993), occurring as early as when the prescription is first written or read. Given the seriousness of these errors, some NMTPs request that consumers be given the actual medication upon discharge from a facility, rather than a prescription that is more subject to error (Johnson, Butta, Donohue, Glenn, & Holtzman, 1996). The most common types of medication errors are due to illegible handwriting, improper transcription, inaccurate dosage calculation, and inappropriate abbreviations (ASHP Report, 1993). In addition, drug product nomenclature of look-alike and sound-alike names can lead to incorrect filling of prescriptions (Allan, Barker, Malloy, & Heller, 1995). Tracking of this problem has revealed that filling the prescription with the wrong medication occurs much too often for comfort and can result in dangerous health situations for consumers (Cohen, 1994; Allan et al., 1995). Medication errors and interaction effects are tracked through large databases that compare and contrast the medications that a consumer is taking, thereby detecting drug interaction effects, allergies, contraindications, side effects, duplicate therapy, as well as ensuring the safety and efficacy of the medications utilized (De Angelo, 2000; *Physicians' Desk Reference*, 2004). It is hoped that comparison services such as these can help to reduce medical and prescribing errors and better protect the consumer.

Furthermore, approximately 125,000 deaths occur each year as a result of consumers not taking medication as directed (Buppert, 2000). NMTPs need to assume an active role in protecting consumers from a lack of information or from misinformation. Office overbookings are one reason why consumers may not be given the time needed to ask questions of MTPs. Yet many of these prescribers are very willing to answer questions and clarify concerns. NMTPs need to check if this information has been obtained, whether it has been received from the prescriber or from other supportive

QUICK TIPS:
Websites to Assist
with Comparison

- Drug Digest
  www.drugdigest.org//DD/Interaction/ChooseDrugs/14109,,00.html

- Health Discovery
  www.healthdiscovery.com/encyclopedias/checker/checker.jsp

medical personnel, such as pharmacists, nurses, or other members of the health care team (McGrath, 1999).

Consumers need to be warned not to accept everything they read or hear about a drug, unless the available information is well-referenced. At times television advertisements and pamphlets promoting specific products can be misleading. When NMTPs are unsure whether the medication claims made are valid, they should not hesitate to admit this to the consumer and offer to help him or her to find out more or refer him or her to another interdisciplinary team member.

QUICK TIPS:
Helping to Reduce Prescription Errors

- Be sure that the prescriber has the medical record or an accurate history and update of all medications a consumer is taking, including a listing of any known drug allergies.

- The practitioner can help the consumer to create an index card that lists current and past medications; the card should be available for review at every appointment with a health care provider.

- Be sure that all pertinent information is listed for each medication, including the name, dose, number, and date of last refill.By ensuring that all providers are aware of what a consumer is taking, problems with duplicate prescriptions, drug interactions and side effects, contraindicated medications, and errors in dosages can be avoided.

- Help the consumer to write down information about when refills and medication changes were ordered and why these changes were made. This information should be given to the prescriber to assist with making informed medication decisions.

- Each time the NMTP has a session with a consumer, it is important to ask what medications he or she is on and if any changes have been made. Don't forget to ask about OTC and herbal preparations as well.

continued

continued

- When a consumer reports that he or she has been given a new medication, ask the following questions:

  "What is the medication for?"

  "Did you get any written information about the side effects or interaction effects?"

  "Would you like to review the information you were given with me?"

  "Do you know what to do (or what may happen) if you miss taking a dose or decide not to take the medication anymore?"

- For documentation purposes, be sure to note that this information has been discussed.

- Ask female consumers of childbearing age if they are using birth control and about the probability of pregnancy. Some medications can delay menses, and women may not know they are pregnant. If medications are harmful to fetal development, they tend to cause the most damage in the first trimester (3 months), so early detection is critical. Making sure that the consumer has given her MTP any pertinent information in this area is a proactive and protective step.

Note: Suggestions provided by Buppert (2000) from the Gold Sheet.

Consumers need to be warned not to accept everything they read or hear about a drug unless the available information is well referenced. At times, television advertisements and pamphlets promoting specific products can be misleading. When NMTPs are unsure whether the medication claims made are valid, they should not hesitate to admit this to the consumer and offer to help him or her find out more or refer him or her to another interdisciplinary team member.

INCREASING COMPLIANCE

Noncompliance with medication regimen is a problem that occurs for most practitioners. To increase compliance with medications, NMTPs should explore, examine, and document the conditions or situations that might lead to noncompliance. Something as straightforward as high cost may stop the consumer from purchasing the medication. Or, if a consumer is

QUICK TIPS:
Helpful Information

- The National Institute of Mental Health (NIMH) provides a user-friendly publication for consumers, NMTPs and MTPs, that gives basic information about numerous mental health medications. The full text for NIMH Publication No. 95-3929 is also available online at *www.nimh.nih. gov/publicat/medicate.cfm*.

- Information for NIMH Publication No. 95-3929: You can order the booklet from NIMH Public Inquiries, Room 8184, MSC 9663, 6001 Executive Boulevard, Bethesda, MD 20892-9663, or fax a request to 301-443-4279.

instructed to take several prescriptions at different times throughout the day, the routine can become confusing (ASHP Report, 1993). For example, when a prescription is given twice a day (BID), what exactly does that mean? Should the consumer take the medication every 12 hours or upon awakening and before going to sleep at night? Even physicians often disagree about the exactness of these prescribed schedules, so it is no surprise that consumers taking these medications can also become confused. In addition, consumers may be unsure of what aspects of the medication or treatment regimen are most important to learn (Airaksinen, Ahonen, & Enlund, 1993). Or they may be confused, especially when first beginning the medication, about instructions to lower or increase their dosage depending on their feelings or symptoms. Consumers may not trust their own feelings and take either too much or too little of the needed medication.

Over the last 15 years, a host of new psychotropic medications have become available, accompanied by unprecedented spending on prescription drugs (Frank, Conti, & Goldman, 2005). When cost is an issue, consider advising the consumer to switch to a generic medication or determine whether the consumer would benefit from a pharmacy assistance program (through governmental agencies or pharmaceutical companies). Some of these companies may provide medications directly to physicians for use with consumers who cannot afford them. (Buppert [2000] warned, however, that it is illegal for a health care provider to sell samples, even at a reduced cost, or to give a consumer the full dosing supply of free samples.) The primary criteria for participation in these programs are financial inability to purchase the medications and (2) absence of health insurance coverage. Because other eligibility requirements vary depending on the program, it is best to call the specific program and find out the requirements (see Table 2.1).

TABLE 2.1
Pharmaceutical Companies That Provide Assistance

Bristol-Myers Squibb	800-444-4106
DuPont	302-992-5000
Jansen, Inc.	800-652-6227
Merck	800-727-5400
Pfizer, Inc.	800-646-4455
Roche Laboratories	800-443-6676
Upjohn Co.	616-323-6332

Purchasing Medications on the Internet

Recent advances in computer technology have facilitated the purchasing of medications via the Internet (Costello, 2000), which may foster compliance. Purchasing medications via a computer appeals to many individuals, especially those who cannot leave their homes or who live in rural areas (Henkel, 2000). With a simple faxed prescription or an online request, medications can be delivered directly to a consumer's door. But this convenient mode of purchase can be problematic when consumers are allowed to purchase a medication prescription simply by requesting one. This type of transaction can result in problems for the consumer that range from misdiagnosis to receiving incorrect medication (Carey, 2000).

Imagine everyone's horror when Chen (1999) described an official crackdown on one such site where the person authorizing the prescriptions was a veterinarian in Mexico! Starting with the Clinton administration, monies have been allocated to crack down on illegal drug sales online; however, foreign-based sites are almost impossible to regulate (Carey, 2000). The rules and regulations for sites located in other countries are not the same as in the United States, but the services are available to anyone with Internet access (Henkel, 2000). Unfortunately, cases such as these give a bad name to the reputable electronic pharmacies that provide a valuable service.

QUICK TIPS:
Increasing Consumer Compliance

First, create an atmosphere for compliance:

- Develop a trusting relationship with the consumer. If the consumer feels comfortable with the NMTP he or she will be more likely to address compliance issues honestly.

- In this trusting relationship it is critical for the NMTP not to give inaccurate information; when unsure, clearly acknowledge your uncertainty as well as your willingness to help the consumer get the information needed.

- Be sure to empower the consumer to build his or her own knowledge and skill toward competent medication self-management. This type of empowerment helps the consumer feel more in control of his or her own care and medication regimen. When consumers are educated in regard to their medication regimens, they are far more likely to comply.

Second, obtain the information that contributes to compliance:

- Ask the consumer why he or she is taking the medication.

- Ask the consumer if compliance has been an issue in the past or is currently one.

- Review the prescribed regimen with the consumer.

- Ascertain to what degree the prescribed regimen is being followed.

- Help the consumer identify factors that would contribute to compliance.

- Ask the consumer to identify potential problems that could hamper compliance, such as cost or side effect profiles.

- Ascertain to what degree noncompliance has had a negative impact on the health of the consumer.

- Does the consumer live alone? If not, are there other caregivers present who could assist the individual with compliance?

- Does the consumer seem receptive to ideas and methods designed to increase compliance? If not, what can the NMTP do to help the consumer feel more comfortable, thereby helping to ensure compliance?

- What types of medication management reminders/devices/services are currently in use, and are others available that are not being used?

- When needed, help the consumer to feel comfortable asking the prescriber to change dosing schedules to meet lifestyle concerns.

Assessing Factors Unique to the Individual

NMTPs need to be sensitive to how each individual's personal situation might relate to the medication regimen prescribed. A person with vision problems may have trouble reading the directions or correctly identifying the different medications prescribed. When this is the case, it can be helpful to advocate for medications that are color coded or that have large, easy-to-read directions and that are placed in easily distinguished containers of different sizes. Providing simple, clear, easy-to-read and easily followed directions can facilitate medication compliance (Kane, Ouslander, & Abrass, 1999).

Creating a Climate of Comfort to Discuss Issues

Consumers need to feel comfortable in asking questions about side effects and discussing sensitive issues (e.g., medication-related sexual dysfunction). Education also needs to extend beyond the consumer to include family members, who can also be instructed on the consumer's medication regimen and can assist with compliance and structure.

The American Society of Hospital Pharmacists (ASHP) contends that the best way to approach the problem of medication errors and noncompliance is through the use of an interdisciplinary team approach. The NMTP can facilitate team interactions and development in this area in the following ways:

QUICK TIPS: Internet-Obtained Medications

Advice to consumers . . .

- Before purchasing anything, be sure to establish the credibility and reputation of the electronic pharmacy.

- Be sure to get the name, phone number, and professional license number of the online pharmacist.

- Once information is gathered, keep it in a safe place in case of any problems.

- Determine whether the site is approved by the National Association of Boards of Pharmacy (NABP), which has developed a seal of approval for sites that meet the appropriate standards (Website: *www.nabp.net*; telephone: 847-698-6227).

- Before using a medication, check the expiration date to be sure it is not outdated.

1. As a team member the NMTP can contribute to the recognition and reporting of medication errors.

2. While spending quality time with the consumer, the NMTP can monitor the consumer's responses to the medications, particularly noting any side effect, excessive sleepiness, and impaired functioning.

3. The NMTP can note any particular problems with dosing schedules or other noncompliance issues that may arise.

4. The NMTP can help educate the consumer and family members regarding all considerations that should be noted when using medications.

5. When a NMTP cannot offer an immediate response to a medication question, he or she should obtain the information (by looking it up in the *Physicians' Desk Reference* or other resources) and give it to the consumer at the next session.

6. To provide consumers with a general understanding of how medications work, NMTPs should encourage consumers to ask for medication information from the physician or local pharmacist (Airaksinen et al., 1993).

UNDERSTANDING NONPRESCRIPTION MEDICATIONS

Many MTPs and NMTPs realize the importance of monitoring prescription medication but fall short in the area of nonprescription medication (often referred to as over-the-counter or OTC medications). The same concerns that were expressed in regard to prescription medications apply to nonprescription medications as well. After all, a considerable number of these OTC medications were previously known as prescription medications. To date, there are over 600 products that were previously available by prescription only but are now available without a prescription (*Physicians' Desk Reference*, 2004). These products range from allergy, cold, and cough preparations to heartburn medications and antidiarrheals (see Table 2.2).

TABLE 2.2
Common Nonprescription Medications

Medications	Side Effects	Interactions
Colds/Flu		
Antihistamines		
Actifed Dristan	Sedation, dizziness, rash,	Increase sedative effects
Benadryl Dixoral I	impairment of coordination,	of other medications
Cheracol-Plus	upset stomach, thickening	
Nyquil	of bronchial secretions,	
Chlortrimeton	blurring of vision	
Sinarest		
Contac Sinutab		
Dimetapp		
Decongestants		
Afrin Nasal Spray	Excessive stimulation,	Aggravate high blood
Sine-Aid	dizziness, difficulty with	pressure, heart disease,
Sudafed	urination, palpitations	and prostate problems
Cough suppressants		
Benylin	Drowsiness, blurred vision,	Increase sedative effects
Robitussin CF/DM	difficulty with urination,	of other medications
Vicks Formula 44	upset stomach etc.	
Diarrhea		
Imodium A-D	Drowsiness, depression,	
Pepto-Bismol	blurred vision	
Pain Relief/Fever		
Aspirin		
Alka-Seltzer	Ringing in ears, nausea,	Increase effect of blood
Bayer Aspirin	stomach ulceration,	thinners
	hyperventilation	
Acetaminophen		
Tylenol	Liver toxicity (in large doses)	
Ibuprofen		
Advil	Upset stomach, dizziness,	
Motrin	rash, itching	
Nuprin		

Most of these medications have multiple ingredients that are intended to treat multiple symptoms. For example, most cold and allergy preparations have more than one ingredient added to address the most common symptoms that someone with a cold or allergy might experience. What if the consumer does not experience all of these symptoms and therefore does not need a preparation with multiple ingredients? In this case the consumer would actually get the greatest benefit from a single ingredient but is forced to take them all because of this premixed combination. Therefore, it is important to advise the consumer to read the labels carefully because the chemical names and the use of multiple ingredients can be confusing (see Table 2.3).

TABLE 2.3
Colds, Coughs, and Allergy Preparations

- *Decongestants*—phenylephrine, ephedrine, phenylpropanolamine; these products address coughs and cold symptoms.
- *Antihistamines*—chlorpheniramine or pyrilamine; these products target the runny nose.
- *Expectorants*—glyceryl guaiacolate and potassium iodide; these products thin the mucous that blocks the air tubes leading to the lungs.
- *Cough suppressants*—dextromethorphan hydrobromide; these products lessen the urge to cough.

There is a myth that use of nonprescription medication cannot be harmful. Yet these medications can produce powerful effects as well as negative interactions with other prescription and nonprescription drugs. Therefore, caution should always be exercised. For example, when treating pain, fever, or headache, aspirin is effective; however, it can also be associated with increased stomach irritation, longer bleeding time, kidney failure, and some kinds of strokes (FDA, 2005). Another common pain reliever, acetaminophen, is reported to have no unusual side effects and, unlike aspirin, does not cause gastrointestinal bleeding; however, taken in large doses or for extended periods, it can cause liver damage. Ibuprofen is advertised as easier on the stomach than aspirin; however, the prescription formula of this product advises that it be taken with food.

A great deal of attention has been paid to the benefits and dangers of OTC medications. Historically, however, the responsibility was given to the manufacturer to provide clear directions and outline risks and benefits. After numerous attempts at regulation, the Durham–Humphrey amendment in 1952 established a clear demarcation between prescription and nonprescription medications (Pray, 2003). The types and sheer numbers of these medications have grown tremendously since 1952. In terms of marketing, consumers are eager to self-diagnose and monitor their own treatment outcomes. This trend has led pharmacies to adopt services such as Healthwatch, which allows consumers to monitor their own medications for side-effects or interaction effects. In addition, blood pressure machines have been added to stores (since 1997) to attract customers and enhance satisfaction (Ralston, 2000). According to the 1992 Heller Research Group study of "Self-Medication in the 90's: Practices and Perceptions," 85% of Americans felt it was important to have OTC medications available to relieve minor medical problems (Heller, 1993). This demand and the expected profit have encouraged drug manufacturers to recognize the importance of marketing nonprescription drugs.

The reason for the choosing an OTC medication over a prescription medication should not be determined by the strength of the medication but by the relative safety. Because OTC medications can be just as potent as prescription ones, they are generally dispensed at lower doses (Nordenberg, 1998). There is a widespread myth that higher doses of a medication are more effective than lower doses; this is a dangerous assumption that can lead to serious problems with drug interactions and the actual worsening of an existing illness (Pray, 2003; Shmerling, 2004).

Overconsumption of OTC medications is a particular problem with consumers over the age of 65. The National Center for Health Services Research and Health Care Technology estimated that in the United States, older adults comprise 13% of the population yet purchase 30% of all prescription drugs and 40% of all nonprescription drugs. Two-thirds of adults over 65 use one or more drugs daily, and older persons use an average of three prescription and nonprescription drugs at any given time (as cited in Beizer, 1994; Cohen, 2000). "Start low and go slow" is a well-known precaution when working with older consumers because adverse drug reactions occur frequently in this population (Williams, 1997). In patients age 60 and older, about one-half (51%) of deaths occur from adverse drug reactions (Cohen, 2000). The bottom line: OTC medications are similar to prescription ones and can interact adversely or cause toxicity when used in conjunction with other medications.

It is also possible for herbal remedies to interact adversely with prescription and nonprescription medications. Chapter 8 provides a detailed discussion of popular alternative medicines.

THE USE OF MULTIPLE MEDICATIONS

Many consumers assume that each prescriber is familiar with the medications they are taking and what will happen when a new medication is added to the intervention scheme. This is an incorrect assumption. Even in the most controlled drug trials, multiple medications are not studied. Therefore, no one can ever be totally sure how adding a medication to a regimen that is being tested will affect results. Furthermore, the simple act of adding another medication can change the entire outcome and result in serious reactions to a drug that, when taken alone, did not occur before (Henkel, 1998). This reality supports the assertion that any substance that creates a desired action in the body can just as easily create an undesirable reaction in the body.

Most prescribers, MTPs, and NMTPs, however, do have an overall awareness of certain drugs, particularly the medications that would fall in the categories of their own specialty. Most prescribers simply look up medications they do not regularly prescribe in order to determine their value and effect on the consumer. Given all the prescription medications available, as well as OTC and herbal medicines, competent and professional practice requires that all providers also identify the interactive effects produced by these medications. This knowledge is especially important when the consumer is taking other medications that can interact with, diminish, or augment the effects of the original medication in question. Polypharmacy (i.e., prescribing multiple medications) increases the risk of medication-related adverse events. It also can create an individualized and complex drug regimen that must be analyzed by the prescriber and monitored by the NMTP. When a consumer is taking more than one medication, it is difficult to determine what caused what; the symptoms or side effects experienced can become blurred. Also, using multiple medications increases the potential for medication-based side effects. The NMTP can assist this complex process by writing down each medication the consumer is taking (including OTC and herbal products). (Chapter 3 discusses how to take a medication history.)

MEDICATION RESPONSE COMPLEXITIES

Finding the right medication for a consumer rests on understanding the potential for individualized responses. Because each consumer's biological and physiological system is unique, each metabolizes and reacts to medication in an individualized manner. Predicting individualized reactions and resulting side effects, as well as handling the consumer's subjective perception of a medication response, can be the prescriber's greatest nightmare (Longhofer, Floersch, & Jenkins, 2003). Each consumer's response is influenced by numerous factors such as age, size, body weight, metabolism, race, gender, and use of generic versus brand name. To complicate this situation, the same consumer can have varied experiences with the same medication over time, based on age and different life experiences (e.g., the death of a loved one, as opposed to a general difficulty getting to sleep). In addition, as an individual ages the metabolism slows and the same medicine can produce a different response than when the consumer was younger. This subjective component means that medication responses to these factors can vary immensely. Some consumers may report mild, temporary discomfort to a particular drug, whereas after experiencing a trauma, they may have a different, longer-lasting response.

In the mental health setting, for example some consumers are prescribed a medication to reduce or eliminate violent or self-destructive behaviors. The medication's sedative effect calms some consumers immediately and may even produce sleep. Yet other consumers with similar characteristics (e.g., weight, height) remain extremely combative. In order to achieve the same calming result observable in the first situation, a second consumer might require a subsequent dose to get a similar calming effect.

Why does this variability occur? There are no definitive explanations of consumer responses to medications. The combination of the consumer's unique biological system and the variability of medications underscores the reality that medication use and application is far from an exact science. Older and younger consumers present additional challenge for the clinician (see Chapter 9 for a detailed discussion of these two populations).

Simply stated, the clinical trials of a medication are not comprehensive or inclusive enough to adequately address all individualized reactions and the medication-related problems, issues, and interactions that may develop (Henkel, 1998; Sadavoy, 2004). In clinical trials, drugs are studied only for the use the company is pursuing. Furthermore, the primary information yielded comes from marketing studies—and in such studies there is a profit motive, which should never be ignored.

Preventing and anticipating all the possible side effects a person may encounter is a clinical impossibility. According to the FDA, if it had to approve a drug that had no side effects, "we wouldn't approve any drugs . . . every single drug that has an effect on the body will also have side effects" (Nordenberg, 1999b, p. 9). So the real issue for the NMTP is to help the consumer become aware of the probable side effects and how many are tolerable. And even though trials of medications are conducted and monitored by the FDA, it is only long after the medication has been used by millions of consumers that the full spectrum of its effects are known (Henkel, 1998). This lacuna has given rise to postmarketing programs such as MedWatch. MedWatch was developed by the FDA as a reporting system to track adverse reactions to prescription and OTC medications (Nordenberg, 1999b). Information is put into a computer database where it is analyzed and tracked for occurrences. Programs such as MedWatch are effective only if health care providers such as doctors, dentists, psychiatrists, and NMTPs pass along information of serious adverse reactions, so that they can be clearly documented and avoided in future use.

AN UNHOLY ALLIANCE

Mosher (1999) warns of an "unholy alliance" wherein psychiatrists and other medication prescribers are persuaded by drug companies to utilize a particular type of medication. These prescribers are typically befriended by the drug company's representatives and given free services or rewards for prescribing the medication (e.g., free lunches, books, and other types of perks). Unfortunately, this alliance between the drug companies and prescribers can determine the prescriptions that are written, rather than the condition of consumers. This alliance may be less evident with NMTPs, but when it occurs, it is nonetheless problematic. More and more pharmaceutical companies realize that prescribers listen to NMTPs' suggestions regarding what medication to use as well as on modification adjustments and changes. This collaboration can lead to more "sponsorship" opportunities, whereby goods and services are provided as knowledge is increased for the sponsored product. Because this negative form of collaboration can create such an unhealthy alliance, many hospitals and other health care facilities clearly discourage it.

TERMINOLOGY FOR MONITORING MEDICATION

To better understand the basics of medication use, NMTPs need to become aware of basic medical terminology. Some common terms for medication dosing and monitoring include *medication half-life, time-release tablets, scored tablets, dosing of liquids, medication potency, therapeutic index,* and *drug tolerance prescribing.*

Simply stated, *medication half-life* is the amount of time it takes for one half of a drug's peak plasma level to be metabolized and excreted from the body (Kaplan & Sadock, 1990; Schwartz, 1998). If the half-life of a medication is estimated to be 4 hours, then the peak concentration of the medication in a consumer's system occurs within 4 hours of ingestion. After 4 hours the level of medication will have decreased by 50% of the original amount. In 8 hours the medication in the system is reduced by another 50%, and so on. The original 50% that was left continues to be divided, so that 12 hours after taking the medicine, 12.5% (one-eighth of the original dose) would be left. It is critical to remember that many medications remain in the system long after the medication has been ingested.

The half-life of a medication has serious implications for consumers who combine medications or who take another medication before the first drug has cleared from the system. This practice can create the potential for hazardous reactions. Therefore, if a medicine is said to have a *long half-life* and a consumer misses a dose, it is considered best not to take the missed dose immediately but to wait till the next dose is due. Simply put, when a consumer takes the missed dose of a drug with a long half-life, an overdose might result. Conversely, a missed dose of a medication that has a *short half-life* can be taken whenever the oversight is noticed because the medication is eliminated more quickly from the system.

The NMTP can often be involved in monitoring a consumer's medication regimen. A working knowledge of medications helps the NMTP to prepare for potential problems related to medication usage and misuse. This supportive role can involve educating consumers and their families on basic issues related to medication use. Although some of the basics of medication use seem simple, often they are not. For example, some consumers may not realize it is best not to chew a *time-release* medication because these medications are generally coated so that part is released first and the remainder is released later when the additional inclusive coating breaks. Chewing this type of medication would defeat the purpose of a time-release dosage. Furthermore, consumers should be informed that it is best not to split capsulated medications.

Many medications are expensive, particularly those required for maintaining mental health. In desperate attempts to save money, some consumers may try to split tablet medications in half. Often health providers may agree that, in practice, this should work. However, misdosing can occur when a consumer splits a nonscored tablet. A *scored tablet* has a line down the middle for easy splitting, and the dose is equally distributed. Often there is no uniform dose distribution in a nonscored tablet. Therefore, the consumer who splits a nonscored tablet, thinking that he or she is getting half the prescribed dose, may be misdosing him- or herself. Unless specifically addressed in the product literature, the precise amount of medication in each side of a split nonscored tablet cannot be determined.

When a practitioner is not sure whether a medication has been internally scored, he or she should make sure that the consumer knows the importance of only splitting medication tablets that have the manufacturer's line across the tablet. Such a simple mistake could cause serious problems in the consumer's medication regimen that might not be easily detected by the consumer, the prescribing practitioner, or the supportive interdisciplinary team.

In addition, *dosing problems* can occur with liquid medications. For example, many consumers might simply use a kitchen spoon to dispense medication—but all spoons are not the same size. Common tableware teaspoons come in various sizes, from 2.5 to 9.5 milliliters. The average measurement for a teaspoon is set at the 5 milliliter mark (Kurtzweil, 1994), so using everyday tableware could create variability in the dosage taken. To assist consumers, various types of standardized measuring devices are available, including oral syringes, oral droppers, cylindrical dosing spoons, and plastic medicine cups. Remind consumers who use instruments such as oral syringes or droppers to remove the cap to prevent injury from accidentally swallowing it (Kurtzweil, 1994).

> **QUICK TIPS:**
> **When the Consumer Is Taking Liquid Medications . . .**
> - Remind the consumer to remove caps from hypodermic or oral syringes and, once used, to throw them away.
> - Remind the consumer to use only standardized measuring devices, such as the plastic dosing cup that comes with the product and not one from another product.

Dosing problems of this nature can be avoided with a simple explanation or demonstration of how to measure liquid medicines more accurately. For the most part, a dosing cup is assumed to be the most accurate and effective way to ensure that the consumer is receiving the correct medication dosage. The NMTPs role can be central regarding the education of consumers about possible dosing problems.

The term *medication potency* refers to the relative dose needed to achieve a certain effect (Kaplan & Sadock, 1990). For example, Haldol (haloperidol, at a dose of 5 mg), a drug used to treat psychosis, is a high-potency medication because the dose needed to produce a therapeutic effect (5 mg) is much lower than its counterpart, Thorazine (chlorpromazine, at a comparable dose of 100 mg). In this case, 100 mg of Thorazine would be required to achieve the same effect achieved by 5 mg of Haldol. The concept of medication potency helps to explain why consumers are prescribed varying doses, and why one pill is given at 50 mg and another at 2 mg. Inadequate knowledge of potency can also confuse family members who are trying to be supportive but are struggling to understand the medication regimen a loved one is expected to follow. Furthermore, if the consumer or family member is unaware of medication potency, and the individual is switched from a low-potency medication such as Thorazine to a high-potency medication such as Haldol, serious consequences can result. For example, if the consumer took several pills of Haldol (totaling 15 mgs), thinking that this is less than the usual dose of Thorazine (which is 50 mgs), a serious toxic response could result.

The *therapeutic index* of a drug is computed by determining the ratio of the toxic dose of the drug to its therapeutic dose—in short, the toxicity or safety level for the consumer. Some drugs have small therapeutic windows—that is, only a small amount above the therapeutic dose could become toxic—and therefore must be monitored carefully.

Lithium (Eskalith), often used to treat the bipolar disorders, is a good example. Because the toxic levels of lithium are so close to the therapeutic levels, consumers and family members should be cautioned to watch for early toxic symptoms and, when noted, to discontinue the drug and contact the MTP as soon as possible (*Physicians' Desk Reference*, 2004).

As noted in Chapter 1 consumers can develop drug tolerance, which refers to lower levels of responsiveness to a medication over a period of time. The therapeutic index of a drug should be monitored to maximize the drug's effects as well as to detect an emerging tolerance. Tolerance generally occurs when the person becomes physically dependent on the medication and must take the drug regularly in order to prevent suffering uncomfortable symptoms related to withdrawal (Kaplan & Sadock, 1990). Because the term *withdrawal* might scare some consumers, it is not uncommon to refer to withdrawal symptoms simply as *discontinuation effects*. This softer term appears in both the lay literature as well as the professional literature (Schweitzer, 2001). Regardless of what it is called, the definition for both terms is the same, and generally the symptoms are unpleasant to experience.

NMTPs need to stay abreast of medical terminology and jargon. To read and interpret consumer information, records, and written prescriptions, NMTPs need to be aware of the symbols and abbreviations commonly used in the medical profession, and how these are applied in the health and mental health care of consumers. Table 2.4 provides examples of common medical abbreviations.

TABLE 2.4
Medical Abbreviations

Abbreviation	General Meaning	Abbreviation	General Meaning
a	Before	oz	ounce
ac	before meals	pt	pint
ad	to; up to	pr	through the rectum
ad lib	as desired	prn	as needed
aq	water	pc	after meals
bid	twice a day	pv	through the vagina
BP	blood pressure	q	every
c̄	with	qh	every hour
/d	daily (per day)	quid	four times a day
gtt	a drop/drops	qt	quart
hs	take at bedtime/	s̄	without
	hour of sleep	ss	a half
liq	a liquid solution	sq	subcutaneously
mg	milligram	tab	tablet
ml	milliliter	tid	three times daily
mm	millimeter	tin	three times a night
os	mouth		

MEDICATION REGIMENS

In understanding the basics of medication regimens, two time frames regarding administration should always be considered: acute and maintenance administration.

Acute intervention efforts may be needed for active problems. For example, a consumer may need to take a medication quickly to keep the symptoms from causing disruption in functioning. When a consumer is experiencing hyper or fearful states on unpredictable behavior, he or she may not be able to respond to verbal intervention. Often the medication helps calm the consumer, so that later verbal attempts at treatment can be made. This benefit is most evident in the treatment of people with anxiety disorders. It is difficult to work with a person (which requires focus) when he or she is anxious. Therefore, acute intervention with a medication can help to calm the consumer, and once the medication takes effect, he or she can better concentrate on the verbal intervention presented.

If *maintenance* of the medication is needed, prevention is highlighted and medications are added as symptoms arise (acute intervention) or in an ongoing manner to prevent recurrences of the disorder (maintenance intervention). The NMTP can help monitor when a consumer starts to feel better, leading him or her to either discontinue the drug entirely or to devalue the importance of taking the medication regularly to maintain the current steady state. For example, soon after taking an antidepressant medication, the depressed individual may start to feel better. Paradoxically, it is when energy returns that the consumer is most likely to act on impulsive behaviors that might be dangerous. Consumers in this maintenance phase who are not open to working with an NMTP can be difficult to assist. These consumers may require more time and effort from multiple sources, such as physician, nurse, home outreach programs, individualized education and care, or weekly or bimonthly supportive telephone contacts. The additional time and monetary costs in working with this group are easily offset by the reduction in hospitalization and other emergency services.

MODES OF MEDICATION ADMINISTRATION

NMTPs need to be aware of how medications are administered. The route of administration can directly affect whether a regimen is followed, because consumers are most likely to take a medication when it is both convenient and quick acting (Goode, 1992a). There is a clear link between the medication regimen (acute vs. maintenance) and the route of administration used for the medication. The best route of administration is determined by the effect desired and how quickly it is needed.

Taking a medication through *oral administration*—taking the pill by mouth—can be a very easy and desirable way to ingest the drug. Unfortunately, however, there is generally a time delay for the consumer to feel the results, because the pill must pass through the stomach before being slowly absorbed in the intestines. The same is true of taking a medication through the *nasal route* (snorting or sniffing): There is an expected time delay between actually taking the medication and feeling the effect, because the product must be absorbed gradually through the mucous membranes. Taking medications in this form of administration is most effective when coupled with a maintenance regimen. Although taking a medication orally or nasally may be quick and convenient, these modes of administration may be problematic when immediate relief is needed (e.g., when a consumer is extremely agitated and hostile, or is threatening to harm him- or herself or others). The best route of administration in these situations, might be one that provides more immediate relief, such as a sedative that is administered via *injection* (Goode, 1992a). Injections, referred to as *depot preparations* (long-acting, injectable medications), can be invaluable when working with chronic consumers who have difficulty with compliance (Lehne & Scott, 1996).

IDENTIFYING USER-FRIENDLY INFORMATION ABOUT REACTIONS AND SIDE EFFECTS

NMTPs should be aware of the potential reactions outlined for a medication by becoming familiar with the precautions that apply to each drug. This means that it may be helpful to know how to reference medications in the *Physicians' Desk Reference* (2004). What appears most helpful for NMTPs, however, is a call to the local pharmacist, who can provide information on medications as well as reading bottle or package inserts. The pharmacist can provide printed information that is much more user friendly than the descriptions in the PDR. All consumers are encouraged to read these inserts completely before beginning their medication regimens. The *Physicians' Desk Reference for Nonprescription Drugs and Dietary Supplements, 25th Edition* (2004), may also be helpful; it provides pictures and clear explanations of the medications and possible adverse reactions, similar to the PDR for prescription medications.

TAPERING MEDICATIONS

Many consumers ask questions about how to best cut back or taper off their medications. It is always best to refer these types of questions directly to the prescriber, because of the complications that can result from discontinuing or reducing the levels of certain drugs. Consumers should be cautioned on the perils of stopping medication abruptly or even weaning off medication without proper medical advice and monitoring. For example, Xanax, which is used to control anxiety, should never be discontinued suddenly because of the risk of seizures.

Tapering off a medication requires constant monitoring, and there are no firm rules for all medications. If a consumer states that he or she is going to discontinue a medication without seeking medical advice, it is best to recommend a slow tapering-off process, decreasing by no more than 10–15% of the medication given each day. When a plan for tapering has been established by the prescriber, the NMTP can assist the consumer in identifying any side effects that occur during the weaning period.

MEDICATION EXPIRATION DATES

The expiration date of a medication indicates how long the active ingredients remain in an active state. If asked about using medications that are past the expiration date, the NMTP should advise the consumer to call the pharmacy before discarding the medication. Many times pharmacists stamp their own expiration date with a date that occurs before the one assigned by the manufacturer (Prufer, 1996), giving the medication a more limited shelf-life than the manufacturer originally intended. This practice can be costly for consumers who are on limited budgets. At the same time, consumers should be reminded that old medications could prove ineffective and might have to be discarded (after consultation with the pharmacist). If there are two dates on a prescription bottle, the older date is most likely the drug manufacturer's date and is the one that should be followed.

Care should always be taken when disposing of medications; the best way to dispose of expired medication is to return it to the pharmacist for appropriate disposal. The second best way is to flush it down the toilet. It is never a good idea to simply throw it in the trash, because someone might retrieve it, try to use it, and be harmed by it in some way.

MEDICATION COSTS AND GENERIC VERSUS BRAND NAMES

The cost of medication is both a personal and political issue. There is wide recognition that medical costs must be brought under control, although much debate remains as to the best way of doing so (Serafini, 2000a). As the cost of medication increases, so does interest in using less expensive generic formulations over the more expensive brand-name products. Although switching sounds simple enough, there are many issues that need to be addressed in order for consumers to make educated decisions. For the most part there remains widespread confusion over whether there is a difference between brand name and generic medications, and whether one medication might be more effective than the other. For many consumers, the decision to go with the generic brand is based on the simple fact that they cannot afford the brand-name medication, or they were given the generic without being consulted. Many companies and public agencies (e.g., the Veterans Administration and military-based pharmacies) are now buying medications in bulk, making use of cheaper generic alternatives over brand-name medications a common practice. According to the principles of this cost-saving feature, the switch is justified because the generic is considered equally effective therapeutically when compared to the brand name. Other system variables that support the switch include predetermination based on insurance reimbursement, related to the formulary of the plan. Regardless of the reason for utilizing or changing to a generic medication, many consumers, as well as MTPs and NMTPs, do not understand what the difference really is between the two products.

What exactly *is* the difference between the brand name and the generic? Creation of a brand-name medication starts with original proprietary research and testing, as well as marketing investments that can be quite costly for the manufacturer (Watson-Heidari, 2000). The average cost, taking into account regulatory requirements and funding the research, to bring a new medication to the market is estimated at $350 million (O'Malley, Trimble, & Browning, 2005). In exchange for this expense and all of the work, the manufacturer hopes to receive FDA approval and a specified time period for exclusive use of the drug patent. During this period of time, no generic drugs that utilize the same ingredients originally under patent can be created. Some manufacturers have been allowed to extend their patent or reward time on the grounds that newer, more extensive testing periods are required. Serafini (2000b) warns that granting this extension violates the Drug Price Competition and Patent Term Restoration Act (commonly referred to as the Hatch–Waxman Act), which allows the generic to be made available when the brand-name market time has expired. The fear is that these increased patent protection periods for brand-name medication manufacturers will lead to increased medication prices, because there will be no competition from generic drugs (Banta, 2000).

The FDA was first to approve two-thirds of the new drugs that have been introduced worldwide (Deyo, 2004). In addition, the FDA is trying to speed up the review period so that what used to take 2–3 years now takes 12 months. The actual process, however, of how a medication is approved was considered a mystery until the FDA became the focus of some critical medical attention: It was accused of accepting gratuities from pharmaceutical companies to expedite approval of their new brand-name medications (Heller, 1993). However, representatives of the FDA argue that the actual clinical trial time for a drug to be tested has really increased because clinical trials must now include women, older adults, people with kidney failure, and other population groups that previously were not included in the testing process. The FDA's drug approval process has come under even further scrutiny as Canada moves closer to beginning concurrent drug reviews. During 2005 and 2006 it is expected that drug manufacturers will be allowed to submit materials at the same time to both the United States and Canada in an attempt to speed up the drug approval process (Regulatory System, 2005).

Generic drugs that are less expensive copies of the brand-name medication are always called by their chemical name. The use of this chemical name can cause some confusion among consumers because the chemical names are not nearly as "catchy" and easy to remember as the brand name, and the brand name (which is different) is generally discarded. The

Federal Trade Commission in Washington, DC reported that generic versions are available for about one-half of all the medications on the market (Watson-Heidari, 2000). The production cost of a generic drug is so much less because all the drug research and development has been completed; almost all of the initial testing and marketing information generated by the original manufacturer carries over to the generic manufacturer. Once open for replication, several different manufacturers may seek approval of these generic medications (see Table 2.5). The FDA only requires that the generic formulation have the same active ingredients, strength, and dosage form of the brand-name medication it duplicates (Watson-Heidari, 2000).

TABLE 2.5
Protocol for Approval of Brand-Name Prescription Medications and Generic Equivalents

1. Brand-name drug is developed.
2. Drug company conducts testing and submits results to the FDA.
3. Company receives time-limited patent with exclusive production rights from FDA.
4. Time limit ends and patent expires.
5. For drugs approved by the FDA and now available to the publish, application for active-ingredient-equivalent generic drugs can now be filed and approved.

The equivalency between generic and brand-name drugs is a statistical one. Simply stated, "There is no difference between generic and brand name drugs on the odds that there will be something found wrong with the amount of the active ingredient or the purity" (Public Citizens' Health Research Group, 1993, p. 679). Keeping this information in mind, are brand-name and generic medications truly equivalent? From a statistical perspective, they are. Generic drugs are required to have the same active ingredients, dose, and strength of the brand-name drugs they replicate. The generic medication can be thought of as a "no frills" version, and the differences may not seem obvious to consumers until they actually use it. For example, a brand-name medication might be coated to mask the taste of the pill, whereas the generic may not have the same coating or any coating at all. For the consumer who is used to taking the brand-name pill with a specific coating, the lack of coating or the noted difference between the tastes of the two may trigger aversion. In addition, the brand-name fillers are not included in the generic, and the resulting taste difference can trigger a reaction, and the assumption that this is not the same proper medication as before. This taste issue is particularly relevant for the consumer who is reluctant to take the medicine in the first place.

Because the FDA requires that only the chemical composition of active ingredients be the same, the color, shape, and size of the generic medication may differ. It is the *inactive ingredients* that are used to hold the pill together or to maintain shape (Watson-Heidari, 2000). These changes can be outwardly noticeable to the consumer; something as seemingly simple as switching from a brand-name to a generic medication could create compliance issues that could go virtually unanticipated by the intervention team. For other consumers, switching the medication from a brand name to a generic, either with or without their consent, could surprise them and cause increased worry about different or additional side effects that might result. NMTPs, similar to MTPs, need to educate themselves about the differences between generic and brand-name medications in order to make educated choices and anticipate reactions to pills perceived as being different.

In virtually all U.S. states, there are laws that allow pharmacists to substitute generic drugs for brand-name products. Some states actually require that, if a generic is available, it must be substituted (Watson-Heidari, 2000). If a consumer does not want a generic medication, or the health care provider does not want the consumer to have one, the prescription should be specific in stating this fact. If no changes are permitted, the prescription should say, "Dispense as written" or "Do not substitute"; these words require the pharmacist to fill the prescription with the brand-name product requested.

When working with consumers or their family members, clarifying insurance and medication reimbursement potential is critical. This can mean helping consumers to interpret pamphlets that outline their insurance coverage or to call the insurance benefits office to clarify its policy. Often simply helping to determine what, when, and under which circumstances medication(s) will be covered by insurance facilitates informed practice. Caution is advised, however: although becoming aware of, and utilizing, information such as cost is crucial to practice reality, it should not be expected as standard practice.

If the cost-saving incentive to switch from a brand-name to a generic brand is accepted, the rationale is simple. On the surface, it is clear that the generic medications are less expensive and are generally considered as equally effective therapeutically as the brand name. For others the selection process may be predetermined by insurance reimbursements that dictate which medications are included in the plan's formulary and are covered under a current health care plan. Regardless of the reason, the desire to save money should never override the need for efficient and effective medication.

Medication use is a major economic enterprise in the United States. Recent estimates place medications/pharmaceuticals as a $40 billion/year industry, with an additional $7 billion spent on OTC drugs (Goode, 1992b). When looking specifically at mental health, in 2003 spending on antidepressant and antipsychotic medications increased 11.9% and 22.1%, respectively, whereas overall medication spending only increased 11.5% (IMS Health, 2005). When seeking medical care, it is estimated that three out of four doctor visits result in prescriptions. This high demand, in turn, reinforces the power of the pharmaceutical companies in setting prescription prices.

In summary, to help control medication costs, consumers should be reminded to read and interpret pamphlets that outline their insurance coverage, and when concerns are noted, they should be encouraged to call their insurance benefits office for clarification. Helping consumers determine what, when, and under what circumstances medication will be covered by insurance helps them make informed self-care decisions. When consumers cannot afford to pay for medication, they will try to cut corners or simply avoid taking it altogether; hence, it is important to discourage a practice of letting cost completely determine prescribing patterns. Still, cost is an important issue in deciding whether to use a generic or brand-name medication and should always be considered within the therapeutic decision-making process.

QUICK TIPS:
Using Medication Wisely

- When working with a consumer who is taking medications, be sure to remind him or her to carefully read the label on a new bottle or the package insert. With prescription medications, be sure that the consumer has received a written synopsis of the drug, including usage and side effects. Because manufacturers are always updating ingredients, encourage the consumer to read the printouts or bottles each time the prescription is refilled.

- Cost of a medication is always a concern for the consumer. Encourage the consumer to ask the pharmacist to clarify information regarding the cost and dosage of medications.

- Advise consumers to discard outdated medications properly. Instead of flushing the medication down the toilet, return it to the pharmacy for disposal or dispose of it so that it will not be used improperly if found.

- Advise consumers to follow the recommended dosing guidelines. This guidelines is particularly important for those who self-medicate and use nonprescription or herbal preparations.

- When consumers are taking multiple medications, encourage them to create a chart outlining what and when medications should be taken, and post it in a visible place. Once taken, the consumer can check off the daily dose.

- Encourage consumers to never skip doses, share medicines, or take pills or other medications without being aware of their possible effects.

- Empower consumers and their families to ask relevant questions related to medication use, such as

  —What is the name of the medication?

  —Why is it being taken, and what food and beverages should be taken, or must be avoided, with use?

  —Is there a generic available? What is the cost when compared to other similar medications in its class?

- Be sure to educate consumers on the warnings that may accompany OTC drugs and herbal preparations and that it is possible to become addicted and develop tolerance to nonprescription medications.

3

The Role of the Non-medically Trained
Mental Health Provider

Consumers are diverse in many ways—age, gender, education, personal experiences, cultural mores and values, and personal tastes and choices all account for distinctive differences between individuals. This makes the role of the NMTP essential in gathering information that supports understanding the *whole* person.

UNDERSTANDING CULTURE AND PERSON-IN-SITUATION

Helping professions such as social work have long stressed the importance of the "person-in-environment" perspective because it allows practitioners to understand some of these differences from the perspective of a cultural lens (Colby & Dziegielewski, 2004). Integrating this framework when addressing a consumer's medication regime in the therapeutic relationship becomes a crucial component of the intervention and ensures that any medication difficulties related to cultural or religious beliefs are addressed. The more a consumer trusts the helping providers, the more the consumer will comply by following the routine and taking medications as prescribed. Because neither the use of psychosocial interventions nor medications is an exact science, both types of intervention will require professional application and ongoing monitoring. Medication use as a sole modality of treatment is not recommended; situational or environmental factors always need to be considered. To put it simply, the consumer may be feeling better, but he or she still needs to address, with the NMTP's help, the cultural, religious, or other situational factors that will continue to arise and influence his or her life.

The person-in-environment or person-in-situation approach is an important stance for NMTPs to take. From this viewpoint the consumer is seen in context, as connected to the environment or situation, and any type of intervention or strategy that does not include this perspective will fall short of the ideal. The consumer's total biopsychosocial and spiritual environment is considered. In the psychological domain, the consumer suffering from mental health symptoms experiences feelings of anxiety, self-doubt, frustration, hopelessness, inadequacy, and many other difficult emotions. Although medication may alleviate the physiological symptoms of the mental illness, the individual still must be able to identify, understand, and resolve the psychological and emotional remnants of the illness. Not only can psychosocial intervention (in combination with medication) help the consumer with this process; it can also assist him or her in developing new coping skills to handle similar situations and stresses in the future. Consumers experiencing mental health symptoms often report feeling alienated and isolated from friends, social support systems, and their spiritual frame of reference. Again, medication can address their biological symptoms but not necessarily their social and spiritual functioning.

To address the person-in-environment or person-in-situation perspective, the NMTP must first recognize the influence of culture. Culture is the sum total of life patterns passed from generation to generation within a group of people, and includes institutions, language, religious ideals, habits of thinking, artistic expressions and patterns of social and interpersonal relationships (Colby & Dziegielewski, 2004). During the assessment process, the NMTP must be careful not to base the assessment on his or her own values, beliefs, societal biases, or stereotypes. Just as the consumer can have biases, so can the NMTP. Be sure, as an NMTP, that you identify your own cultural beliefs and biases and ascertain whether these might influence the needs of the consumer.

Readers are encouraged to seek out additional information pertaining to clinical practice and medication therapy with a focus on special populations, including minority consumers. Although there is extensive literature on medications, more information is needed about how special populations (e.g., women, certain minority groups, children, older people) respond to medications. When addressing women, in particular, most individuals remember the thalidomide tragedy that occurred in the 1950s. This drug trial resulted in abnormalities in the babies of women who had been exposed to diethylstilbestrol (DES). In response to this tragedy in clinical drug use, the FDA prohibited women of childbearing age from being engaged in any further type of clinical drug testing. Although the National Institute of Health Revitalization Act of 1993 changed that policy and now drug trials include mandates that women of childbearing age be included in these studies, the literature on this population still remains limited (Hendrick & Gitlin, 2004). This conservative approach regarding women in their childbearing years has led to gaps in our understanding of gender differences in dosing, metabolism, and the impact of the female menstrual cycle on medication efficacy.

> **QUICK TIPS:**
> **Understanding Culture**
>
> - When you interact with any consumer, be sure to be aware of your own cultural expectations or biases.
>
> - As you identify the problem a consumer is having, be sure to take a moment to write down what you believe about the consumer's condition.
>
> - Review your interpretation of the consumer's problem and be sure to answer the question as to whether your beliefs could cloud your ability to facilitate consumer self-determination and provide services from a nonjudgmental position.

The beliefs of consumers about the role of drug therapy in curing or controlling their disease or in promoting their health are intimately linked to their beliefs about disease causation (Eisenhauer, 1998). Providing care without regard to cultural sensitivities, or practicing therapeutic interventions while utilizing a narrow cultural lens, could possibly result in erroneous interpretation of a minority consumer's traditions and problem-solving processes as abnormal or dysfunctional (Colby & Dziegielewski, 2004).

For instance, in some countries in the old "iron-curtain" era, psychiatric intervention was sometimes used to control or silence dissenters;

**QUICK TIPS:
Incorporating Cultural
Influences**

- Ask the consumer about his or her personal beliefs in regard to individuals who suffer from mental health problems.

- Ask the consumer what types of mental health treatment cause him or her the most concern.

- Ask the consumer what would stop him or her from following the medication regimen outlined.

- Ask the consumer if he or she has an informal support system that could provide nontraditional therapeutic services (e.g., some consumers may request a spiritual counselor or member of the clergy to provide support as well as specific rituals and possibly herbal remedies to cure the emotional and psychological ills that they feel accompany the illness).

some people from those lands may have a fear of psychiatry that seems at odds with the more benign image of it in Western cultures. Some traditional societies consider some conditions (such as pregnancy) or illness (such as cancer) to be highly embarrassing; people from these cultures may find frank discussion of these matters to be rather shocking, whereas an American or European might discuss these quite casually. It is always important to assess whether cultural or religious preferences, and other contextual factors, could affect medication regimens and response. For the most part, the most important clinical tip for the NMTP is to be careful not to use a cookie-cutter approach to the challenge of understanding how cultural expectations and biases can affect the helping relationship.

PROFESSIONAL AND NONPROFESSIONAL SOURCES OF INFORMATION

With the abundance of information now available on the Internet to the professional and nonprofessional/lay community, NMTPs need to verify that all information comes from realistic, trusted, and comprehensive sources of information. These responsible sources need to provide the consumer and NMTP with a working knowledge on the basics of how medications can and should work. From a professional perspective, as mentioned in the previous chapter, medication use is not an exact science. When information is gathered from non-peer-related sources such as the Internet or self-help nonreferred pamphlets, misconceptions and bias can result (Sadavoy, 2004). Even using a more professional source can have drawbacks. MTPs frown on the practice of merely lifting information about a particular drug verbatim from the PDR. Most of the drug information listed in this book is compiled and supplied by drug manufacturers. This relationship makes researcher bias a primary concern because much of the information gained from drug development and testing is used for marketing purposes. All those engaged in research agree that researcher bias is a factor that must always be acknowledged and controlled, whenever possible. When the person who makes the money does the testing, constant controls and healthy skepticism of the results should be expected. Bottom line: The information gathered from professional source material that is manufacturer-promoted and supported should be supplemented with professional peer-reviewed sources.

A second area of concern is the vast and sometimes conflicting information available to the public on medications increases the possibility for misinformation or misinterpretation. Acquiring self-help information via the Internet is now commonplace and allows consumers and NMTPs to have easier access to a wealth of information on medication. The Internet has also become a supplier of prescription and nonprescription and herbal medications; no physician's visit is necessary (Associated Press, 1998). Although this type of access reinforces the consumer's right to information and control over his or her own health and mental health, it also makes it easier to bypass professional oversight and safeguard. In short, ensuring competent and effective use of medications remains a complicated challenge (Friebert & Greely, 1999; Pray, 2003). Although consumer self-determination is always highly encouraged, consumers should also be advised to approach all information with caution—especially when it is from non-peer-reviewed sources such as newspapers, television, or the Internet (Larkin, 1996; Sadavoy, 2004). Many Internet sources are essentially anonymous, and some have obscure or eccentric agendas; and many reporters lack expertise. Therefore, it is not uncommon for some of the informational claims found on these Websites to be misleading and unsubstantiated (Dziegielewski, 2003; Larkin, 1996).

The market is now filled with non-peer-related sources designed to help consumers make choices about a medication. When a consumer self-diagnoses a problem, however, he or she has no objective help to investigate whether a particular medication is appropriate for his or her specific and unique situation. The NMTP can play a critical supportive role in helping consumers to secure accurate and relevant product information and to assist them in interpreting it. Ethical professional practice responsibility mandates that all MTPs and NMTPs help consumers obtain the most recent and updated information possible, to enable them to determine the credibility of the information and the appropriateness of the medication for them. Consumers are asking more informed questions, and those in the helping services are being expected to have the answers. To assist consumers in determining the reliability of the information gathered from disparate sources, the FDA suggests asking the following six questions (Larkin, 1996):

1. *Who maintains the site from which the information is gathered?* It is suggested that government or university-based sites offer the most scientifically sound information. Remember that private sources may have their own entrepreneurial agenda for promoting or marketing a product that may not be appropriate for each and every consumer. This caveat is particularly important when reading and interpreting information on herbal remedies offered for preventive or therapeutic purposes. The FDA does not (generally) monitor these products and the claims made of them (Zink & Chaffin, 1998).

2. *Is there a professional body responsible for reviewing the contents of the Website?* Do the health care providers who review the site have a direct connection to the site? (i.e., are they hired by, or work as employees of, the site?) Or are they considered independent professionals? An independent provider is more likely to review the contents of the site from a more objective perspective. Are other references made to professional journals or researchers that support what the site is saying? Can the professional individual(s) or researchers scientists who review the site be contacted for additional information or clarification?

3. *Is there a link to other sources of information that can be used to support or supplement what is provided in the site?* Again, be sure these referral sources are also reputable and well established.

4. *How often is the site updated?* All sites that describe medications or other medical information should be updated at least monthly. As Henkel (1998) noted, so much of what we know about medication reactions, in particular, comes from what we learn after a product is marketed.

5. *Does the site supplement medical information with any type of multimedia presentation that can facilitate understanding and interpretation of the product?* The more ways information is presented (e.g., brief video, flyers, article download), the more understandable it will become for the consumer.

6. *Does the site charge a fee for access?* Before paying such a fee, be sure to determine if it is really worthwhile to pay for such a service, given that so many sites are available to the public free of charge. In addition, it is important to remember that just because a fee is attached to the accessing of certain information does not mean the information is trustworthy. All providers need to warn consumers to remain cautious about purchasing products that and advertised as "the miracle cure" or promise that simply taking a pill can solve their problem(s). Exaggerated statements or false claims about medications can set up a climate of false pretense and doomed expectation; any claims that seem unrealistic should be scrutinized thoroughly.

Investigating whether all information has been shared is as important as evaluating the information obtained. Many consumers will take OTC medications/herbal treatments and not inform the health care worker responsible for their health care. It is common to think of herbal preparations as "natural and safe" and therefore harmless; consumers take these preparations because they believe they will lead to improved health. However, many OTC medications/herbal treatments may interact negatively with prescription medications. For example, some herbal preparations such as St. John's wort can create mild serotonin poisoning when mixed with prescription medications such as SSRIs for depression, creating highly undesirable herb–drug interactions (Fugh-Bergman, 2000). Consumers should be reminded to write down all the medications and treatments they are taking and the source of their information on products. This information should later be shared with the health care provider or the interdisciplinary team in order to determine whether the products are indicated for a particular consumer and compatible with his or her medical, mental, social and environmental situation.

TAKING A MEDICATION HISTORY

As part of the assessment process, MTPs and the NMTPs are expected to take a medication history that includes information on the consumer's pattern of medication use, preferences, and abuse. Identifying a pattern of high risk or a potential for medication abuse allows the NMTP to share important information with the medication prescriber, who, in turn, can anticipate possible problems and determine the most effective medication and dosage. When taking a medication history, it is important to elicit *all* medications that a consumer is taking, including prescription and nonprescription drugs, as well as drugs for chronic conditions. For example, a consumer may take aspirin for arthritis pain and not consider it important enough to mention. Recording aspirin as a medication is important because it can interact with certain blood pressure or anticoagulant medications (e.g., Coumadin), diabetes medications (e.g., Diabenese), and mood stabilizers (e.g., valproic acid; *Physicians' Desk Reference*, 2004). Also ask the consumer if he or she is taking any herbal preparations or nontraditional drugs that are (perhaps incorrectly) assumed to be safe.

In addition, consider substances that consumers may not consider worth mentioning. For example, caffeine has been noted to decrease the antipsychotic effects of medications. Cigarette smoking has been linked to decreased levels of antidepressant and antipsychotic medications in the blood. OTC medications should also be documented, particularly antacids, which may lead to decreased absorption of antipsychotic medications. Needless to say, it is important to document *all* medications and herbal products that a consumer is taking, even the ones that may not be considered "real" medications—including vitamins and diet supplements. (It can be convenient to ask consumers to fill out a form such as the one shown on page 58.)

Although the formats have changed, documenting medication history for maintaining case continuity remains a professional priority

(Dziegielewski, 2002a, 2004; Kagle, 1995). Good record-keeping can provide a map of where the consumer and worker have traveled in their intervention journey. Understanding and recording the consumer's problems (in a culturally sensitive way), the counseling and medication interventions used, and the consumer's progress enable the NMTP to assess the interventions, recommend adjustments in medications, and make necessary changes in the counseling strategies.

Among the various methods of record-keeping, health care facilities frequently use a problem-oriented format. Developed first in medical settings, this method of record-keeping was used to encourage interdisciplinary collaboration and to train medical professionals (Weed, 1969). Providers who work in interdisciplinary health care and mental health settings find that problem-oriented record-keeping enables them to comply with the facility's documentation requirements. This format emphasizes worker accountability through brief and concise documentation of consumer problems, services or interventions provided, and consumer responses. With its emphasis on brevity and its numerous formats, problem-oriented record-keeping is compatible with the increase in consumer caseloads, the increasing need for rapid assessments, and the time-limited treatment of managed care (Dziegielewski, 1998).

By taking brief, informative notes, the NMTP can provide comprehensive summaries of treatment progress. As part of good record-keeping, the NMTP should ask consumers, on a regular basis, about the positive and negative effects of their mental health medications. Following is a list of sample questions:

- Are you taking the medication as prescribed?
- Did you make any changes in dosage or frequency directions?
- When was the last time you took the medication?
- Have you noticed any positive or negative effects from the medication?
- Are you clear on what the medication is supposed to accomplish?
- How do you feel about taking medication?
- Do you believe your family and/or friends support your medication use?

Sample Medication Assessment Form

Name: _____

Practitioner's Name: _____

Date: _____

Medication/ Preparation	Dose	Times/Day	When Taken	Why Taken (what is it for?)
Prescription Medications				
_____	_____	_____	_____	_____
_____	_____	_____	_____	_____
_____	_____	_____	_____	_____
Over-the-Counter Medications				
_____	_____	_____	_____	_____
_____	_____	_____	_____	_____
_____	_____	_____	_____	_____
Herbal or Natural Preparations (including caffeine)				
_____	_____	_____	_____	_____
_____	_____	_____	_____	_____
_____	_____	_____	_____	_____
Vitamins and Mineral Supplements				
_____	_____	_____	_____	_____
_____	_____	_____	_____	_____
_____	_____	_____	_____	_____

Medications that are currently being taken should be distinguished from those that have been taken in the past. Generally, a time frame of at least 3 months is recommended for documentation of past medication use. Because many consumers may have trouble remembering, especially when they have taken multiple medications, be supportive and encourage them to search for any medication bottles, prescriptions, or product descriptions that will provide more accurate information.

NMTPs are not usually responsible for documenting the medication history. Nevertheless, I cannot overemphasize the importance of keeping careful records that support the work of the interdisciplinary team. It is anticipated that the increased emphasis on effective treatment and outcome by managed care and regulatory organizations will require NMTPs to include specific medication information in counseling documentation (Dziegielewski & Leon, 2001).

An Exercise for NMTPs

Complete a medication assessment for either yourself or a family member.

1. Write down all medications that are being taken on a 3" x 5" index card or create a computer file of the information.
2. Describe the purpose of the medication, how the drug works, its potential side effects, the dosage being taken, the expected dosage range, and any precautions that must be noted.
3. List any medication benefits or side effects experienced.
4. Explain how the side effects were handled.

In addition, consumers should be given opportunities to ask questions about their medications and to express any concerns. Having consumers explain their understanding of the medication therapy can increase their compliance with the medication regimen. Addressing these questions also provides important information that is then documented in the consumer's record and is available to the medication prescriber and other health care team members for coordinating and maximizing the treatment experience.

The primary care physician or nurses are generally responsible for documenting medication progress notes. According to Ouslander, Osterweil, and Morley (1998), these MTPs often gather the following information: the clinical effectiveness of the drug and any side effects; periodic measurement of various clinical parameters (e.g., pulse, blood pressure, postural blood pressure); and periodic laboratory studies.

One of the most valuable function of this documentation process is to alert team members to possible problems in how the consumer is responding to the medication. For example, let's assume that a consumer has been prescribed a pain medication to be taken prn (only as needed). During a visit with his NMTP, the consumer reports that he is in so much pain that he is taking the medication every 2–4 hours. This information is immediately documented and shared with the intervention team. The team and prescriber can then decide if this 2–4-hour schedule is the best way to administer the medication, if the medication is really needed on such a regular basis, whether another stronger medication might be more beneficial; and if there is any potential for abuse or dependence.

The key to documenting medication and counseling strategies is to maintain brevity yet still provide informative data. Only the most salient issues relevant to consumer care and progress should be recorded. Information should focus directly on the content covered in therapeutic sessions and on the interplay of the consumer's progress with the medication and counseling interventions. Always link the therapeutic interventions to the original problems, goals, and objectives. Providing brief, accurate, and informative documentation that includes both counseling and medication interventions requires skill and training. These honed observation skills will assist the medication prescriber and other health care and mental health team members in providing the most effective interventions.

LESSONS LEARNED AFTER ADVERSE EFFECTS

Lessons can be learned—indeed, should be learned—from prior misuses of medication. Redux and fenfluramine were distributed and prescribed repeatedly for weight loss, even after warnings that not enough was known about them. The FDA approved fenfluramine as safe for short-term use in 1973. The assumption for its use was that it would be prescribed for severely obese consumers who were not responding to other forms of treatment. Contrary to this assumption, the drug was prescribed to many consumers who were not obese but were seeking a quick fix to address their weight problem. With this increased attention, many physicians readily obliged and dispensed prescriptions for this purpose (Lumpkin, 1997). Then studies reported that the combination of fenfluramine and phentermine (an anorexiant) (fen/phen), would help shed the pounds faster and with fewer side effects. Although the FDA had not approved this drug "combo," it became one of the hottest selling remedies for overweight consumers in the drug industry. When Redux (the brand-name version of the fenfluramine–phentermine combination) was approved by the FDA in 1996, it was not long before 2.5 million prescriptions had been written, and the number of people exposed to the drug rose to 60 million worldwide. In July of that same year Mayo Clinic researchers reported serious heart-valve damage in 24 Redux users. Eventually 30% of the 291 users of the drug combination reported the same problems (Golden, 1997). After this news the drug was recalled. Golden (1997) raises interesting points when he questions who should be held accountable for this serious error. The FDA is particularly to blame for approving it, given that initially it received a vote of 5 in favor to 3 against, and serious misgivings from researchers had been reported. Also, the drug companies that produced, tested, and marketed the drug promoted the pills while knowing that more research was needed (Pray, 2003). The physicians and diet/weight control programs eagerly dispensed them, even prescribing the medications to consumers for whom they were never intended. The blame could also be placed with those marketing the medication, who depicted and promoted the pills as miracle combinations. Regardless of where the blame is placed, consumers were harmed; and manufacturers, who were assumed to act in the best interest of consumers, did not.

As providers, we need to develop a risk–benefit ratio for each consumer, always keeping in mind the possibility of individualized, even idiosyncratic, responses and that prescribing is not an exact science.

MedWatch: Filing a Professional or Consumer Report

MedWatch is a program sponsored by the FDA that conducts postmarketing surveillance. Through this program, health care providers can share safety concerns on products that may require formal action (Henkel, 1998, 1999). Because initial testing for medication side effects prior to market release is limited, programs such as MedWatch are needed to follow up on medication reactions that take place once the product is on the market.

Purpose of MedWatch Program

- To clarify the parameters of what should be reported to the FDA.
- To increase awareness about serious reactions caused by drugs or medical devices, and make it easier to report adverse drug reactions.
- To give the health community a continuous feedback mechanism for reporting product safety issues.

Note: Information from Henkel, 1999.

A report is filed when there is a suspicion or evidence that a serious adverse reaction has occurred (Henkel, 1999). Generally, the type of reaction to report is one that was not evident during initial drug trials, was not expected to be a common side effect, and therefore does not appear in the product handout.

When to File a MedWatch Report

An immediate report to MedWatch is considered warranted if one or more of the following occurs:

- *Death*: If you believe that using a medication or medical device is the suspected cause of a consumer's death.
- *Life-threatening hazard*: If a consumer were at risk of death due to the adverse reaction, or if it is suspected that continued use of a product could cause death (e.g., pacemaker failure, an intravenous pump that could cause excessive drug dosing).
- *Hospitalization*: If a consumer is admitted to a hospital because of a severe reaction to a prescribed medication.
- *Disability*: If the adverse reaction results in a significant or permanent change in a person's previous level of functioning.
- *Birth defects, stillbirth, miscarriage, or birth with disease*: If a consumer is exposed to a medication or medical device that leads to any of these problems in the birthing process.
- *Intervention*: If a consumer needs intervention to avoid permanent damage.

Note: Information from U.S. Food and Drug Administration MedWatch, 2005.

A MedWatch report can be filed by mail, fax, or online.

- *By mail.* Use the postage-paid MedWatch form, which includes the address. To obtain copy of the form, call MedWatch at 800-332-1088 and request that one be sent by mail or fax.
- *By fax.* The fax number for MedWatch is 800-332-0178. Be sure to use the form. Any serious or adverse reaction can also be reported to the product manufacturer, who by law is required to report it to the FDA.
- *Online.* Go to the MedWatch Website at *www.fda.gov/medwatch/* and follow the directions for submitting a report electronically.

The reporter is not required to demonstrate or substantiate the reaction, but he or she needs to determine, based on his or her professional expertise, that it has occurred and that future incidents are possible. Because the FDA usually asks for technical follow-up information on a report, it prefers that a trained health care provider, rather than a nontrained consumer, makes the report.

Once a MedWatch report has been filed, the FDA may take any of the following actions:

- *Issue medical alerts.* Medical alerts provide valuable product safety information to physicians, pharmacists, and other health providers or practitioners as well as to trade and media groups.
- *Require label changes.* The manufacturer may be required to add or change product information on all current product labels.
- *Create prominent or boxed warnings on packaging and product information.* The FDA can require that these warnings be placed in a prominent place so that physicians, health care providers, and consumers are aware of their important information.
- *Withdraw product.* When warranted, the FDA has the power to require the company to withdraw its product from the marketplace immediately and permanently.

Part II

MENTAL HEALTH
PRESCRIPTION MEDICATIONS

4

Medications Used to Treat Depression Disorders

It is estimated that approximately 20% of the population will suffer from clinical depression at some point in their lifetime (Ables & Baughman, 2003). Symptoms relating to depression are reported so often during routine medical visits and throughout the course of psychological treatment that many in the medical community have come to refer to depression as the *common cold of mental health*. In the primary care setting, up to 30% of all consumers report seeking help for depressive symptoms (Tierney, McPhee, & Papadakis, 1997). "Clinical depression" can be defined, simply, as a condition wherein the depressive symptoms are severe enough to affect the consumer's daily activities. In clinical depression the consumer experiences a lack of desire, coupled with an inability to perform everyday social and occupational tasks. For instance, the consumer may lose his appetite and lose weight rapidly. Or the consumer may report having so little energy that he or she neglects basic hygiene needs, such as bathing. Working with this population can be frustrating, because many times these individuals have complaints that are generally somatic in nature (e.g., vague aches and pains that cannot be explained medically). But when given a medical exam, the results are negative and reveal no physical causes for the problem. This multifaceted disorder provides fertile ground for misunderstandings and frustration for consumers, providers, and family members alike. To complicate the matter, many individuals who suffer from clinical depression once can expect a recurrence (Mauri et al., 2003).

When dealing solely with depressive symptoms, the term *unipolar* depression is used. In all forms of clinical depression, the degree of depression must clearly disrupt an individual's daily activities and significantly affect most areas of the individual's social and occupational life. Traditionally, this type of depression has been referred to as major depression, or, according to the *DSM-IV-TR*, major depressive disorder (American Psychiatric Association, 2000).

Two types of major depression have been postulated. The first is often referred to as *endogenous* (previously melancholic) depression. In this type, symptoms of depressed mood are related directly to internal biological factors, such as neurotransmitter dysfunction (Kaplan & Sadock, 1990; Tierney et al., 1997). Electroconvulsive therapy (ECT), referred to historically as shock therapy, has been used to treat this type of depression. Direct (biological) stimulation of the neurotransmission process can be an effective treatment strategy. The use of ECT to treat endogenous depression is explored later in this chapter. The second and the most common method of addressing endogenous depression is the use of antidepressant medications. Similar to ECT, medications also address depression from an endogenous or biological perspective; the major difference is that medications affect neurotransmitter pathways chemically rather than electrically (Maxmen & Ward, 1995).

A second type of depression, often referred to as *exogenous, environmental,* or *reactive* depression, is generally linked to a precipitating event involving psychosocial stressors such as divorce, unemployment, or injury (Tierney et al., 1997).

Exploring the type of depression can be helpful in determining treatment intervention. If the symptoms can be clearly related to exogenous or external factors, solely psychopharmacological treatment would be short-sighted. For MTPs and NMTPs alike, it is always helpful to differentiate, as much as possible, between depression that is related to internal causes versus one that is related to external or environmental causes. Although both conditions may have similar symptoms, individual attributions are likely to differ. In endogenous depression the individual might report low self-esteem that is marked by a sense of worthlessness and guilt; in contrast, in exogenous depression the consumer is less likely to suffer from low self-esteem and more likely to suffer from a sense of hopelessness or helplessness in regard to a certain life event or circumstance. Exogenous or reactive factors such as depression related to medical conditions (e.g., HIV) can clearly complicate the diagnostic picture (Pieper & Treisman, 2005).

Understanding clinical depression is further complicated by the varied symptoms and course the disorder may follow. This variation in course and symptoms makes it difficult to determine exactly what constitutes depressive behaviors. Clearly established criteria reflect consistent clinical patterns, signs, and symptoms relative to a mood disorder (Gitlin, 1996). Furthermore, some form of depression (often referred to as dysphoric mood) is present in virtually all mental health conditions, with the possible exceptions of mania and certain forms of schizophrenia (Gitlin, 1996).

RECOGNIZING DEPRESSION-RELATED SIGNS AND SYMPTOMS

The first step toward providing effective intervention for the consumer suffering from depression is to apply a criteria-based assessment to the symptoms of depression described by the consumer. The second step is to evaluate the degree to which the symptoms affect the consumer's activities of daily living (ADLs). When the symptoms exceed what is considered tolerable or normal, clinical depression exists, and direct professional help on how to best deal with these symptoms is warranted. For example, say the consumer reports difficulty sleeping. The NMTP must determine how much difficulty this lack of sleep is actually causing; that is, the level of impairment must be clearly identified. Is it stopping the consumer from going to work or from wanting to socialize with friends or family? How much of this impairment can the consumer tolerate, and what is he or she willing to do to try to reduce it? Sleep disturbances include trouble falling asleep (insomnia) or the opposite, sleeping too much (hypersomnia), in which the person reports sleeping up to 12 hours a night and awaking exhausted.

Many consumers with depression present with dysphoria (a disturbance in mood) or anhedonia (a loss of pleasure or interest in normally enjoyable activities; Maxmen & Ward, 1995). This reduced ability to feel often leads to a wide range of complaints that include feelings of guilt, an inability to concentrate, feelings of worthlessness, helplessness, and hopelessness, and various types of anxiety. In terms of appetite, individuals may complain of having no or little desire to eat, often referred to as *anorexia*; or the opposite, they may report having an increased desire to eat, with an insatiable appetite that propels the ingestion of large quantities of food, often referred to as *gluttony*. When ideas of worthlessness are coupled with changes in sleeping and eating patterns, as well as numerous nonspecific physical complaints, it is no surprise that the consumer may further suffer from chronic fatigue and a lack of desire to participate in forms of physical and sexual activity.

Symptoms reported by the consumer and evaluated by the NMTP must always be viewed in context, in relation to the cultural and stress-related environmental influences that can affect behavior. For example, the probability of experiencing extreme life changes and transitions is high for many older individuals. Loved ones may die or suffer from health issues that either directly of indirectly impact their lives. These individuals may feel uncomfortable revealing their feelings related to this loss, and these feelings may then manifest via the signs and symptoms of depression. The supportive role of the NMTP is essential in identifying the situational factors that might mitigate an overly hasty perception that the mental health symptoms are related to clinical depression. Life transitions and subsequent losses are a normal part of life, but if they are addressed in isolation, they may provide an assessment that is both short-sighted and incomplete.

DIFFERENCES IN ASSESSMENT BETWEEN MALES AND FEMALES

Historically, there has been little differentiation between how males and females experience depression. This view has been challenged, however. For example, Hendrick and Gitlin (2004) outlined several differences between males and females in the expression of depression-related concerns. They reported that females are more likely to express anxiety, guilt, and indecisiveness, whereas males are more likely to express self-criticalness. In addition, males tend to experience the classic signs (also known as *neurovegetative symptoms*) of insomnia and diminished appetite, whereas females often experience atypical signs (also known as *reverse neurovegetative symptoms*), such as increased sleep and appetite. Furthermore, women seem to have more seasonal-related symptoms (e.g., heightened symptoms during the winter months) and symptoms that increase during the childbearing years (Hendrick & Gitlin, 2004). As with any mental health problem, taking into account all relevant factors such as gender can facilitate the formulation of an accurate diagnosis of clinical depression. The complete diagnostic assessment requires that the consumer's cognitive, behavioral, and somatic complaints be clearly documented.

DIFFERENTIATING DEPRESSION FROM BIPOLAR DISORDER

The criteria and definition utilized in this text closely resemble the one outlined by the *DSM-IV-TR* (American Psychiatric Association,

> ### QUICK TIPS:
> #### Comprehensive Screening Questions to Determine Severity of Depression
>
> - Ask the consumer if he or she has been feeling down, depressed, or hopeless during the last month. If so, have these feelings been severe enough to impair routine activities of daily living (i.e., eating, sleeping, focusing on work or chosen task)?
>
> - Ask the consumer to describe several activities that he or she found enjoyable in the past. Next ask if each pleasurable activity, if performed in the present, could still bring enjoyment.
>
> - Ask the consumer what his or her usual day is like. What tasks are completed during the day? Are the depressive symptoms severe enough to affect social or occupational functioning? Do these symptoms represent a change from a previous level of functioning?
>
> - Help the consumer identify all related depressive signs and symptoms. Read a list of these features and ask which ones he or she is experiencing (e.g., appetite disturbance, significant or unintentional weight loss, sleep disturbance, an inability to concentrate, and persistent thoughts of death or suicide). Help the consumer identify the intensity and frequency of each symptom.

2000), in which the diagnosis of depression is based on a history of one or more depressive episodes without the presence of manic or hypomanic symptoms (see Chapter 5 for the bipolar disorders). In assessing depression, it is essential to know the similarities and differences with which consumers who suffer from depression or the bipolar disorders may present. The distinctions are critical and will become clearer after reading the next chapter. Stated simply, if a consumer is misdiagnosed with depression and treated with a medication for such when he or she actually has some type of bipolar disorder, a manic or hypomanic phase could be triggered. This misinterpretation could place the consumer in distress. See Table 4.1 for the symptoms most likely to be present in both the depressive and manic/hypomanic phases.

TABLE 4.1
Differentiating between Depressive and Manic or Hypomanic Symptoms

Symptoms common to both the manic/hypomanic and depressed mood states:
- Disturbances in sleeping and eating habits/patterns: In depressed mood there can be either a lack of appetite or increased appetite; in the hypomanic or manic state, the symptom is almost always decreased appetite or lack of appetite (sometimes referred to as anorexia).
- Disturbed levels of energy: In depressed mood the energy level is often low and sluggish, whereas in the manic or hypomanic state, the opposite will occur—the consumer is often elated and has boundless energy.
- Increased levels of restlessness
- Problems concentrating, easily distracted
- Increased irritability and impatience with others
- Disorientation
- Incoherent speech
- Impaired judgment
- Lack of interest in personal relationships

Symptoms rarely seen in depression but that often occur in manic/hypomanic states:
- Instances of extreme feelings of happiness
- Laughing inappropriately, usually accompanied by agitation
- Pressured talking

continued

TABLE 4.1 (*continued*)

- Racing thoughts—the consumer may report he or she cannot keep up with the influx of thoughts
- Grandiose thinking
- Inflated self-esteem
- Easily excitable
- Indications of violent behavior, or increased activities that are risk taking or destructive
- Bizarre hallucinations (in the manic phase, not the hypomanic)
- Symptoms of panic, including rapid heartbeat, tremor, dizziness, chest pains, nausea, and breathing problems

SELECTING AN MTP

Even with the increased incidence of reporting of depressive symptoms, there are those in the professional practice community who continue to believe that depression is still seriously underdiagnosed (Shell, 2001). However, it is important to question what has driven this increase in reported cases (Currie, 2005), as well as the effectiveness of the medications used to treat the condition. In some cases the medications are associated with a worsening of symptoms related to the disorder (Melander, Ahlquist-Rastad, Meijer, et al., 2003; U.S. Food and Drug Administration, 2004). Selecting the best MTP can be a very difficult process for the consumer. The NMTP can help the consumer to decide from whom or where to seek treatment, what questions to ask, as well as the type of treatment that is best.

Consumers should ask their MTPs the following questions:

- What training and experience does the MTP have in treating depression?
- What is the MTP's basic approach to treatment?
- How long will the consumer need to be treated for depression?
- How long are treatment sessions, and how often will the consumer need to have them?
- What lifestyle changes can help him or her manage depression?
- What resources are available to help the consumer with:

> —Eating a healthful diet
> —Exercising regularly
> —Finding social support
> —Managing stress

- What fees will be charged by the MTP?
- What health insurance does the MTP accept? (If the MTP does not have this information, a referral to the person who does is needed.)
- Does the MTP offer sliding-scale fees to accommodate various financial circumstances?

If the MTP has little experience treating depression, consider asking for referral to an NMTP who is trained in diagnosing and treating depression and can supplement the care the prescriber is giving.

Consumers are bombarded with messages that tout the merits of using antidepressant medications, while playing down the side-effect profiles that are often attached. The message is given that these antidepressant medications, in addition to helping the truly depressed, can provide a type of "cosmetic psychopharmacology" for those who are not *quite* depressed but in need of a personality change (Montagne, 2002). The following clinical tips are intended to help the NMTP guide the consumer. Often the depressed individual cannot easily express what he or she is feeling, so planning for the supports needed to communicate what is being experienced is essential.

MEDICATION INTERVENTIONS FOR DEPRESSION

In this book antidepressant medications are classified into four major groups: (1) tricyclic antidepressants and TCAs, (2) monoamine oxidase inhibitors, or MAOIs, (3) the newer generation of antidepressant drugs, such as selective serotonin reuptake inhibitors (SSRIs), and (4) the newer combination antidepressants, such as selective serotonin and other norepinephrine inhibitors (SSNRIs), (Hendrick & Gitlin, 2004; Tierney et al., 1997). The popularity of these medications, especially the SSRIs and the other newer-generation antidepressants, has risen dramatically. The trend to medicate all depressive symptoms continues to rise, even after current medical treatment guidelines have recommended that depression associated with reactive or external environmental pressures (i.e., exogenous depression) may not require drug therapy (DeGrandpre, 2004). Also, 2004 MedWatch warnings have identified several of the newer SSRI antidepressant medications as of particular concern (U.S. Food and Drug Administration, 2004).

TRICYCLIC ANTIDEPRESSANTS AND CHEMICALLY SIMILAR MEDICATIONS

The first major group of antidepressant medications—tricyclics and chemically related compounds such as the tetracyclics (TCAs) (see Table 4.2)—were discovered in the late 1950s. These drugs, along with monoamine oxidase inhibitors (MAOIs), are considered the oldest drugs in the treatment of depression. The tricyclics were historically used as the first line of medication intervention for unipolar depression (Austrian, 1995). SSRIs and SSNRIs, with their lower side-effect profile, have replaced the tricyclics and TCAs as first-line medications in the treatment of depression (Anderson & Tomenson, 1995). Although tricyclics or TCAs are still

QUICK TIPS
Advice for Consumers

- Recommend that the nervous consumer bring a friend, spouse, or companion to appointments so that this person can make sure important questions get asked. Help the consumer to formulate his or her questions ahead of time so as not to forget them.

- Rehearse what will happen when the consumer meets with the MTP and asks the questions. In reviewing the questions, make any needed clarifications. Sample questions the consumer might ask the prescriber about depression and treatment options:

"What do you see as a possible cause for the symptoms related to depression? What specific things can be done when the symptoms interfere with my ability to function in personal relationships, at work, or in the home life?"

"Could the symptoms I am feeling be related to a physical cause? If so, can I have a physical exam to look for other causes?"

"What are my chances for recovery from depression, with or without treatment?"

"What are the chances of my depression recurring, and is there anything I can do to prevent that from happening?"

prescribed, often they are considered a second- or third-line alternative for the treatment of depression (Diamond, 2002).

Dosage and Course

Tricyclics inhibit the uptake of neurotransmitters such as serotonin, norepinephrine, and dopamine. The tetracyclics, such as Ludiomil (maprotiline), are often classified along with the tricyclics, although the neurochemical response they provoke is slightly different. For example, when specifically using maprotiline at high doses (greater than 225 mg), the risk of seizures would discourage this medication for routine use (Maxmen & Ward, 2002).

When using medications that fall in the class of tricyclics/tetracyclics, Maxmen and Ward (2002) warn that the major mistakes to watch for are inadequate doses and inadequate trial time, so patience with the course of trail and error may be required. Taking into account cautions such as noted with maprotiline, the therapeutic dose generally does not start working for 10–30 days. For most consumers a trial of 10–14 days is usually needed to get the full therapeutic dose, and the full affect might not occur for up to six weeks. Short-term effectiveness is noticeable in most consumers within 2–4 weeks, and the tricyclic drug can be evaluated through changes in blood levels. An increase in the medication is appropriate if the consumer has not experienced any changes in symptoms and is reporting minimal side effects (Gitlin, 1996).

Side-Effect Profiles and Special Considerations

Tricyclics have many side effects because they bind to multiple unrelated receptors (Kent, 2000). Therefore, monitoring the consumer placed on a tricyclic medication should be done carefully. Special attention should be given to whether the medication was effective if used previously, and whether the side effects experienced were tolerable. The most common side effects (that seem to occur across all medications in this class) include constipation, urinary retention, dry mouth, sedation, postural hypotension, cravings for sweets, and weight gain (Gitlin, 1996; Kent, 2000). See Table 4.3 for a comprehensive list of potential side effects. Although tricyclic medications can decrease the symptoms of depression, NMTPs need to educate their consumers on the uncertainty of the potential long-term effects that taking these drugs can have on the body. Some of these side effects can vary among users, so in the assessment process each symptom experienced needs to be identified, reviewed with the list of the most common side effects, and monitored, while the consumer adjusts physiologically and psychologically to the medication.

TABLE 4.2
Overview of Tricyclics and TCAs

Medication	Sedative Effect	Daily Dosage Range[a] (mg)
Elavil, Endep (amitriptyline)	Strong	100–300
Tofranil (imipramine)	Moderate	150–300
Pamelor/Aventyl (nortriptyline)[b]	Mild	75–150
Norpramin/Pertofrane (desipramine)[b]	Mild	150–300
Asendin (amoxapine)	Mild to moderate	200–400
Surmontil (trimipramine)	Mild to moderate	150–300
Ludiomil (maprotiline)[c]	Moderate	150–225

[a]Dosage range suggestions are for adults. All information uses guidelines from Maxmen and Ward, 2002.
[b]These tricyclics have the lowest incidence of side effects and have been considered first-choice medications when selecting from this class of antidepressants.
[c]Ludiomil (maprotiline) is generally listed as a tetracyclic and inhibits norepinephrine reuptake.

One of the greatest concerns with this class of medications is that overdose can be fatal. This possibility is probably the reason that many prescribers now seem to steer away from them, especially because consumers who are severely depressed generally need increased and prolonged dosages (Fugh-Bergman, 2000). Furthermore, there is increased potential for substance abuse among those prone to suicide, so prescriptions dispensed for more than a week at a time should be viewed carefully (Diamond, 2002). Because tricyclics magnify the effect of alcohol, the consumer is likely to feel the effects of alcohol more quickly. Also, when alcohol is combined with these medications, potentially nonfatal doses of the medication can become fatal. In terms of sexual side effects, use of tricyclics has been linked to a decreased libido (sex drive) and impotence.

It is always best to advise consumers not to discontinue this medication without consulting a physician, because rapid withdrawal can produce nausea, vomiting, abdominal cramps, diarrhea, chills, insomnia, and anxiety lasting anywhere from 3 to 5 days (Diamond, 2002).

TABLE 4.3
Possible Side Effects of Tricyclic Antidepressants

Complications	Interactions
• Reactions may vary	• Thyroid hormones
• Can complicate heart problems	• Antihypertensive medications
• Sweating, dryness of the mouth, headache	• Oral contraceptives
• Increased appetite for sweets	• Alcohol and tobacco
• Weight gain, unpleasant taste in mouth	• Some blood coagulants
• Difficulty urinating	• Some sleeping medications
• Changes in sexual desire and decrease in sexual ability	• Antipsychotic medications
• Muscle twitches, fatigue, and weakness	• Diuretics
	• Aspirin
	• Vitamin C
	• Antihistamines
	• Bicarbonate of soda

MONOAMINE OXIDASE INHIBITORS

Monoamine oxidase inhibitors (MAOIs) constitute a group of antidepressant medications that have historically been used to treat severe depressive symptoms (see Table 4.4). According to Diamond (2002), these drugs work by blocking the action of the enzyme that deactivates neurotransmitters that have a single amine group. This is why they are called mono (one) amine oxidase inhibitors. Monoamines stimulate effects that occur in the central nervous system, and by blocking their uptake, more monoamines remain available to the system. Monoamines are divided into two subtypes, A and B (MAO-A and MAO-B), which differ in their substrate specificity (i.e., how the subtype is acted upon in the biochemical reaction).

This classification of medications is considered a third-line treatment for depression (Brophy, 1991; Tierney et al., 1997). There are times, however, that this group of drugs can be utilized as the first line of treatment, but only when the depression is of an atypical nature (i.e., increase in appetite or weight gain as opposed to decreased appetite and weight loss, as in typical depression), or the consumer has not responded to the other classes of medications (Diamond, 2002; Tierney et al., 1997). Early observations suggested that MAOIs were not as effective for consumers with severe depression, and that their side effects were serious and at times life-threatening (Gitlin, 1996). Both these concerns overshadowed later information that indicated that this group of antidepressants can be effective in the treatment of both typical and atypical depression. With the development of the newer antidepressants, the MAOIs have become the third choice of antidepressants. When this group of drugs is prescribed, consumers should be carefully educated about one of the major side effects (hypertension, i.e., high blood pressure) and about specific dietary restrictions: the importance of avoiding foods containing *tyramine* (e.g., herring, aged cheese, salami) and *sympathomimetic* drugs (e.g., cocaine, amphetamines, decongestants) (Maxmen & Ward, 1995) to avoid toxic interactions. For the most part, practice wisdom dictates that MAOIs, with their dangerous treatment-effect profiles, should only be considered after the newer antidepressants and TCAs have been tried (Tierney et al., 1997).

Dosage and Course

The two most commonly used MAOIs are Nardil (phenelzine) and Parnate (tranylcypromine). Both of these medications are often considered useful for the treatment of panic disorder as well as depression. The most frequent complaints with Nardil are weight gain and postural hypotension. Each tablet is 15 mg and the initial dose is usually 15 mg or less, and then gradually increased to 30 mg daily, in divided doses. Most consumers need a minimum of 45 mg daily with a maximum dose of 90 mg (Maxmen & Ward, 2002). Parnate evidences less consumer weight gain and sedative effects. According to the product information in the *Physicians' Desk Reference* (2004), the potential for a hypertensive crisis or problems with hypotension should be monitored closely. The starting dose for this medication is one to two 10 mg tablets, with dosage increases every 3–4 days. Generally, the maintenance dose is 30–60 mg in one or two doses in the morning or early afternoon.

QUICK TIPS:
Recommendations
NMTPs Should Make to Consumers of MAOIs

- Use of this medication should be reevaluated if the consumer has trouble understanding, following, or maintaining the dietary and drug restrictions.

- Be aware of, and immediately report, the abrupt occurrence of any of the following symptoms: occipital headache, palpitations, neck stiffness, tachycardia (i.e., abnormally rapid beating of the heart), bradycardia (i.e., heart beats slower than normal), or other atypical or unusual symptoms not previously experienced.

- Always remind consumers, especially hypertensive consumers, to be cautious and avoid excessive consumption of foods that are high in tyramine content.

Marplan (isocarboxazid) is used similar to the other MAOIs to treat depression. Generally, dosing starts with one tablet (10 mg) given twice a day up to four tablets daily by the end of the first week (Hoffmann-LaRoche, 2005).

Another MAOI, Eldepryl (selegiline), is similar to the others in class. The recommended dose of Eldepryl is 10–20 mg per day, up to 50 mg, generally taken with meals (e.g., breakfast and lunch). Of all the MAOIs, Eldepryl has received the most attention related to its use with individuals who suffer from Parkinson's disease (Waters, 1991). Parkinson's disease involves the progressive degeneration of a particular type of nerve cell that results in muscle rigidity and difficulty walking and talking. At times this medication may be prescribed with Sinemet (levodopa/carbidopa) when Sinemet no longer seems to be working well.

The newest of the medications in this class is Manerix (moclobemide), a short-acting medication that is a reversible inhibitor of monoamine oxidase (MAO or MAOI) (Merriman, 1999). Similar to the other medications in its class, this medicine is often used as an antidepressant; however, it is recommended that depressed consumers in whom agitation is the predominant clinical symptom should not be treated with Manerix.

For adults the average initial dose is 300 mg a day, and generally it is divided: given after meals and divided into two or three equal doses. If needed, the dosage can be increased gradually to a maximum of approximately 600 mg a day. The initial dose is usually given a trial period of approximately a week or so before considering an increase. MTP assessment determines whether the consumer has any type of hepatic disease or is taking drugs, such as cimetidine, that inhibit hepatic microsomal enzymes. Cimetidine blocks the activity of acid-producing cells in the stomach and thereby controls stomach acid. If a consumer is taking an acid-blocking medication, he or she is asked to reduce the daily dose by one-third or one-half of the standard dose.

TABLE 4.4
Monoamine Oxidose Inhibitors

Medication	Daily Dosage Range[a] (mg)
Marplan (isocarboxazid)	10–30
Nardil (phenelzine)[b]	45–60
Eldepryl (selegiline)	20–50
Parnate (tranylcypromine)[b]	20–40
Manerix (moclobemide)	150–600

[a]Dosage range suggestions are for adults. All information uses guidelines from *Physicians' Desk Reference*, 2004, and Maxmen & Ward, 2002.

[b]Nardil and Parnate are the two most commonly used medications of this type (Lehne & Scott, 1996).

NMTPs also need to be aware of the "washout" time that is required if there are plans to switch from one medication in this category of antidepressants to another, particularly when the change involves taking a newer-generation antidepressant, such as an SSRI (Tierney et al., 1997). Not being aware of this washout period could have serious consequences: the development of a hyperserotonergic syndrome, consisting of excitement, diaphoresis, rigidity, hyperthermia, tachycardia, hypertension, and possibly death (Perry & Lund, 2004). To avoid this type of interaction, a 5-week washout period is recommended when switching a patient from an SSRI with a long half-life, such a Prozac (fluoxetine), to an MAOI.

The other SSRIs have shorter washout times due to their shorter half-lives (see Table 4.5 below). Observing these specified periods of time can assist with the discontinuance and can allow for complete elimination of the SSRI from the consumer's system. When the opposite direction is considered and the individual goes from an MAOI to the SSRI, a standard washout period of 10 to 14 days is necessary regardless of which SSRI is used to allow regeneration of monoamine oxidase (Perry & Lund, 2004).

TABLE 4.5
SSRI–MAOI Drug Interaction/Washout Period

	Prozac (fluoxetine)	Luvox (fluvoxamine)	Paxil (paroxetine)	Zoloft (sertraline)	Celexa (citalopram)
SSRI to MAOI	5 weeks	1–2 weeks	1–2 weeks	1–2 weeks	14 days
MAOI to SSRI	10–14 days	10–14 days	10–14 days	10–14 days	14 days

Note: Table adapted from Perry and Lund, 2004.

Side-Effect Profiles and Special Considerations

MAOIs carry a risk of serious reaction, and consumers must be warned about the high potential for interaction with other medications (Kent, 2000). Table 4.6 provides a summary. NMTPs should remind consumers to provide prescribers with a complete account of the different medications they are currently taking, so that prescribers can determine whether an MAOI should be used at all. Information on which dietary and drug products to avoid is essential, because MAOI (those marketed for the treatment of depression) leave consumers vulnerable to exogenous amines (e.g., the tyramine in food items). Dietary and drug restrictions should be reviewed by NMTPs and monitored periodically. Foods to be avoided include most cheese products (except cottage cheese, cream cheese, and fresh yogurt), any fermented or aged meats (e.g., salami, bologna), liver of all types, pickled herring, broad bean pods and Chinese pea pods, meat and yeast extracts, raisins, pineapples, overripe bananas, and chocolate. Beverages to be avoided include red wine, beer, ale, vermouth, cognac, sherry, and coffee (Maxmen & Ward, 2002). Drugs to be avoided include products containing phenylpropanolamine, phenyle-phrine, meperidine, dextromethorphan, and pseudoephedrine. The presence of many of these compounds in OTC cold and allergy preparations makes it all the more essential to ensure that consumers know the danger from toxicity that can occur through drug interactions.

In the limited research available on the newest MAOI medication, it does appear that the blood pressure increase observed during administration of Manerix together with tyramine-enriched food was less than what would be expected after the administration of other currently marketed MAOIs. Because this medication is so new, however, the research remains limited, although it does appear that taking this medication before meals or immediately after meals should be considered. Treatment with Manerix does not necessitate the special dietary restrictions required for other available MAOIs. Regardless, until further studies are carried out, consumers should be cautious and avoid the consumption of excessive amounts of aged or overripe cheese and yeast extracts.

TABLE 4.6
The Most Common Side Effects and Drug Interactions for MAOIs

1. Dizziness and rapid heart rate when changing position (especially when moving from sitting to standing).
2. Interaction with certain food additives, especially monosodium glutamate (MSG).
3. Interaction with OTC cold and allergy preparations, antihistamines, amphetamines, insulin, narcotics, and antiparkinsonian medications.
4. Reactions may not appear for several hours and can include rapid heart rate, high blood pressure, seizures, stroke, or coma.

THE NEWER ANTIDEPRESSANT MEDICATIONS

Compared to other forms of antidepressant medication treatment, the SSRIs and other newer compounds identified to treat depression, such as Effexor (venlafaxine), Remron (mirtazapine), Serzone (nefazodone), and Edronix (reboxetine), are newcomers in the fight against mental disorders (Kent, 2000). This class of drug has rapidly become the most prominent form of antidepressant medication. For example, Prozac (fluoxetine), which was first approved in 1987, has now become one of the most popular antidepressants in use (Jann, Jenike, & Liberman, 1994). With the advent of this class of drug and its ability to target the neurochemical serotonin, it is not surprising that numerous other similar medications, such as Zoloft, Paxil, Celexa, and Luvox, soon followed. With the increased number of antidepressants available, the fear as to whether this trend could have a negative affect, by discouraging alternate and equally effective forms of treatment, continues to grow (Moore, 2002). Some critics state that these newer antidepressants have the potential to become "as familiar as Kleenex and as socially acceptable as spring water" (Cowley, 1994, p. 41).

Selective Serotonin Reuptake Inhibitors

Several different types of medications fall into the classification of selective serotonin reuptake inhibitors (SSRIs), which are commonly referred to as second-generation antidepressants (see Table 4.7). The SSRIs— Prozac (fluoxetine), Paxil (paroxetine), Zoloft (sertraline), Luvox (fluvoxamine), Celexa (citalopram), Lexapro (S-citalopram)—all work by inhibiting the reuptake of serotonin (Kent, 2000) and preventing the nerve cells from reabsorbing this neurotransmitter, thereby increasing its presence at the synapses in the central nervous system (Jann et al., 1994; Lemonick, 1997).

TABLE 4.7
Selective Serotonin Reuptake Inhibitors

Medication	Maximum Daily Dose (mg)	Daily Dosage[a] (mg)
Prozac, Sarafem (fluoxetine)	80	20–40
Paxil (paroxetine)	50	20–40
Zoloft (sertraline)	200	50–150
Luvox (fluvoxamine)	400	100–300
Celexa (citalopram)	80	20–40
Lexapro (S-citalopram)	40	10–30

[a]Dosage range suggestions are for adults. All information uses guidelines from from *Physicians' Desk Reference*, 2004, and Maxmen & Ward, 2002.

Prozac, Sarafem

Following Belgium's approval in 1986, the FDA made Prozac (fluoxetine) the first SSRI approved for use in the United States for the treatment of depression (Elli Lilly, 2001). Prozac revolutionized the treatment of depression because of its ability to raise serotonin levels in the brain. Increased availability of this neurotransmitter has been directly related to the alleviation of symptoms prevalent in depression. Because of less unpleasant side effects than the tricyclics, Prozac, and the newer brand-name version of Prozac known as Sarafem (and the other SSRIs), have gained in popularity when treating depressed adults (Szegedy-Maszak, 2001).

Other uses include such conditions as bulimia nervosa and obsessive–compulsive disorder (*Physicians' Desk Reference*, 2004). In addition, Prozac can be used for the treatment of panic disorder (with or without agoraphobia). Sarafem, marketed by Eli Lilly for use in treating premenstrual dysphoric disorder, demonstrates another application for this profitable medication.

This drug is a white or off-white crystalline solid, and fluoxetine hydrochloride is its active ingredient. Prozac is sold by prescription in different oral dosages, ranging from 10 to 20 mg tablets; Prozac weekly comes in a 90 mg capsule, and a liquid solution is available as well (*Physicians' Desk Reference*, 2004). In 2001 alone, it was sold in more than 90 countries and used by more than 40 million people (Prozac makes history, 2001). When using Prozac, the general daily dosage is 20–60 mg. This drug is eliminated through the urine and feces. There is still no firm guideline as to how long a consumer should take the medication for maximum effectiveness. For the most part, it appears that when beginning use, a consumer can experience improvement in symptoms within 1–2 weeks. However, it can take as long as 4 weeks or more to get the full benefits of the drug (Safety Facts, 2001). If the drug causes discomfort such as nausea, it can be taken with food. Prozac has been found to be effective in consumers with severe depression who receive 12 weeks of acute treatment and an additional 38 weeks for more long-term use. For consumers with obsessive–compulsive disorder or bulimia nervosa, a course of 16 weeks or less is recommended (Prozac, 2001). Terminating the medication requires a tapered disengagement (Eisner, 2000).

Because Prozac has a long half-life of approximately 7–15 days, it is not recommended that missed doses be taken. Furthermore, the long half-life of Prozac is why it is sometimes found in breast milk, in low concentrations. Therefore, mothers using this drug are discouraged from breastfeeding their infants. The drug has been found in the plasma and tissue of infants; during the first months of life, this presence can be extremely detrimental to the growth of the child.

One illegal use of Prozac is the "ecstasy–Prozac cocktail," which is now being used in dance clubs where ecstasy (MDMA) is taken. Ecstasy increases the amount of serotonin in the brain by preventing serotonin reuptake. Once the levels of serotonin decrease, the user experiences depression. To eliminate the "down" effect, the user then takes a Prozac "chaser" (Dotinga, 2002). The NMTP should be aware of this potential for abuse and educate the consumer about the danger that can occur with this combination. It appears that this overstimulation of the neurotransmitter serotonin can leave the body vulnerable. The excess serotonin could be absorbed into the system and linked to the absorption of other toxic substances derived from either the use of the compounds in the ecstasy itself or other brain neurotransmitters such as dopamine. Either way, until more research identifies what actually happens when these two drugs are combined, it is best to discourage the use of any SSRI in combination with the drug ecstasy.

Paxil

Paxil (paroxetine) is similar to the other SSRIs; it works by inhibiting the reuptake of serotonin. Paxil was introduced on the market in 1992 and has become one of the leading treatments for depression and anxiety disorders in the country. According to Sifton (2001), Paxil is prescribed for chronic depression that interferes with the person's ability to function appropriately. It can also be used to treat major depressive disorder, generalized anxiety disorder (GAD), social anxiety disorder (SAD), panic disorder, obsessive–compulsive disorder (OCD), and posttraumatic stress disorder (PTSD) (*Physicians' Desk Reference*, 2004). Other uses include the treatment of depression in children (an off-label use; Paxil is not labeled for pediatric populations). It was also approved for the treatment of premenstrual dysphoric disorder (PMDD; Danner & Kipp, 2003).

(Paxil CR [control-release] is particularly helpful) with another off-label use for women in the treatment of hot flashes. Paxil is considered one of the more potent SSRIs.

Paxil can be taken with or without food; however, it is best when taken with water. In its CR form, the medication should be swallowed whole and not crushed, because it is specially formulated to be released slowly into the body. Given the risk of suicide when using Paxil CR, the prescription should be written for the smallest quantity possible for sound medical care to reduce the risk of overdose (*Physicians' Desk Reference*, 2004). Paxil also comes in the form of a liquid suspension that should be shaken well and measured accurately. The average daily dosage for adults is 10–50 mg and is usually taken approximately the same time each day (the most common the dosage is at 20 mg). The half-life of this medication is 12–20 hours, if a dose is missed, the individual should omit the forgotten dose and continue the regular schedule with the next dose; it is recommended not to take a double dose to compensate for the one forgotten (*Physicians' Desk Reference*, 2004).

Zoloft

Zoloft, like the other SSRIs, is generally used in the treatment of depression. It can also be used for anxiety disorders such as OCD and for the treatment of PMDD. The average daily dose of this medication ranges from 50 to 200 mg a day. Like Paxil, the half-life of Zoloft (around 26 hours) is much less than that of Prozac (7–15 days); therefore, it does not stay in the system as long (Diamond, 2002). Caution should always be exercised when using other medications, because Zoloft (like the other SSRIs) can elevate the serum levels of other medications. The route of elimination for this medication is through the urine and feces.

Luvox

Luvox (fluvoxamine) is used in the treatment of depression as well as the anxiety-related condition of OCD. The average dose is 25–300 mg daily. The dosage is generally given at night because it is a more sedating than the other SSRIs; however, it is believed to be less likely to cause agitation. The half-life of this medication is approximately 17–22 hours (similar to Paxil and Zoloft). The route of elimination is through the urine.

Celexa

Celexa (citalopram) is used for the treatment of depression, OCD, and panic disorder, and it can be used to assist with chronic schizophrenia and dementia. Close monitoring of this and all SSRIs is critical because of the potential for triggering mania or suicidal ideation (Fernandez & Calix, 2004).

Lexapro

Lexapro (escitalopram oxalate, S-citalopram) was approved by the FDA in 2001. It was created with the same ingredients as those in Celexa (citalopram); therefore, if a consumer has an allergic reaction to Celexa, he or she might also have one to Lexapro (Lexapro, 2004). Other uses of Lexapro include GAD, based on the results of three separate studies (Lexapro, 2004), and kleptomania (Wood, 2002). In terms of cost, Lexapro is only $69 for a 1-month supply, compared to $80 for Zoloft, and $84 for Paxil, and $85 for Prozac (Masilamani & Ruppelt, 2003). Consumers should note that because of the similarity of the names, Lexapro has been confused with Loxitane, an antipsychotic drug (Cohen, 2004). Lexapro is taken orally once a day; due to its high potency, the dosage prescribed for adults is not usually more than 20 mg a day. It may be taken with or without food and can take 1–4 weeks to become fully effective (Escitalopram, 2003a, 2003b).

Side-Effect Profiles and Special Considerations
Common side effects of SSRIs include:
Constipation, diarrhea, dizziness, dry mouth, ejaculatory delay, decreased appetite, nausea, stomach pain, gas in the stomach, heartburn, indigestion, diarrhea, inability to have or keep an erection, impotence, increased sweating, loss in sexual ability, desire, drive or performance, insomnia or sleeplessness, trouble sleeping, sleepiness or unusual drowsiness, dizziness, dry mouth, fatigue, flu-like symptoms, runny nose, sinusitis.

Less common side effects include:
Chills, cough, decreased appetite, fever, general feeling of discomfort or illness, headache, joint pain, muscle aches and pains, pain or tenderness around eyes and cheekbones, runny nose, shivering, shortness of breath or trouble breathing, sneezing, sore throat, stuffy nose, sweating and vomiting.

Rare side effects include:
Coma, confusion, convulsions, decreased urine output, and a fast or irregular heartbeat. Also consumers should seek immediate treatment if they start having unusual excitement or see or hear things or voices that do not exist (i.e., hallucinations) (Escitalopram, 2003b).

Extreme caution should be taken when mixing any SSRI with any MAOI. Consumers should never take an MAOI at the same time as an SSRI. There should always be a 10–14 day buffer between the discontinuation of an MAOI and the beginning of any SSRI. When switching from an SSRI to an MAOI, 5–6 weeks washout is needed for Prozac.

Because the safety of these medicines in pregnant women is not clearly established, it is best to avoid use. The effects of SSRIs on breastfeeding mothers and their infants are also not known. According to the *Physicians' Desk Reference* (2004), some of these medications (e.g., Prozac, Paxil) have been shown to pass into breast milk and can potentially cause drowsiness, weight loss, and decreased feeding in the infant. The presence of the SSRIs in infants can be measured in their plasma and urine. Major problems were not found in the area of fetal malformations or pregnancy-related complications. Data on the long-term developmental outcomes of children exposed to SSRIs in utero and during breastfeeding are limited (Misri, Burgmann, & Kostaras, 2000).

For all the SSRIs, particularly Prozac, concerns of medication-associated suicide and violent behavior are growing (DeGrandpre, 2004). Wooltorton (2003) noted three unpublished trials involving pediatric consumers with major depressive disorder who had suicidal thoughts, suicide attempts, and episodes of self-harm—which became more frequent when using Prozac. Over 200 lawsuits against the makers of Prozac have been filed since 1988, mostly concerning violent behavior of consumers to others or to themselves during early use of the medication (Prozac, 2001). Eli Lilly refutes this claim. However, Dr. David Healy, director of Cardiff University's North Wales Section of the Department of Psychological Medicine, reported in 2002 that Prozac produced akathisia, which was linked to an increase in the potential to attempt suicide (Raphael, 2002). Dr. Joseph Glenmullen, author of *Prozac Backlash* and clinical instructor of psychiatry at Harvard University, discusses suicidal preoccupation and other potential side effects of Prozac in his book.

Concerned about the negative consequences related to this medication, he urges that the medication and subsequent risks be monitored carefully by physicians and other prescribers while it is being taken (Raphael, 2002). On October 15, 2004 the FDA directed the manufacturers to add a "black box" warning describing the increased risk of suicidality in children and adolescents being given antidepressant medications. The black box warning is the most serious warning that can be required in the labeling of a prescription medication. On October 15, 2004 the FDA launched a multipronged strategy to strengthen safeguards for children and adolescents by issuing this warning on all the commonly used SSRIs such as Prozac, Sarafem, Celexa, Laxapro, Luvox, Paxil, and Zoloft. The new warning language does not prohibit the use of antidepressants in children and adolescents. Rather, it warns of the risk of suicide and encourages prescribers to balance writing the prescription and associated risk with clinical need. These new warnings recognize the need for caution and advise close monitoring of consumers as a way of managing the risk of suicidality. Later in the chapter, the increased risk of suicide is discussed as it now pertains to all antidepressant medications (FDA News, 2004).

Medical conditions that could affect the use of SSRIs are diseases affecting metabolism or blood circulation, a history of drug abuse, severe kidney or liver disease, mania or hypomania, or a history of seizure disorders. Special precautions should be taken when a consumer is taking other medications such as anticoagulants, antihistamines, sedatives, sleeping pills, tranquilizers, or Focalin (desmethylphanidate, a CNS stimulant). There are no general or special dietary restrictions.

Overall, the SSRIs have been found to have fewer side effects than the older classes of antidepressants. The most common side effects of SSRIs include gastrointestinal complaints, nervousness and agitation, sexual dysfunction, and weight gain with long-term use (Kent, 2000).

The results from recent studies using Lexapro seem the most promising for decreased problems in sexual desire (Ashton, 2004). Being aware of potential side effects is important because many times the discomfort will lead the consumer to stop taking the medication. Most prescribers know that one of the greatest dangers in using TCA medications is that an overdose is often fatal; this is not the case with Prozac and the other SSRIs (Morris, 1999). Withdrawal from these medications is always a concern. Because Prozac stays in the body longer than the other SSRIs, it is probably easier to stop taking; many doctors do not realize this difference (Eisner, 2000).

Other Antidepressants

Although the SSRIs are said to have revolutionized the treatment of depression, there are several new medications that have gained in popularity. These other antidepressants are said to be equivalent to the SSRIs or even better in terms of efficacy (Kent, 2000). A major advantage to using these newer antidepressants is that a gradual dosage increase is not required to reach a therapeutic level. Because the newer medications differ from the SSRIs in their mechanism of action, their side-effect profiles also differ, providing improved tolerance. It is beyond the scope of this book to explain the precise action of these newer medications. Simply stated, they differ from the SSRIs because they activate other neurotransmitters in addition to serotonin, and do so differently, depending on dosage. Based on previous research on this category of newer antidepressants, and despite all the methodological issues relative to limited testing of consumer responses, there are probably only minimal differences in clinical efficacy among these four newer antidepressants (see Table 4.8 below; Kent, 2000).

TABLE 4.8
Other Antidepressants

Medication	Daily Dosage Range[a] (mg)
Effexor (venlafaxine)	150–300
Wellbutrin (bupropion)	300–450
Serzone (nefazodone)	400–600
Remeron (mirtazapine)	15–60
Desyrel (trazodone)	150–400

[a]Dosage ranges from Hendrick & Gitlin, 2004. Maximum recommended daily doses might vary slightly based on the source.

Effexor

Effexor (venlafaxine), one popular medication in this category, is a serotonin/norepinephrine reuptake inhibitor (SNRIs). Effexor is particularly convenient because it comes in an extended-release form, which allows consumers who may have difficulty complying with multiple dosing to take the medication only once a day (Kent, 2000). For the older consumer with impaired liver or kidney functioning, Effexor must be used cautiously, because this type of impairment may not allow the medication to be absorbed and filtered properly (Kent, 2000). Consumers on this medication are generally given 75 mg a day in two or three divided doses. Similar to the SSRIs, MAOIs should not be taken with these SNRIs because fatal reactions have occurred with such a combination. Furthermore, this medication should be avoided in pregnancy because it often appears in breast milk. It is also important to avoid taking Effexor when taking Crixivan, a drug used in the treatment of HIV and AIDS, because it can reduce blood levels of Crixivan. On June 28, 2004, the FDA posted a warning on MedWatch (2004) that children and adolescent consumers with major depressive disorder who have been prescribed this antidepressant (and other SNRI antidepressants) need to be monitored closely for increased risk of suicide. This monitoring is critical at the beginning of the course of therapy, as well as whenever the dosage is adjusted or changed. Some of the most common side effects with consumers taking this medication are nausea, lack of appetite, anxiety, nervousness, headache, insomnia, and fatigue. Other side effects include constipation, weight loss, sexual problems, increased blood pressure, and increased heart rate (*Physicians' Desk Reference*, 2004).

Wellbutrin

Wellbutrin (bupropion) is a more activating, rather than sedating, medication and the only antidepressant that works directly with dopamine, a neurotransmitter. This drug is similar to the structure of amphetamines and can serve to suppress the appetite. Because this medication passes into breast milk, breastfeeding while taking this drug is not advised. Common side effects include headache, nausea, agitation, and insomnia. One of the most notable aspects of this medication is that, unlike the SSRIs, it does not generally cause sexual side effects. Given this low incidence of sexual side effects, it has been used in conjunction with the SSRIs to decrease the potential for SSRI-related sexual side effects (Diamond, 2002). Similarly to Effexor, the FDA posted a warning on June 22, 2004 on MedWatch (2004) that children and adolescent consumers with major depressive disorder who have been prescribed Wellbutrin (and other anti-depressants of this type) need to be monitored closely for increased risk of suicide. This monitoring is critical at the beginning of the course of therapy, as well as whenever the dosage is adjusted or changed.

Serzone and Desyrel

Serzone (nefazodone) is most similar to Desyrel (trazodone), and both of these medications are used to treat depression. Although both of these medications can cause sedation, trazodone is considered very sedating and is generally given at night. Both Serzone and Desyrel have short half-lives. Because Desyrel is the more sedating, the short half-life (3 hours) makes it desirable as a means of helping consumers to overcome sleep problems without a hangover effect (Diamond, 2002). On June 23, 2004, the FDA recommended a comprehensive risk–benefit analysis of Serzone to determine the potential for hepatic failure. Also, MedWatch (2004) indicated that, similar to the other antidepressants, users of Serzone should be monitored for the intensification of depressive symp-toms and for the potential for suicide. Side effects these medications share in common are headaches, dry mouth, and nausea. One serious side effect with Desyrel, however, is a condition called *priapism* (very painful and long-lasting penile erection that can require surgery to achieve relief and may result in impotence).

Remeron

Remeron (mirtazapine) is a noradrenergic and specific serotonergic anti-depressant (NaSSA). This medicine comes with a warning regarding its use with older people who have decreased liver or kidney function. Because Remeron is so new to the market and long-term studies have not been conducted, physicians should periodically reevaluate this medication for the individual consumer (*Physicians' Desk Reference*, 2004). Common side effects related to this medication are sedation, increased appetite, weight gain, dizziness, dry mouth, and constipation.

Side-Effect Profiles and Special Considerations
Most of the side effects caused by this group of medications are typically mild and tend to disappear within 1 to 2 weeks. Sexual side effects, however, are experienced by 20–60% of consumers; these side effects can occur with all antidepressants but are most prominent with the SSRIs (Gitlin, 1996; Labbate, 1999). Sexual difficulties can be long term and involve decreased libido or arousal and difficulties with achieving erections and with reaching orgasms (Marano, 1999). Consumers who experience sexual side effects should be informed that normal sexual functioning may return after their body has adjusted to the medication. Prescribing additional medications may be helpful in alleviating sexual side effects. For example, in one study, Viagra (sildenafil) was found to be effective in increasing sexual arousal in women taking SSRI antidepressants (Psychopharmacology Update, 2000). The NMTP should be aware that several of these supplemental types of treatments are available. As noted, both Serzone and Wellbutrin hold promise for helping consumers who experience sexual side effects with the SSRI (*Physicians' Desk Reference*, 2004).

MEDICATION DISCONTINUANCE

Regardless of the type of antidepressant medication a consumer is taking, he or she should be advised to stay on it for a minimum of 16–20 weeks or until the stressors in his or her life are under control (Maxmen & Ward, 1995). Psychiatrists recommend that consumers with severe and frequent episodes stay on the newer antidepressants (with their milder side effects) for longer periods of time. Consumers should be cautioned that discontinuing an antidepressant is a medical matter requiring a gradual and monitored tapering of the drug. This is especially true for tricyclics, which may cause severe withdrawal symptoms that include nausea and sleeping problems if stopped abruptly (*Physicians' Desk Reference*, 2004).

Because the risk of depression increases at certain times of the year (e.g., holidays, anniversary dates), NMTPs should work closely with their consumers to select the least disruptive time to begin decreasing the medication. Consumers should be aware that they have the option to return to earlier dosages if depressive symptoms reappear. As consumers prepare to discontinue the use of antidepressants, NMTPs should keep the following in mind: (1) encourage and reinforce the consumer's awareness and identification of recurring depressive symptoms; (2) ensure that the consumer has a good support system; (3) encourage the consumer to continue counseling after discontinuing the medication; (4) help the consumer develop a plan of action for the possible return of depressive symptoms; and (5) involve family and significant others in the early identification of relapse.

ELECTROCONVULSIVE THERAPY

The ECT performed in the past (and depicted so heinously in films such as *One Flew Over the Cuckoo's Nest*) is a far cry from the process used today in the treatment of major depressive disorder. In ECT, a generalized central-nervous-system seizure is induced by means of an electric current. The objective is to achieve a full seizure threshold until therapeutic gains can be established. The exact process by which ECT works is unknown; however, the shock results in an increase in different neurotransmitter responses at cell membranes. Four to twelve treatments are generally needed to achieve therapeutic results (Sachs, 1996).

ECT is considered one of the most effective treatments (75–85% efficacy) for endogenous and psychotic depression (Maxmen & Ward, 2002), and, when compared to medications, ECT is often considered as effective (Tierney et al., 1997). ECT may also benefit those individuals suffering from severe depression who cannot take antidepressant medications due to underlying medical conditions, or when a nonresponse to traditional antidepressant medication therapy is noted. Despite the prominent gains evidenced by the practice of ECT as a treatment modality, the most significant drawback remains the general lack of acceptance for the technique based on the public's misperception of, and skepticism about, the procedure (Maxmen & Ward, 1995; Tierney et al., 1997).

For the most part, electrical stimulation is reliable, simple to use, and cost-effective, and in many states, psychiatrists perform ECT on an outpatient basis, which greatly reduces inpatient hospital stays. The relapse rate after the discontinuation of ECT is high, however, and to combat this high relapse rate, continued psychopharmacological treatment is usually suggested (Sackeim et al., 2001). At times, maintenance ECT may be recommended to provide ongoing stability.

The major side effects of ECT are memory disturbance and headaches (Maxmen & Ward, 2002). Memory loss is related to two factors: the number of treatments and the oxygenation provided during the treatment experience (Tierney et al., 1997). Unfortunately, some memory loss may be permanent, but often awareness returns within several weeks of termination of the treatments. The NMTP working with consumers who receive ECT must be aware of the possible side effects, especially memory disturbance. During this process, the consumer may feel a conflict between the expectation that he or she continue verbal interventions and the reduced capacity to express him- or herself while the memory is disturbed. To avoid unwanted pressure and strain on the consumer, it may prove helpful to encourage the consumer to decline verbal therapy until the ECT treatments are discontinued.

RELAPSE AND INCREASED RISK OF SUICIDE

One issue of particular concern for NMTPs working with consumers on the newer antidepressant medications is the increased risk of suicide (Teicher, Glod, & Cole, 1990; MedWatch, 2004). Research results have been mixed; some clearly support a correlation between risk of suicide and the uses of these medications (Jann et al., 1994; Kapur, Mieczkowski, & Mann, 1992), whereas others conclude that there is no convincing or consistent evidence that particular classes of psychotropic drugs provoke suicidal behavior in predisposed consumers (Baldwin, 2000; Conference Report, 2003). Regardless of the outcome of the controversy suicide potential should always be monitored (deVane, 1994; Gitlin, 1996;

Hamilton & Opler, 1992; Mann & Kapur, 1991; Tollefson, Ramphey, Beasley, Enas, & Potvin, 1994).

As mentioned previously in this chapter, this risk was brought to the public's attention with a press release on October 15, 2004, when the FDA directed the manufacturers of all antidepressant medications to add a black box warning. This warning is among the strongest types of warnings the FDA can issue. The warning describes the increased risk of suicidality in children and adolescents being given antidepressant medications. Furthermore, it outlines the signs and symptoms that are of most concern, such as increased anxiety, agitation, panic attacks, insomnia, irritability, hostility (aggressiveness), impulsivity, akathisia (psychomotor restlessness), hypomania, and mania. Although a direct causal link between the emergence of such symptoms and either the worsening of depression or the emergence of suicidal impulses has not been clearly established, there is concern that such symptoms may represent precursors to emerging suicidality. In the drug trials the risk of suicide increased significantly when compared to placebo (no-medication group), but no participant actually died as a result. The identified symptoms can serve as a warning of increased risk for suicidal thinking and behavior, and they indicate a need for very close monitoring and possibly changes in the medication regime. Although originally linked solely to SSRIs, the SNRIs have also been targeted for the same warning of increased risk of suicidality (FDA News, 2004).

For the most part, antidepressant medications work very effectively in treating endogenous types of depression and result in positive mood changes that are usually visible within 2–6 weeks. However, it is important to remember that these medications are still fairly new and more testing is needed before there are definite answers. Until that time, NMTPs are advised to err on the side of caution. Depressed consumers are most vulnerable when they have more energy to act on their negative thoughts and feelings. As a rule of practice, it is recommended that when a consumer is taking an antidepressant medication, especially if it is in the newer category (SSRIs and SNRIs), he or she should be thoroughly assessed for suicidal ideation and intent. Because hospitals and other mental health facilities continue to discharge consumers after very short stays,

QUICK TIPS:
Assessing Suicide Potential

- Assess whether the symptoms of depression and anxiety would respond well to medication.

- Ask direct questions to elicit signs and symptoms of suicidal ideation or intent. Record reports of depression, anxiety, difficulties in eating or sleeping, psychological numbing, self-mutilation, flashbacks, panic attacks or panic-like feelings, as well as increased incidences of substance use.

- Assess the consumer's living situation and identify members of his or her support system that can help to assure that the individual is out of danger.

- Assess any unrealistic interpretations from the consumer, such as ideas related to abandonment or punishment.

- Assess feelings of self-blame and the degree to which they limit the individual's capacity for trust, which may be reflected in a negative self-image or poor self-esteem.

- The NMTP should encourage consumers and their families to be alert to the emergence of adverse signs such as increased anxiety, agitation, panic attacks, insomnia, irritability, hostility, impulsivity, akathisia, hypomania, mania, other unusual changes in behavior, worsening of depression, and suicidal ideation, especially early during antidepressant treatment and when the dose is adjusted up or down.

- When these symptoms occur, be sure the consumer or his or her family member immediately reports the onset to the MTP, especially if the symptoms are severe or onset is abrupt, and especially when the symptoms are not part of the consumer's original presenting symptoms.

NMTPs are in a position to recognize, assess, and actively address any potential suicidal situations that may emerge prior to a consumer's leaving the hospital or facility. For those NMTPs in private practice, this means that the potential for suicide must be carefully assessed when a consumer is referred directly from a psychiatric hospitalization. Ask the consumer directly if he or she is having any suicidal thoughts and has access to means, and determine whether a concrete plan exists. If the potential for suicide is suspected, regardless of the level of intent, a no-suicide agreement should be initiated directly with the consumer and maintained in the consumer's record. Once symptoms of depression lift, consumers may want to discontinue their medication regimen. Although consumers have the right to self-determination in medication and other aspects of their treatment, it is the NMTP's responsibility to educate them about the triggers for, and risk of, relapse (Dziegielewski & Leon, 2001).

When medication is used as a sole modality, caution should always be emphasized. For example, the newer antidepressant medications have a quicker response rate, helping the depressed individual to feel better and have more energy. When energy returns, the individual may be more likely to act on suicidal thoughts or feelings. Prescribing medication without counseling may unintentionally deprive consumers of the proper care, leaving them in a potentially dangerous situation.

PREGNANCY AND ANTIDEPRESSANTS

Because limited information is available on the effects of antidepressants on pregnancy, it is a good idea, when working with pregnant consumers who are currently being prescribed antidepressants, to ask their prescriber about potential risk or harm to the baby in utero and postnatal, via breast milk. Most studies have shown that the amount of antidepressant medication found in the milk is very low to undetectable, particularly from SSRIs (Stowe et al., 2000). Although research does not appear to show a direct correlation between medication in the milk and infant behavior, consumers should still be advised that these medications are fairly new and that conclusive and long-term effects have yet to be determined. Women who are deciding whether to continue taking antidepressant medications during pregnancy and whether to breastfeed are in special need of informed guidance.

AVOIDING ADVERSE DRUG INTERACTIONS

To help consumers avoid drug–drug interactions with antidepressants, it is critical to take a comprehensive history of all the substances they are taking. The history should include prescription and OTC medications, herbs, nutritional supplements, alcohol, tobacco, and illegal substances. For example, many consumers may not be aware of potential interactions between Prozac and an OTC cough remedy that contains dextromethorphan, which can increase reactions such as dizziness, sedation, and confusion (Morris, 1999). St. John's wort, an herbal preparation used to treat depression, should never be used in conjunction with the newer antidepressants, especially the SSRIs (Morris, 1999). Taking this herbal medication with an antidepressant can raise serotonin transmission to toxic levels, which may result in a serotonin syndrome. Another herb that can cause interaction effects is *Panax ginseng*, primarily used to assist with balancing metabolism and increasing vitality, which, when combined with antidepressants, may cause manic symptoms (Fugh-Bergman, 2000). Both the NMTP and the consumer need to be aware of adverse effects that may occur from combining OTC and herbal products with prescription medication used to treat depression.

COUNSELING AND OTHER SUPPORTIVE INTERVENTIONS

Talk therapy remains an important and viable treatment for depression, creating changes in the brain similar to antidepressant medications (Davis, 2004). Traditionally, regardless of the type of talk therapy used, many in the counseling professions used a biopsychosocial approach to assist depressed individuals in dealing with the exogenous or reactive stressors. The difficulties experienced by consumers are examined from this perspective, which emphasizes empowering them to take charge of their lives and strive for new and improved levels of health and mental health (Dziegielewski, 2002a, 2004).

Cognitive–Behavioral Therapy

Cognitive–behavioral therapy (CBT) investigates how specific cognitive processes influence an individual's emotions and behavior. Beck and his colleagues postulated the use of this form of intervention in addressing numerous mental health problems, including depression (Beck, 1991; Beck, Emery, & Greenberg, 1985; Beck & Freeman, 1990; Beck, Rush, Shaw, & Emery, 1979; Beck, Wright, Newman, & Leise, 1993). From this perspective, CBT is considered to be a number of related theories that all focus on the salient role of cognitions in the psychological process (Vonk & Early, 2002).

Often, medication alone is not sufficient, particularly for people with exogenous depression. Cognitive–behavioral therapy addresses depression by helping the person identify the *schemas* he or she has developed (Beck & Weishaar, 2000; Beck & Freeman, 1990). Negative schemas in key areas (e.g., relationship, work, self) are believed to contribute to the depressed state. The NMTP who use CBT helps the consumer identify negative schemas (e.g., "Nobody will ever love me," "I'll always be a loser") that produce cognitive distortions when the person interprets a current situation or event (Beck et al., 1979).

When treating the depressed consumer, cognitive–behavioral (CB) therapists focus on the present and seek to replace distorted thoughts and their associated unwanted behaviors with positive thoughts and desired behaviors (Fanger, 1994; McMullin, 2000). In the CB approach, the setting of goals and objectives are crucial for measuring the effectiveness of the intervention provided. Once identified, goals should always be stated positively and realistically to increase motivation for completion (Dziegielewski & Powers, 2000). In addition, to facilitate the measurement of effectiveness, objectives must be stated in

QUICK TIPS: Application of Cognitive–Behavioral Therapy for Depression

- Help the consumer identify distortions and dysfunctional patterns of thinking that are factors in the development and maintenance of the depressed mood (e.g., "I am useless," "I am worthless").

- Discuss how these dysfunctional patterns are related to expectations of the environment, self, and future that contribute to the depressed mood.

- Guide the consumer to evidence and logic that test the validity of the dysfunctional thinking.

- Help the consumer identify expectations and activities that seem unsatisfying or unrealistic.

- Assist the consumer in identifying repeated thoughts that occur spontaneously and contribute to the distorted affect (e.g., "I am always feeling sad, lost, and alone" [personalizing], or "Either I complete this task, or I will fail at everything I try to do." [all-or nothing thinking]).

- Help the consumer to identify more functional patterns of thinking.

concrete and functional terms. In setting the appropriate objectives, the focus is not on process but on the outcome that is desired (e.g., helping the consumer complete his or her activities of daily living (ADLs), such as taking a shower). By rethinking distorted perceptions, the consumer can gain a sense of perspective and have an alternative course of action; the ADLs can be cognitively reexamined and completed.

Crisis Intervention for the Depressed Individual
Depressed individuals often have incongruent descriptions of the current crisis situation that can further complicate their responses to a crisis. When an individual suffers from depression, situations that previously would have been perceived as manageable become unmanageable and may push the individual into a crisis state (Dattilio, 2001). James and Gilliland (2001) describe a crisis as both a danger and an opportunity; on one hand, the crisis may overwhelm the individual, but on the other hand, opportunities that are masked as crises can push the individual toward the discovery of new ways of being. The growth that comes from having successfully endured a crisis enhances the individual's feelings of self-worth. In terms of the depressed individual, a crisis is viewed as an intense emotional response that lasts from 6 weeks to 6 months and compromises his or her steady state (Dattilio, 2001; Roberts, 1990; Roberts & Dziegielewski, 1995). The intense emotional response may result from interpersonal sources (Brewin, 2001), intrapersonal sources (Lois, 2001; Roberts & Dziegielewski, 1996), or environmental concerns. What constitutes a crisis for the depressed individual is subjective and depends on his or her mood and coping skills (Roberts & Dziegielewski, 1995).

When the individual feels a lack of control, medication can be helpful to start the therapeutic process and allow the individual to recover the energy needed to work toward resolving the immediate issue. In addition to the use of psychopharmacology, Roberts's (1991) seven-stage crisis intervention model can be applied to working with the consumer who experiences depression within the crisis response. This model includes (1) assessing safety needs, (2) establishing rapport and communication, (3) identifying the major problems, (4) dealing with feelings and providing support, (5) exploring possible alternatives, (6) formulating an action plan, and (7) providing follow-up. In the process, the NMTP needs to remind the consumer that both pleasure and pain are a necessary part of growth and adaptation. The person who is depressed must realize that both states can co-exist, as well as fluctuate, throughout the healing process.

SELF-INITIATED TREATMENTS FOR DEPRESSION

In today's evolving health care climate, many consumers are taking an active role in their own physical and mental health treatment. Consumers often want to rely less on traditional medications and more on alternative or holistic means (Dziegielewski, 2003). These alternate approaches can include anything from acupuncture and exercise to nutrition, herbal medicines, meditation, spirituality, self-help support groups, imaging and affirmations (Lee & Carlin, 1997). Among the most popular self-treatment preparations are herbs designed to treat depression. St. John's wort is one example of a natural herbal remedy for depression that has gained in popularity across the United States. In Europe, it is reportedly outselling Prozac. St. John's wort (*Hypericum perforatum*) is a lush green herb with bright yellow flowers that has traditionally been used to heal wounds and as a tea to soothe nerves and relieve "melancholy." The natural antidepressant effect that results enhances the neurotransmitter levels of serotonin, norepinephrine, and dopamine, with few side effects (Lemonick, 1997, 1999). The herb is native to Europe, western Asia, and northern Africa, and is available at many health stores in the United States. It costs much less than prescription antidepressant medications. Although studies have been carried out in Europe that support the efficacy of this product, in the United States there is a scarcity of clinical trials on maintenance and long-term use of the product. There are no studies with regard to the herb's effectiveness in the treatment of severe depression, or the ideal dosage levels. One side effect noted with the herb is a tendency to be more vulnerable to sunburn.

Although the FDA monitors many of the claims made for traditional medicines, it does not impede access to alternative forms of medicine. In short, working with consumers who self-medicate is a practice reality (Lee

& Carlin, 1997). Attitudes within the medical community are changing, and physicians and other health care providers are becoming more aware of alternative medicine strategies (Lee & Carlin, 1997); it may become common in the future to include these strategies as part of the consumer's health and mental health treatment regimen (Dziegielewski, 1998). But until then, NMTPs should remain aware that consumers may conceal their use of herbal medications for fear that it will be viewed in a negative and disapproving manner. Discussion about herbal preparations should take place in an open, supportive, and nonjudgmental environment (Fugh-Bergman, 2000).

CONCLUSION

The second half of 20th century brought tremendous progress in the treatment of depression, beginning with the discovery of the neurotransmitters norepinephrine, serotonin, and dopamine, and the medications that affect them (TCA, MAOIs, and later the SSRIs and SNRIs). No one, however, could have predicted the changes and treatment gains from 1995 to 2005. The phenomenal advances made possible by the discovery of the SSRIs and SNRIs have revolutionized traditional treatments for the depressed consumer (Moller, 2000). This new pharmacological emphasis on mental health treatment makes the knowledge of medications a practice necessity.

When addressing the depressed consumer, it is critical to identify whether the symptoms are related to exogenous factors, and if so, the importance of these external factors needs to be made clear for all members of the health care team. Medications alone may be a simple and easy course of action, but medications alone may not be enough to bring about positive results. It has been estimated that 70–80% of all visits made to primary health care providers are made by consumers suffering from psychophysiological, or mind–body, illness (Corbin, Hanson, Happ, & Whitby, 1988). The importance of the interdependent relationship between the sociopsychological aspects of an illness and those that are physical, medical, or biological should not be underestimated; and though antidepressant medications often have a positive effect on cognition, mood, and behaviors, they do not change the underlying disease process (Gitlin, 1996).

Whenever a consumer shows depressive symptoms, he or she should be thoroughly assessed for suicidal ideation and intent. Direct questions should always be asked to determine the consumer's potential for suicide, and any current or past suicidal gestures should be documented. The documentation of potential suicidal behavior is particularly important with the use of the newer antidepressant drugs (SSRIs and SNRIs) that help to lift depression quickly, because depressed consumers are more likely to harm themselves when the depression lifts and energy returns.

QUICK TIPS:
Role of NMTPs in the Treatment of Depression

- Become aware of the different types of antidepressant medications that can be used to treat the symptoms the consumer is experiencing.

- Learn what can be expected in terms of behavioral change in consumers who take medication, and how the medication can affect the counseling relationship.

- Monitor consumers for medication compliance and make recommendations when it appears that changes or adjustments in medication dosage or class are needed.

- Help to gather and interpret information for consumers and their families with regard to medication and potential side effects.

- Help consumers identify and express needs and concerns about using medication.

- Complete a social–environmental assessment to identify the factors and support systems that can facilitate medication compliance and ensure treatment efficacy.

- Help the consumer develop the ability to recognize, accept, and cope with feelings of depression.

- Help the consumer improve depressed mood enough to return to previous levels of functioning.

- Help the consumer develop cognitive patterns and beliefs about self that will lead to control or alleviation of depressive symptoms.

- Clearly assess for suicidal thoughts and feelings and ensure that a plan for action is available to the consumer if a crisis erupts.

NMTPs can educate consumers and their families so that they do not develop a false sense of security with regard to the "curative" nature of a pill for treating depression (Marano, 1999). The allure of a quick fix is strong when compared to engaging in supportive counseling that often takes substantial time, emotional energy, and effort. The mistaken belief that antidepressants can cure creates unrealistic expectations for all. In the treatment of depression, NMTPs are important to the interdisciplinary team and assist with improved communication, coordination, and referral among primary health, mental health, and community-based programs.

5

Medications Used to Treat
Bipolar Disorders

There are two categories of mood disorders; *unipolar* mood disorders, which all involve some type of depression, and *bipolar* mood disorders, in which individuals experience both the "lows" characteristic of depression and the "highs" related to an elevated mood. Another name for bipolar disorder that lay individuals are most familiar with is *manic–depressive* illness (National Institute of Mental Health, 2002). Bipolar disorder involves unusual shifts in mood and energy levels, causing high and lows severe enough to impair normal daily functioning (American Psychiatric Association, 2000). Once they are recognized, the varied symptoms can indeed be difficult to understand and medically manage—not just for consumers, but for their relatives, coworkers, and friends. As is the case with all mental illnesses, family members may feel embarrassed by the behaviors of their loved ones with bipolar disorder. They often believe that the extreme mood fluctuations and behavioral difficulties that accompany their loved one's illness occur voluntarily and purposefully. This chapter discusses how NMTPs can better assist consumers with bipolar mood disorders and their characteristic mood swings.

According to the National Institute of Mental Health (NIMH, 2002), more than 2 million American adults (or about 1% of the population age 18 or older) suffers from this disorder. In addition, another 2% struggles with *cyclothymic disorder*, which is a milder but more persistent type of mood disorder (Regier et al., 1993). Bipolar disorder is most likely to develop in late adolescence or early adulthood. The onset of symptoms in this disorder can vary; some consumers report symptoms that started in childhood, whereas others do not experience symptoms until much later in life (National Institute of Mental Health, 2002). With the variability in the course of the disorder and the unpredictability of its symptoms, it is no surprise that the bipolar disorder is ranked worldwide second only to unipolar depression as a major cause of mental disability (Young, Karine, Macritchie, & Calabrese, 2000).

MOOD EPISODES

To better understand the highs and lows associated with this disorder, this chapter reviews what is meant by a *mood episode* and relates this information to the four primary diagnostic categories identified in the *DSM-IV-TR*: bipolar I disorders, bipolar II disorder, cyclothymic disorder, and bipolar disorder not otherwise specified (NOS); (American Psychiatric Association, 2000). Mood episodes are considered the building blocks for the mental health disorders that follow. There are four types of mood episodes: manic, hypomanic, major depressive, and mixed episodes (American Psychiatric Association, 2000).

In the first type of mood episode, referred to formally as the manic episode, the consumer's mood is persistently elevated, and he or she exhibits at least three of the following symptoms: increased psychomotor agitation, distractibility, flightiness of ideas, decreased need for sleep, and grandiosity. During this type of episode, the individual may also experience positive symptoms, which are psychotic features that involve either hallucinations (i.e., false sensory perceptions) or delusions (i.e., false beliefs held with extreme conviction, even when evidence to the contrary is demonstrable). (These terms are defined further in Chapter 7.) To qualify for a diagnosis, the manic episode and its characteristic symptoms must be persistent and last approximately 1 week (American Psychiatric Association, 2000).

In a *hypomanic episode* the symptoms may initially appear similar to those of a manic episode but much less severe, along with the absence of positive symptoms. For all practitioners, whether MTPs or NMTPs, the identification of what constitutes "less severity" makes this the most subjective component of the distinction (Bowden, 2002). Careful documentation of the signs and symptoms is mandatory for a thorough assessment. Because it is common for a consumer with hypomania to report persistently elevated and expansive or irritable mood, what is *significant* about the individual's level of functioning must be identified. Specifically, what makes this behavior different from previous levels of functioning? Given that the symptoms are not nearly as severe as those of a manic episode, inpatient hospitalization is rarely needed. That is, many of the symptoms of mania can exist within a hypomanic episode, but because they are not as severe and obvious as those during a manic state, less intense forms of treatment are applied.

Furthermore, individuals experiencing a hypomanic episode do not show evidence of psychotic features (such as hallucinations and delusions) and are generally aware that something is "not right"—that the behaviors they are exhibiting are uncharacteristic (American Psychiatric Association, 2000). The time frame for this type of mood episode which lasts approximately 4 days, is a little shorter than a manic episode, which generally lasts 1 week.

The *major depressive episode* generally involves at least five characteristic signs: appetite disturbances that occur on a daily basis (consuming either too much food, resulting in weight gain [5% of the body weight in 1 month], or too little food, resulting in weight loss), sleep disturbances (either too much sleep [hypersomnia] or too little [insomnia]), daily bouts of depressed mood, markedly diminished interest or pleasure in activities that are usually pleasurable, psychomotor agitation or retardation nearly every day, fatigue or loss of energy, and other related symptoms. In addition, the symptoms experienced must be significant enough to impair occupational and social functioning, involve either depressed mood or loss of interest or pleasure, and last for a period of at least 2 weeks (American Psychiatric Association, 2000). When in a depressive phase, individuals may consider suicide. As discussed in Chapter 4, a thorough assessment of the potential for committing suicide in this depressive phase is always indicated.

The last type of mood episode is referred to as a mixed episode because it generally meets the criteria for both the manic and depressive episodes. In a mixed episode the individual often experiences changing moods, in which feelings of sadness, irritability, and euphoria may alternate rapidly. The time frame is shorter than the major depressive episode; individuals experiencing a mixed episode generally report an active phase lasting approximately 1 week.

To be diagnosed with a mood disorder, the individual must exhibit one or a combination of these episodes. Identifying the characteristic symptoms of a bipolar mood disorder can be a difficult task because the variability of symptoms and inconsistent time frames (i.e., the major depressive episode lasts longer than 2 weeks) can complicate the assessment of the type of episode being exhibited. This overlap of symptoms can be especially confusing to the beginning professional. For example, a consumer may appear either euphoric (i.e., elated or happy) or dysphoric (i.e., dissatisfied or angry) during either a manic or hypomanic episode (Cassidy, Murry, Forest, & Carroll, 1998). When feeling *euphoric*, there is often an abundance of energy, and the individual may talk very rapidly and be unaware that his or her thoughts are racing, a false feeling of self-confidence can leave him or her feeling in complete control. When feeling *dysphoric*, the consumer may also experience a "high" state, but it is one in which his or her thoughts and activities reflect agitation, rage, anxiety, or panic. Yet, similarly to the euphoric state, the individual in the dysphoric state can present with rapid and pressured speech and quickened thoughts. Dysphoria can also accompany depression; when these symptoms are combined, the individual would likely meet the criteria for the mixed episode.

DISTINGUISHING AMONG BIPOLAR DISORDERS

Once the type(s) of mood episode is identified, the NMTP can apply this information to the assessment of the mood disorder the consumer is experiencing: one type of bipolar I disorder, bipolar II disorder, cyclothymic disorder, or bipolar disorder NOS (American Psychiatric Association, 2000). When specifically addressing consumers with *bipolar I* disorders, there is a potential for the development of either depressive episodes, manic episodes, or mixed episodes (Maxmen & Ward, 1995). Practitioners should keep in mind that these consumers often report full depressive episodes accompanied by symptoms of agitation and hyperactivity. Between episodes, 20–30% of consumers continue to have labile (fluctuations) mood significant enough to disturb interpersonal or occupational relations. In some cases the development of positive (psychotic) symptoms may occur; when this happens, subsequent manic episodes are more likely to have similar psychotic features (American Psychiatric Association, 2000).

In the *bipolar II* disorder the consumer has alternating experiences with major depressive episodes and periods of hypomania but no history of either a manic or mixed episode (Maxman & Ward, 1995). As stated earlier, hypomanic symptoms include increased levels of energy and mood that are not as intense as manic episodes. Furthermore, the consumers with bipolar II disorder generally do not require acute hospitalization (American Psychiatric Association, 2000).

In both bipolar I and bipolar II disorders, symptoms of persistent depressed mood, loss of interest in activities, poor concentration, feelings of hopelessness, and changes in eating and sleeping patterns characterize the depressive phase. Bipolar disordered individuals are generally considered at high risk for suicide (McElroy, Strakowski, West, & Keck, 1997). The consumer with hypomania related to bipolar II usually exhibits increased levels of energy, irritability, and pressured verbalization; and decreased appetite and need for sleep (American Psychiatric Association, 2000).

According to the *DSM-IV-TR*, consumers with the diagnosis of cyclothymic disorder have milder experiences than those who suffer from bipolar disorder. Cyclothymic disorder is considered chronic; even though the mood swings are less severe, the symptoms are generally ongoing, and the individual is not symptom-free for more than 2 months over a 2-year period (Austrian, 1995).

The diagnosis of *bipolar disorder NOS* is generally used with consumers who do not meet all of the criteria described for the bipolar disorders, yet still exhibit some of the basic symptoms evident in manic, hypomanic, major depressive, or mixed episodes (American Psychiatric

Association, 2000). Table 5.1 summarizes the requirements of a diagnosis of bipolar mood disorders.

TABLE 5.1
Bipolar Mood Disorders

- *Bipolar I disorder*: one or more manic episodes, usually with a history of depressive episodes
- *Bipolar II disorder*: one or more depressive episodes, with at least one hypomanic episode
- *Cyclothymic disorder*: persistent mood disturbance lasting at least 2 years; symptoms do not abate longer than 2 months; less severe than bipolar I or bipolar II disorder.
- *Bipolar disorder NOS*: does not meet the criteria for any specific mood disorder and has symptoms similar to depressive disorder NOS.

Note: Diagnostic categories based on the *DSM-IV-TR* classification system (American Psychiatric Association, 2000).

RECOGNIZING BIPOLAR-RELATED SIGNS AND SYMPTOMS

Bipolar disorders can be diagnosed in early adolescence or in adulthood through the age of 50 (Austrian, 1995). Because the symptoms of bipolar disorders vary, assessment should be related directly to the symptoms that cause major problems in functioning. Individuals with these disorders are often overwhelmed by their symptoms and feel despair over their fluctuating moods. NMTPs need to understand the intricacies of the bipolar disorders so that they are equipped to educate consumers and their families. Bipolar disorder is not an "all-or-nothing" (i.e., either feeling depressed or not) mental health condition. Indeed, consumers themselves need help in gaining a greater understanding of the overlapping and cyclical nature of the mood states they experience as well as the course of the illness.

NMTPs need to track two separate sets of symptoms within one illness: those that arise during a manic (hyper) state, and those reflected in the depressive state. During the manic or hypomanic state, consumers may be resistant to seeking and maintaining treatment; consumers often avoid or refuse support during this "up" phase of the illness, because they believe nothing is wrong. Changes in behaviors and energy level can occur gradually or quite suddenly. Some individuals cycle rapidly, experiencing four or more complete mood cycles within a year's time, within days, or in some cases, within hours (Badger & Rand, 1998).

There is also a possibility that the consumer may suffer from mood swings related to alcohol or drug-related problems (Carlson, Bromet, & Jandorf, 1998). Therefore, the initial assessment needs to outline the consumer's difficulties comprehensively, including assessing for an alcohol and/or other substance abuse history. Failing to assess for substance abuse can be dangerous if the consumer is mixing medications with these substances.

Once bipolar disorder is confirmed, the following should also be assessed: suicide potential, history and risk of violence, psychotic symptoms, and risk-taking behaviors (including acting out sexually).

Mood swings can lead to serious problems, even suicide attempts or successful completion. Symptoms that often plague consumers with bipolar mood disorders are listed in Table 5.2.

TABLE 5.2
Symptoms of Bipolar Disorders

- Changes in sleeping and eating habits/patterns
- Changes in levels of energy
- Erratic behaviors
- Changes in levels of restlessness
- Psychomotor agitation
- Increase in activities, especially in those considered risk-taking or destructive
- Problems concentrating (whether excited or depressed) and easily distracted
- Severe fluctuations in mood
- Extreme feelings of happiness and hopelessness
- Laughing inappropriately, usually accompanied by agitation
- Increased talking, or an inability to talk or express oneself
- Talking takes on a pressured quality
- Incoherent speech
- Racing thoughts

continued

TABLE 5.2 (continued)

- Disorientation
- Impaired judgment
- Grandiose thinking
- Inflated self-esteem or self-defeating feelings that cannot be shaken
- Increased irritability and impatience with others
- Easily excitable
- The possibility of bizarre hallucinations or delusional thinking
- Lack of interest in personal relationships or highly self-interested and focused
- Depressed feelings that can lead to suicidal ideation
- Difficulty managing feelings of anger, irritability, hostility, explosive outbursts, and violent behaviors
- Periodic antisocial behaviors
- Violent behaviors leading to child abuse and domestic violence
- Feelings of low self-esteem evident in fear of rejection, feeling disliked, and self-blame

In clinical situations, consumers often describe the course and severity of these symptoms as being on a roller coaster and not knowing when to expect the next drop (Hilty, Brady, & Hales, 1999). NMTPs can explain bipolar disorder to consumers as an illness that involves overlapping mood states and accompanying symptoms. It is also important that NMTPs recognize that consumers with bipolar disorders can concurrently suffer from other forms of mental illness, such as alcoholism, drug use, and anxiety disorders (Cassano, Pini, Saettoni, & Dell'Osso, 1999). Finally, knowledge of the diagnostic criteria (to avoid misdiagnosis) as well as knowledge of the types of medications and psychosocial treatments appropriate for both the highs and lows of bipolar disorders are essential (Kasper, 2003).

A comprehensive assessment involves a thorough account of the consumer's present and past history in regard to suicide potential, violence, risk-taking behavior, psychotic symptoms, alcohol and drug use, especially if the consumer is in a depressive episode (Marlatt, 1998). The immediate plan for the bipolar consumer who exhibits acute symptoms in any of these areas should be to rapidly assess what appears to be occurring, protect the consumer from harm, refer him or her to an MTP to begin a medication regimen, and stabilize the dangerous symptoms. Usually hospitalization is recommended because it can help ensure an environment in where these objectives can be met, and the consumer can continue the therapeutic work. Always allow time for the adjustment of medications in a supervised setting, because the greater the medication tolerance, the greater the compliance upon being discharged to a less restrictive environment. The period of hospitalization can also serve as a time when consumer and family members are educated on the nature of the illness and the treatment alternatives. Family understanding and support can help to facilitate discharge.

Identification of the problems a consumer is experiencing should lead to the targeting of appropriate objectives and action steps that will decrease or eliminate these problems. For example, if one goal of the treatment were to decrease discomfort by increasing the capability for restful sleep, then one of the objectives would be to help the consumer establish a plan that created the most conducive environment for fostering a specific number of hours of sleep per night (Jongsma & Peterson, 1995). In the case of bipolar disorders, effective treatment planning must include a medication regime that enables the consumer to follow through on objectives, such as ensuring adequate sleep. The objective of ensuring a specific amount of sleep also needs to indicate the time period for accomplishing this goal and the specific way in which the consumer will monitor the activity (e.g., via a sleep log). To assist consumers who suffer from bipolar disorder, a strategy that employs medication and some type of psychosocial intervention is often the suggested treatment of choice (National Institute of Mental Health, 2002).

DIFFERENCES IN ASSESSMENT BETWEEN MALES AND FEMALES

Mood disorders affect both men and women, although there appear to be some differences. Arnold (2003) believes that the onset of bipolar disorder tends to occur later in life for women than men, and women more often have a seasonal pattern to the mood disturbance. He also reports that bipolar II disorder, which is predominated by depressive episodes, also appears to be more common in women than men. Yet, although the course and clinical features of bipolar disorder differ between women and men, there is limited evidence to support the idea that gender affects the treatment response to the medications that are used to treat the disorder.

MEDICATION INTERVENTIONS FOR BIPOLAR DISORDERS

Brotter, Clarkin, and Carpenter (1998) and the National Institute of Mental Health (2002) advocate for the importance of providing medication therapy to consumers with bipolar disorders, either before psychosocial interventions are utilized or concurrently. Controlling the various symptoms with the help of medication enables the individual to concentrate on psychosocial strategies. Because medication use is not an exact science, it may take careful monitoring before the best regimen for the individual is identified; and once found, the small therapeutic window for these medications may require regular monitoring to ensure that both the drug choice and dosage remain appropriate. In addition, a clear diagnostic assessment is required to avoid a misdiagnosis of depression and a prescription for medication that could trigger a manic or mixed episode concurrent with the effective resolution of the depressive symptoms (Bowden, 2002).

Because the bipolar disorders are recurring illnesses, consumers often experience repeated episodes that require an ongoing regimen of medication. Treating the varied symptoms of bipolar disorders often leads to polypharmacy: the use of many different types of medications. It is not unusual to see medications such as SSRIs (discussed in Chapter 4), which are generally used to treat depression and some types of anxiety, being used to augment treatment of this condition; or antipsychotic medications (discussed Chapter 6), which are used to address the potential for positive symptoms that exists in the manic episode.

Of all of the possible medications to treat this illness, the most likely ones are those generally termed *mood stabilizers* (Dulcan, 1999). Mood stabilizers include lithium and medications that generally fall into the anticonvulsant category. Although mood stabilizers address both the highs and the lows, the most effect is seen when addressing the mania rather than the depression (Young et al., 2000). Because varying moods are intrinsic to this disorder, regulation requires adherence to a strict routine, especially when the consumer is feeling "good" in either the manic or hypomanic phase. The false sense of security that accompanies this phase can lead to medication noncompliance—a development that is particularly problematic for individuals in the manic phase. Giving up the high—the feeling of exhilaration—is a challenge for many individuals with bipolar disorders. Nevertheless, adherence to a strict medication routine is critical to help prevent cyclic recurrences (Boerlin, Gitlin, Zoellner, & Hammen, 1998).

Lithium

Lithium, an element of the periodic table that readily forms salts, has a long history as a treatment for the bipolar disorders, dating back as far as 200 A.D. when the Greek physician Galen prescribed alkaline spring baths for manic patients (Turkington & Kaplan, 1997). In the early 1900s, lithium bromide was used as a sedative—until the fatalities in the 1940s of some heart patients, who used the element as a salt substitute, caused its decline. Originally used in Australia as a medication for mood swings the popularity of lithium grew until it was widely prescribed in the United States. Since the mid-20th century lithium has been used as a primary mood stabilizer (Young, et al., 2000).

Treatment of bipolar disorders during the 1950s, 1960s, and 1970s consisted primarily of *lithium salts* as the medication of choice. Lithium helps to control the mood swings that fluctuate severely from normal, to elated, to depressed (National Institute of Mental Health, 2002). Although scientists are not entirely certain how lithium works, the current belief is that it may correct chemical imbalances in the neurotransmitters serotonin and norepinephrine, which influence emotional status and behavior (Turkington & Kaplan, 1997). Maj (2000) stated that the research continues to make lithium the first choice for long-term treatment.

Dosage and Course

There are two major types of lithium salts: lithium carbonate (Eskalith and Eskalith CR) and lithium citrate (Lithane, Lithobid, Cibalith-S).

Maxmen and Ward (2002) reported that there are no major differences between these two medicines, although lithium citrate may have fewer gastrointestinal problems and allergic side effects than lithium carbonate (see Table 5.3).

TABLE 5.3
Brand-Name Versions of Lithium Salts

Medication	Dosage and Form
Eskalith (lithium carbonate)	300 mg tablets, 300 mg capsules
Eskalith CR (lithium carbonate)	450 mg tablets
Lithane (lithium citrate)	300 mg tablets
Lithobid (lithium citrate	300 mg tablets
Cibalith-S (lithium citrate)	8 mEq/5 ml syrup

Lithium can help to provide symptomatic control of both the manic and the depressive phases of bipolar disorder in all age groups, and its use can also assist in long-term prophylaxis against condition recurrence. Generally, lithium use can diminish manic symptoms within 5–14 days, but it may take days to months longer before the condition is fully controlled (Dulcan, 1999). Lithium has a short half-life because it is rapidly excreted. The drug is highly toxic, however, and must be monitored regularly, along with other recommended tests such as white blood cell count, calcium level, kidney function, thyroid function, urinalysis, and pregnancy (Maxmen & Ward, 2002). This medication has a limited therapeutic range, which results in a fine line between the therapeutic dose and the toxic dose.

Since the amount of lithium needed to treat or prevent manic and depressive symptoms effectively differs greatly from one consumer to another—and can change over time in one individual—blood samples to determine how much lithium a consumer needs are taken periodically. The blood is then analyzed to determine how much lithium is present. Testing for the lithium blood level is a vital part of continued treatment efficacy, because it aids the MTP in selecting and maintaining the most effective therapeutic dose. Similarly, consumers must maintain their pre-scribed dose and be very careful not to take more lithium than indicated. It is imperative that the consumer know how to recognize the signs of lithium toxicity. According to Turkington and Kaplan (1997), early signs of lithium toxicity include diarrhea and vomiting, drowsiness, muscular weakness, and lack of coordination; warning signs of higher toxicity include giddiness/confusion, blurred vision, tinnitus (ringing of the ears), seizures, and staggering gait. Lithium blood levels are always obtained at the beginning of the regimen, and once stable, levels should be checked every few months (Dulcan, 1999).

Because 95% of lithium is excreted through the kidneys, consumers with any type of renal impairment should avoid this medication (Maxmen & Ward, 2002). With its high toxicity and excretion potential depending so heavily on the kidneys, lithium can be particularly problematic in older adults (*Physicians' Desk Reference*, 2004). Only older adults who have a normal salt (sodium) intake and normal heart and kidney function should take it.

Lithium has been known to affect the thyroid gland, causing it to be underactive or sometimes enlarged. That is why the consumer who is on lithium should always be monitored for thyroid functioning. Many times, thyroid hormone will be prescribed along with lithium to restore normal functioning (*Physicians' Desk Reference*, 2004).

The efficacy of using lithium, in general, has been questioned. Kirchner (2000), however, after reviewing the literature, disagreed—reporting that lithium use continues to appear justified. Furthermore, it appears that lithium use continues to become more widespread with all age groups, including children and adolescents. Children and adolescents with bipolar disorder are generally prescribed lithium for up to 2 years; it is generally used in these age groups to control behavioral outbursts or rage. When prescribed for this purpose, however, use of the medication's is temporary until more appropriate ways to control the anger can be found (Dulcan 1999). Although this medication can help control rage, the larger purpose should be to add psychosocial counseling to help the young consumer develop more effective problem-solving and coping skills. Substituting a safer medication should also be considered.

Side-Effect Profile and Special Considerations

Consumers taking lithium are cautioned about excess sweating, because this side effect can deplete the body's storage of salt and water and thereby cause lithium toxicity (Turkington & Kaplan, 1997). Consumers should avoid extremely hot climates and sauna baths, in addition to being careful of any illness that causes fever, sweating, vomiting, or diarrhea. Because elderly consumers have decreased fluid retention, overall, in their system, a lower dose is generally recommended. Furthermore, because lithium absorption and excretion are related to sodium absorption and excretion, consumers need to drink plenty of fluids (avoid caffeinated beverages) and ingest an adequate amount of dietary salt. Too little salt can cause the body to hoard lithium; and too little water will decrease urination, which, again, can lead to lithium buildup.

In regard to pregnancy, experts recommend that lithium use be discontinued during the first trimester of pregnancy—and throughout pregnancy, if possible. Taking lithium during pregnancy has been linked with birth defects, especially in the baby's heart, as well as "floppy infant" syndrome, which includes weakness, lethargy, unresponsiveness, low temperature, a weak cry, and poor appetite (Turkington & Kaplan, 1997). Other concerns are related to the risk of fetal malformation in the newborn (Eberhard-Gran, Eskild, & Opjordsmoen, 2005). It is recommended that consumers stop taking lithium immediately if they are trying to become pregnant or if they have just conceived. Because lithium is also excreted in breast milk in significant amounts, it is recommended that consumers on lithium do not breastfeed their infants.

Initial side effects, listed in Table 5.4, usually go away quickly; however, the hand tremor may remain.

Very toxic effects can be associated with too much lithium (see Table 5.5). According to Dulcan (1999), when these serious side effects occur, the consumer and his or her family should be encouraged to go to a physician's office or the emergency room immediately.

Most consumers do not experience serious side effects when they begin lithium therapy. Initially, the consumer may have slight nausea, stomach cramps, diarrhea, thirst, muscle weakness, and may feel tired, dazed, or sleepy, but generally these effects subside after several days of treatment.

TABLE 5.4
Initial Side Effects of Lithium

General side effects include:	Less common side effects may include:
• Drowsiness	• Acne or skin rash
• Weight gain	• Bloated feelings or pressure in stomach
• Muscle weakness	• Muscle twitching (slight)
• Stomach cramps	
• Nausea	
• Increased thirst	
• Vomiting	
• Diarrhea	
• Fatigue	
• Increased frequency of urination	
• Hand tremor (as doses increase)	

TABLE 5.5
Serious Side Effects of High Lithium Levels

• Irregular heartbeat	• Inability to urinate
• Fainting	• Muscle twitches (pronounced)
• Staggering	• High fever
• Blurred vision	• Seizures (fits or convulsions)
• Ringing or buzzing in the ears	• Unconsciousness

There may also be a slight hand tremor. Because the potential for much more serious side effects does exist, NMTPs should always check to see if the consumer has had a thorough medical examination (including blood work) prior to taking the medication, that a complete medical history was taken, and that other factors such as potential thyroid or renal problems and potential for pregnancy have been assessed. In addition, frequent monitoring (about every 2–3 months) of potential problems needs to be conducted while the consumer is on the medication. Overdosing with lithium can end in death (*Physicians' Desk Reference*, 2004); clearly the seriousness of this rare occurrence cannot be overemphasized, nor can the importance of properly educating consumers and family members to the dangers of using this medication. Luby and Singareddy (2003) remind us, however, that although the side effects from lithium can be daunting, the resulting improvement in quality-of-life issues, the preservation of relationships, work productivity, hospital costs saved, and suffering prevented by lithium may be well worth the risks.

Anticonvulsant Medications

Generally anticonvulsant medications are used as a secondary line of treatment of the bipolar disorders, with lithium considered the most common and the first choice. Yet this trend appears to be changing, and although the mechanism of action of these anticonvulsants remains unclear, popularity of use continues to rise (Young et al., 2000). Of all mental health disorders, the bipolar disorders are the most likely to be treated with polypharmacy. Therefore, it is not uncommon for consumers with this disorder to take other medications (e.g., antipsychotic drugs) to assist with positive symptoms (i.e., hallucinations and delusions) and behavioral outbursts along with these anticonvulsant medicines (Hendrick & Gitlin, 2004).

The most common of these atypical medications are Tegretol (carbamazepine), Depakene (valproate or valproic acid), Depakote and Depakote ER (divalproex, a stable coordination compound of valporate and valporic acid), Klonopin (clonazepam), and Neurontin (gabapentin) (see Table 5.6). This entire class of drugs was first approved to treat seizures and the condition of epilepsy (complex or partial) and to address generalized tonic–clonic and mixed-pattern seizures. Although no one is sure exactly why these medications work for bipolar disorder, the efficacy may be found in the fact that there is a connection or relationship between bipolar disorder and seizure disorders. For example, the psychotic experiences that may accompany bipolar disorder can closely resemble various types of nonconvulsive seizures; this resemblance may help to explain the effectiveness of antiseizure drugs in the treatment of the bipolar disorders. "Seizures" in a bipolar disorder may take the form of a hallucination that is frequently preceded or accompanied by an "aura," as there is with epilepsy. There is a disturbance of the normal chemical/electrical activity in the brain, and a seizure is nothing more than an electrical disturbance. Therefore, it makes sense that these drugs could help with this disorder.

TABLE 5.6
Anticonvulsant Medications Used to Treat Bipolar Disorders

Medication	Dosage and Form
Tegretol (carbamazepine)	100/200 mg tablets
Depakene (valproate or valproic acid)	250 mg capsules
	250 mg/5 ml syrup
Depakote (divalproex)	125/250/500 mg tablets
Depakote ER (divalproex)	500 tablets
Klonopin (clonazepam)	0.5/1/2 mg tablets
	100 mg/5 ml suspension
Neurontin (gabapentin)	100/300/400 capsules

Note: Information from *Physicians' Desk Reference,* 2004.

Tegretol (carbamazepine) was the first anticonvulsant drug used to treat the bipolar disorders, applied particularly for rapid cycling or severe sleep problems. Some of the off-label uses for this medication include diabetic neuropathy, schizophrenia, intermittent explosive disorder and other rage disorders, alcohol withdrawal syndrome, benzodiazepine withdrawal, and posttraumatic stress disorder (PTSD). Special caution, however, should be given to the potential development of carbamazepine drug interactions—such as with hormonal contraceptives and several newer anticonvulsant (valproate) and antipsychotic drugs—that can lead to drug toxicity (Kerry, Wang, Nowakowska, & Marsh, 2004b). Similar to the other mood stabilizers to be discussed in this section, this drug is less likely than lithium to be linked to weight gain.

Of the five medications discussed in this category, Depakene (valproic acid), Depakote (dilvaproex sodium), Depacon (valproate sodium), and Depakote/Depakote ER (divalproex) continue to gain in popularity for the treatment of resistant or atypical bipolar disorder. All of these medications behave similarly as all of them convert, in equivalent doses, to valproate ion in the brain. When valproate was used in the last quarter of the 20th century, it appeared that a proprietary formula could also have its advantages. This led to the formulation and subsequent FDA approval of divalproex in 1994 (Ketter, Wang, Nowakowska, & Marsh, 2004). Depakote ER was approved for the treatment of migraine headaches in 2000.

For the most part, Depakene is prescribed instead of lithium or an antidepressant to prevent a depressive episode. Depakene and Depakote are also used during manic episodes for people who do not respond well to lithium alone. Furthermore, they are considered the second most common mood stabilizer in the United States (Hendrick & Gitlin, 2004). It has also been suggested that for maintenance treatment, combining lithium with an anticonvulsant medication that converts to a valproate ion in the brain may be more effective than simply using lithium alone (Hendrick & Gitlin, 2004). Furthermore, in a review of controlled studies it was found that using an anticonvulsive medication such as Depakote (divalproex), in combination with a newer antipsychotic medicine such as Risperdal (risperidone) or Seroquel (quetiapine), may be superior to using the anticonvulsive medication alone (Ketter, Wang, Nowakowska, & Marsh, 2004).

Klonopin or Rivotril (clonazepam) is often used as an anticonvulsant and prescribed as a mood stabilizer in the treatment of bipolar disorder. Klonopin differs from the other medications in this therapeutic class (i.e., anticonvulsant) because it is the benzodiazepine chemical class. (For more information on the benzodiazepines, see Chapter 6; this medication can also be used for the treatment of anxiety and related conditions.)

Lastly, Neurontin (gabapentin) is a newer anticonvulsant drug, approved by the FDA in 1993, that is often used in inpatient and outpatient settings to help control anxiety and decrease arousal. Sometimes this drug is misspelled as *Neurotin*, so be aware that this mistake can and does happen. Although the information on the benefits of the efficacy of this drug is limited, it is often used as the sole or adjunctive treatment for the highs and lows characteristics of this disorder (Hendrick & Gitlin, 2004). Neurontin, similar to valporate, may lead to sedation, cognitive difficulties, fatigue, weight gain, and possible antimanic or anxiolytic effects (Ketter, Wang, Nowakowska & Marsh, 2004). As of 2002, and with a revision of the *Practice Guidelines for the Treatment of Bipolar Disorder* (2002), the American Psychiatric Guidelines have called this medication into question for treatment of bipolar disorder, and more research is needed to establish its exact role in treatment when related specifically to this disorder.

Table 5.7 summarizes reasons for choosing an anticonvulsant over lithium.

TABLE 5.7
Choosing an Anticonvulsant over Lithium

Preference to anticonvulsant medication is given over lithium when the following is indicated:

- Inadequate response or intolerance to antipsychotics or lithium
- Manic symptoms
- A typical features (an unusual mixture of mania and depression symptoms)
- Rapid cycling of the condition
- EEG abnormalities
- Head trauma (Kaplan & Sadock, 1990)
- History of brain damage

Note: Information from Bezchlibnyk-Butler & Jeffries, 1999; Dulcan, 1999; and Kaplan & Sadock, 1990.

The toxicity associated with lithium use also makes these medications an option for children who have been diagnosed with bipolar disorder (Dulcan, 1999). Generally, when these medications are used, only one from this category is prescribed at a time; prescribers are concerned about drug to drug interactions and overtaxing the hepatic system (Brotter et al., 1998). To avoid problems of this nature, blood tests are often done before starting Tegretol (carbamazepine) and Depakene (valproic acid) to ensure suitability. These tests are continued every month or so to be sure the dosing is correct and that side effects are not overwhelming. Blood tests are not generally needed when Klonopin (clonazepam) (Dulcan, 1999) or Neurontin (gabapentin) (Hendrick & Gitlin, 2004) is taken. When these medications are used to treat bipolar disorders, it is more likely that they will be continued for many years. If they are used to treat impulse control disorders, however, the course of the medication is much shorter and is discontinued when behavioral approaches appear to be helping (Dulcan, 1999).

Side-Effect Profiles and Special Considerations

One of the most important roles of the NMTP when working with individuals on medications is the monitoring of side effects. Common side effects for Tegretol (carbamazepine) that often occur when the medication is first started include double or blurred vision, sleepiness, dizziness, clumsiness or decreased coordination, mild nausea and stomach upset (advise the consumer to take the medication after a light meal or a snack), hair loss, increased risk of sunburn, and skin rash (*Physicians' Desk Reference*, 2004). Some of the emotional or behavioral side effects for practitioners to be aware of include anxiety and nervousness, agitation and mania, impulsive behavior, irritability, increased aggression, hallucinations, and motor and vocal tics (Dulcan, 1999).

Serious but rare side effects listed in the *Physicians' Desk Reference* (2004) include a decrease in the number of blood cells, lung irritation, worsening of seizures, yellowing of the skin, loss of appetite, increased or decreased urination, dark urine or pale bowel movements, sore throat or fever, mouth ulcers, vomiting, and the development of severe behavior problems.

The side-effect profile for Depakene (valproic acid) and Depakote (divalproex) that can appear early in the course of treatment includes upset stomach, increased appetite, thinning hair, tremor, drowsiness, and weight gain (*Physicians' Desk Reference*, 2004). Behavioral and emotional side effects include increased aggression and irritability (Dulcan, 1999). Serious but rare side effects are very similar to Tegretol (carbamazepine), except that Depakene has not been noted to decrease the number of blood cells or to lead to lung irritation. Consumers taking this medication should not stop taking it suddenly, because uncomfortable withdrawal symptoms may occur; a planned course for discontinuance of this medication is needed (Bezchlibnyk-Butler & Jeffries, 1999).

The most common side effects of Klonopin (clonazepam) are difficulty with balance and drowsiness (American Psychiatric Association, 2000). Behavioral and emotional side effects include irritability, excitement, increased anger and aggression, trouble sleeping or nightmares, and memory loss (Dulcan, 1999). These side effects can be disturbing to the consumer as well as family members, making essential family education on how best to control the problem side effects that occur. One of the most serious side effects occurs if Klonopin is combined with alcohol or other drugs; sleepiness, unconsciousness, and even death may follow (*Physicians' Desk Reference*, 2004).

The most common side effects related to the of use Neurontin (gabapentin) are dry mouth, nausea, somnolence, and dizziness or ataxia. One important consideration for using this drug is that, contrary to other anticonvulsant medications, there does not appear to be a need for blood monitoring (Hendrick & Gitlin, 2004).

When working with these anticonvulsant medications to treat the bipolar disorders, it is important to realize the high potential for adverse interactions with other drugs; when a consumer is taking multiple medications, the potential for interaction effects should be explored carefully (Bezchlibnyk-Butler & Jeffries, 1999). Tegretal (carbamazepine), for example, can interact with several types of mental health medications, including antidepressants, antipsychotics, benzodiazepines (often used to treat anxiety), and lithium. It is always best to become informed about potential medication side effects in consumers than to risk the development of an uncomfortable and dangerous interaction effect (Bezchlibnyk-Butler & Jeffries, 1999).

COUNSELING AND OTHER SUPPORTIVE INTERVENTIONS

The previous sections discussed the importance of accurately assessing and diagnosing bipolar disorders and fully distinguishing between the different mood states that individuals with these disorders can experience. This section provides an overview of the supportive types of treatment interventions that are available and often used successfully to manage bipolar symptoms. Although bipolar disorders are long-term illnesses that require monitoring and treatment measures, they can be managed with psychosocial as well as psychopharmacological means (Brotter et al., 1998; National Institute of Mental Health, 2002). These psychosocial interventions, which emphasize supportive therapy as well as active problem solving, appear to be of most help when the consumer's acute symptoms have been stabilized by use of medication. At this point of stabilization, practitioners can introduce various psychosocial treatments, from individual therapy to group therapy, as well as treatment modalities that involve specialized addiction groups designed to treat any coexisting substance abuse disorders that consumers with bipolar disorder often report (Weiss et al., 2000).

The most commonly used psychosocial approaches are cognitive–behavioral therapy (CBT), interpersonal therapy (IPT), psychoeducation, and family therapy. Each of these methods stresses the importance of establishing a therapeutic relationship that will allow the consumer to trust the NMTP. The consumer is always made to feel comfortable in seeking the necessary assistance; this comfort level enables the consumer to receive help as soon as indications of a new episode arise. For example, during the depressive episode, the consumer will need to be assessed for potential suicidal thoughts and behaviors (Austrian, 1995; Maxmen & Ward, 1995). A trusting therapeutic relationship actively involves the consumer in the intervention process, while also allowing the consumer to take responsibility for monitoring a complex mental illness.

Relapses can be a frequent occurrence with this disorder, especially for those who do not comply with the treatment protocol and stop medication abruptly and without consultation (Perry, Tarrier, Morriss, McCarthy, & Limb, 1999). When things appear to be going well, consumers may ignore the chronic, cyclical, long-lasting nature of their illness. In addition, the exhilaration experienced during the manic/hypomanic phase may be appealing to consumers and make them resistant to treatment efforts. Regardless of the type of intervention, this problem needs to be anticipated and planned for; the NMTP needs to point out repeatedly the past patterns and consequences of medication noncompliance, because these individuals often have a tendency to blame others (Nassir, Boiman, & Goodwin, 2000).

Cognitive-Behavioral Therapy
The use of CBT with consumers suffering from bipolar disorder is designed to help them deal with inappropriate or negative thought pat-

terns and the behaviors associated with the illness (National Institute of Mental Health, 2002). There is increasing support for the use of CBT as an adjunct to medication for this population (Scott, 2001). As a psychosocial intervention it appears that CBT may be particularly beneficial for consumers with bipolar disorder. CBT is based on the idea that thinking, mood, and behavior affect one another. Cognitive therapists teach their clients techniques they can use to examine and change thoughts that are unhelpful. When used with bipolar disorder, CBT a collaborative, educational style and a stepwise approach for identifying and addressing irrational thoughts. This type of therapy, similar to the other psychosocial approaches, allows consumers to take an equal and active role in their own therapy. Many consumers with bipolar disorder experience frequent relapses, despite taking mood stabilizing medication; this psychosocial approach can help to address, prepare for, and avoid these recurrences.

Interpersonal Therapy
Interpersonal Therapy (IPT) is becoming one of the most popular forms of short-term psychotherapeutic treatment used in reducing symptoms, preventing relapse, and dealing with interpersonal problems (Dziegielewski, 2004). In addition, it is also viewed as helpful for individuals who are having difficulty relating to significant others, careers, social roles, or life transitions (Karasu et al., 1993). In this model therapists are viewed as an active and supportive contributing factor to therapeutic gain (Fimerson, 1996; Rounsaville, O'Malley, Foley, & Weissman, 1988). IPT treatment generally addresses a person's current situation and maintains a "here-and-now" focus (Rounsaville et al., 1988). The focus of ITP is on helping the consumer monitor mood changes in relation to stressful interpersonal events and identify ways to meet the therapeutic objectives. Through this model the consumer is made aware of subtle changes in mood and how these changes can affect behavior. In addition, the NMTP also becomes aware of these fluctuations and helps the consumer assess and change the problematic behaviors that could result. Sometimes this assessment will indicate the need for a change in medication or an evaluation of medication compliance.

Psychoeducation

The primary intervention goal of psychoeducation as a form of supportive counseling for individuals with bipolar disorder is to prevent or minimize the adverse effects of future episodes. As with other mental illnesses, prevention requires that consumers and their support systems are educated about the cyclical nature of the illness. Consumers are taught basic living functions that enable them to relate to people appropriately, obtain and hold employment, and improve their overall social skills. During the education process, the family should be made aware of the different levels of motivation that may affect the consumer's desire to seek help (Dziegielewski, 2004). For example, consumers often feel that they are "on top of the world" during a manic or hypomanic episode and believe that they do not require any assistance. They may even accuse family members and helping professionals of being overprotective or worrying "for no reason." Many hospitals, agencies, and mental health organizations provide educational pamphlets on bipolar disorders for consumers and their families, and these sources can be integrated into the therapeutic discussions.

Family Therapy

From a family therapy perspective, involving all of the consumer's family members in the treatment of his or her condition is essential. Family members can provide support to the consumer and help him or her monitor the fluctuations in mood episodes. However, to provide effective support, family members need to be educated on the nature and course of the illness, and must be given an opportunity to express their feelings of frustration and anger (Brennan, 1995; Simoneau, Miklowitz, Richards, Saleem, & George, 1999). When consumers begin to demonstrate active symptoms of bipolar disorder, both they and their family members can feel the strain of the changes in their interpersonal relationships. This model is based upon the premise that if both the family and the consumer are helped to understand these illness-related changes and problems, the strain between the consumer and his or her support systems will decrease. In particular, family members need to be helped to understand that consumers with this disorder do not deliberately behave strangely and act inappropriately.

Including the family system in the treatment effort is especially important when striving to increase the individual's medication compliance. The use of journal logs and other tracking mechanisms can help consumers and family members identify and monitor the triggers that precipitate changes in symptoms and moods. Tracking mood changes can also be beneficial when consumers are trying to determine the amount of structure necessary in their lives to control those mood fluctuations. For example, through journaling the individual can see for him- or herself how sleep and rest patterns support overall well-being; and once productive patterns are identified, they can be further pursued or increased. Consumers can also identify and assess problem behaviors and formulate ways to avoid or decrease them (Ellicott, Hammen, Gitlin, & Brown, 1990). Once the triggers for areas of concern have been identified, the practitioner can help the consumer work through the interpersonal dynamics that arise when he or she either confronts or avoids these triggers (Swendsen, Hammen, Heller, & Gitlin, 1995).

The bottom line of all psychosocial interventions for bipolar disorder is the study of acute episodes to prevent future episodes and restore the consumer's functioning. Each of the psychosocial methods discussed above has a strong *educational* component and *relapse prevention* component; in addition, all emphasize the fostering of stable patterns of behavior, particularly in the areas of sleep, work, and social interaction with others.

NMTPs need to recognize that in most cases medication will be prescribed for their bipolar consumers, and so they must gain awareness of the different types of medications, their dosages, side effects, and the potential health problems. These practitioners can provide important information about the consumer's functioning to the prescriber, thereby positively influencing the consumer's medication regimen in this rapidly changing field of psychopharmacology.

Because consumers who suffer from bipolar disorder present with symptoms that affect all aspects of their functioning, flexibility is needed; they may require modified or different counseling interventions to ensure that they maintain a productive level of functioning. These interventions include medical exams, ongoing lab testing to monitor medication

effects, vocational counseling, securing possible disability benefits, identification of specialized support groups in the community, and case management services.

QUICK TIPS:
Creating an Intervention Plan for Consumers with Bipolar Disorder

- Map out an individual intervention plan for the consumer that includes both medication and supportive counseling.

- Invite the consumer and any willing family members to assist with the identification of problem areas and viable strategies to address them.

- Anticipate resistance from the consumer; regardless of the degree of resistance, continue to help the consumer and his or her family members formulate, implement, and monitor the interventions necessary to eliminate the bipolar symptoms.

- Identify the potential for any harmful or dangerous symptoms and how these symptoms can be addressed.

- Document all problems in measurable terms that will allow all involved (i.e., the practitioner, consumer, and family members) to assess if objectives have been met successfully.

- Identify broad goals that will be addressed through a series of objectives; each objective should indicate the target behavior to be changed, who will work on the change, the measurable outcome desired, specific dates by which the change will be made, and the measures or instruments that will demonstrate that the objective has been met.

- Help the consumer and family members to prioritize goals.

6

Medications Used to Treat Anxiety Disorders

Experiencing *anxiety* is a functional part of human growth and development and is generally considered a normal reaction to a threat (House & Stark, 2005). Unavoidable stressful situations may trigger feelings of anxiety that represent appropriate reactions to the stressor. Anxiety is often related to fear. However, there is one major difference between fear and anxiety: Fear is generally the body's response to a real threat, whereas anxiety is an exaggerated response to a threat that is unclear, unrealistic, or unknown (Dziegielewski, 2002). Generally, feelings of fear characterize the normal response to threat and alert the individual to danger, preparing him or her for the challenges that need to be addressed (Rapee, 1996). Anxiety feelings, in contrast, are more diffuse and can be experienced as uneasiness and tension, as well as representing and ambiguous sense of immediate danger or conflict from an unidentified or irrational source.

OVERVIEW OF THE ANXIETY DISORDERS

Anxiety constitutes a subjective emotional and physical state experienced by all people at some point in their lives. Anxiety can be positive because it can motivate individuals by making them uncomfortable enough to act on their feelings, drives, and instincts. It can be negative in the excess, however, leading to problematic behaviors that appear to be beyond the control of the individual (e.g., compulsive hand washing, inability to leave the house). This negative aspect of anxiety is most problematic when it begins to interfere with an individual's ability to work, sleep, or concentrate. Stress that leads to excessive anxiety can be induced by life circumstances such as financial problems, multiple medical problems, death of a loved one, divorce, etc. In the mental health setting it is common to encounter consumers who report anxiety-related problems. Yet despite the obvious symptoms, some professionals do not recognize the serious negative aspects of anxiety, and therefore consumers in need may not receive adequate intervention (Hales, 1995).

QUICK TIPS:
When Anxiety Is Considered
Problematic

- The consumer begins to feel powerless to address what is happening to him or her.

- The feelings of anxiety force the consumer to develop alternative physiological or cognitive strategies to prepare for, or avoid, a threat or danger that is not realistic.

- The person becomes either physically or psychologically exhausted by constantly preparing to face his or her unrealistic fears.

- Anxiety-induced self-absorption prevents the person from responding appropriately to life situations.

The symptoms indicative of anxiety can involve a combination of cognitive, behavioral, and somatic responses that may include nervousness, sweating, irritability, sleeplessness, fear, muscular tension, obsessive thoughts, poor concentration, compulsive actions, feelings of depression, and other types of general discomfort (American Psychiatric Association, 2000). Anxious feelings can help to mobilize individuals into creative action or to engage in problem solving. But when these feelings become so pronounced that they impair occupational and/or social functioning, some degree of attention and concern is warranted. If an individual is so anxious that he or she has to stop and verify that doors are locked 20 times, then he or she has a problem unrelated to physical safety concerns. This repeated obsessive behavior is clearly disruptive to the individual's daily functioning. Anxiety that is so extreme that behaviors become dysfunctional is the focus of intervention in this chapter.

When the symptoms of anxiety become severe enough to interfere with activities of daily living (ADLs) as well as occupational or social functioning, it is possible that an anxiety disorder exists. Experiencing this level of anxiety-related distress produces very uncomfortable feelings, prompting individuals to seek immediate relief. Although psychotropic medications can provide relief from anxiety, these medications by themselves do not address the underlying problems, nor do they provide the coping skills needed to prevent future anxiety (Stein, 1998). The most common anxiety disorders are outlined in Table 6.1.

RECOGNIZING ANXIETY-RELATED SIGNS AND SYMPTOMS

The NMTP needs to quickly and accurately identify the symptoms related to anxious behaviors. Symptoms such as panic with persistent worry and depression can impede counseling efforts and delay a patient's progress.

Panic

When an individual experiences repeated panic attacks, along with anticipatory concern or fear about future impending attacks, a diagnosis of panic disorder is suggested (American Psychiatric Association, 2000).

QUICK TIPS:
Signs of the Anxious Consumer

- These consumers generally seek the assistance of a primary care physician before seeing a mental health professional.

- These consumers rarely report that their problem is related to anxiety, and they often attribute what they are feeling to other things (e.g., unrelated pain, incidences, or happenings not related to the feelings of anxiety).

- The physical symptoms generally reported by these consumers include tremors, difficult or labored breathing, dizziness, sweating, irritability, restlessness, hyperventilation, pain, and heartburn).

- The somatic symptoms of anxiety are similar to those of organic disease; generally, however, the symptoms seem unrelated or involve two or more organ symptoms (e.g., headache and back pain).

- The cognitive symptoms include difficulty concentrating, impaired problem-solving ability, scattered thinking, and trouble prioritizing concerns.

Note: Adapted from Dziegielewski & Leon, 2001.

TABLE 6.1
Types of Anxiety Disorders

- *Panic disorder with or without agoraphobia*: attacks involving intense anxiety and apprehension lasting several minutes, either with or without agoraphobia.

- *Agoraphobia with history of panic disorder*: fear of being in places where escape may be difficult.

- *Social phobia*: persistent fear of one or more social situations.

- *Specific phobia* (previously called simple phobia): fear of a particular object or stimulus (e.g., fear of snakes); not generalized fear.

- *Obsessive–compulsive disorder*: recurring obsessions (repeated inoluntary thoughts) and compulsions (repetitive, driven behaviors) severe enough to affect social/occupational functioning.

- *Posttraumatic stress disorder*: Reexperiencing of past traumatic events involving intense fear and persistent symptoms of avoidance and increased arousal.

- *Acute stress disorder*: a new category in DSM-IV to address acute reactions to extreme stress; this category may help predict the development of PTSD.

- *Generalized anxiety disorder:* undue persistent worry about at least two or more life circumstances.

Note: Adapted from *DSM-IV-TR* (American Psychiatric Association, 2000) and *DSM-IV-TR in Action* (Dziegielewski, 2002a).

In this disorder feelings of panic are spontaneous and unexpected. Brief episodes of anxiety that begin suddenly and peak quickly, characterized by an intense sense of dread and doom and accompanied by other physical symptoms (e.g., racing heart, sweating, hyperventilation), are referred to as *panic attacks*. Although panic attacks appear to come suddenly, "from out of nowhere," they are not truly spontaneous occurrences. Rather, they erupt due to an accumulation of factors: a combination of physical sensations and fearful cognitions that extend beyond the control of the individual and give rise to thoughts of danger and anxiety (Wilhelm & Margarf, 1997).

Panic attacks are different from genuine fear in that the cause of the attack may not be externally precipitated or known. When these panic-like symptoms are combined with *agoraphobia* (literally, a fear of the market-place, i.e., open/public spaces), the results can be traumatic, leaving the individual unable to leave home or perform basic ADLs. In agoraphobia, there is a habitually desperate attempt to avoid the anxiety-producing stimuli of characteristic patterns that cluster around situations such as being outside of the home, in a crowd, in an automobile or other mode of transportation, as well as being on a bridge (American Psychiatric Association, 2000). When panic attacks and agoraphobia symptoms exist in some combination, and these behaviors are severe enough to interfere with occupational and social functioning, the diagnosis of panic disorder with or without agoraphobia or with a history of agoraphobia can be utilized.

Because panic-like symptoms tend to be severe and chronic, assessing the frequency, intensity, and duration of them is crucial. Severity of the symptoms in the pretreatment phase should be measured and compared with those being experienced at the end of treatment. Also, a concrete plan, taking into account the potential for relapse of anxiety symptoms, should always be considered (Jacobson, Wilson, & Tupper, 1988).

Phobias

Intense, unrealistic fears, related to an object, event, or a feeling, are referred to as *phobias* (Plaud & Vavrovsky, 1998). It has been estimated that 18% of the U.S. adult population suffers from some type of phobia; yet exactly how phobias develop, and what triggers and develops the phobic response, remains a mystery (Hall, 1997). When a person suffers from a phobia, simply exposing him or her to an anxiety-provoking stimulus can

---

**QUICK TIPS:
Assessment of Panic Symptoms**

- Episodes of panic attacks should be evaluated for the frequency, intensity, and duration of the attacks (e.g., does the individual have multiple attacks during a single day, or a few attacks a year?).

- Note how the panic or agoraphobia is experienced and record the common characteristics that cause the consumer to misinterpret symptoms, resulting in unrealistic fear(s) or dread of what should be common life situations.

- Note symptoms such as palpitations or the feeling that the heart is pounding in the chest, sweating, trembling, shaking, feelings of choking, nausea or abdominal distress, feeling faint, derealization (the feeling that what is occurring is not real).

result in an immediate anxiety response (American Psychiatric Association, 2000). These reactions are far beyond what would be considered the usual nervousness associated with being in a stressful situation. The fear is intense and generally stops the individual from engaging in many of the usual activities that need to be completed. Phobia sufferers are similar to individuals with panic attacks, in that both groups of individuals engage in avoidance behavior as a desperate means to avoid the feared stimulus (Stein, 1998). Individuals want to avoid panic-like reactions at all levels, so they will often rearrange or abandon activities that could invoke anxiety. If these activities cannot be avoided, they will be endured with significant discomfort and dread. When the fear, anxiety, and avoidance are so great that they interfere with an individual's daily functioning and routine or social and occupational functioning, a *phobic disorder* is diagnosed (see Table 6.2; American Psychiatric Association, 2000; Hall, 1997).

TABLE 6.2
Types of Phobic Disorders

Agoraphobia: the fear of being unable to escape a safe place (e.g., a movie theater)

Social phobia: fear, embarrassment, and avoidance of social situations

Specific or simple phobia: fear of an object or situation (other than social situations)

Obsessions and Compulsions

Eddy and Walbroehl (1998) define *obsessions* as recurring and distressing thoughts, images, and impulses that are perceived as inappropriate, anxiety-provoking, and contrary to an individual's will. Some of the most common obsessions include a fear of contamination; a fear of being harmed or harming others; disturbing visions of a sexual or aggressive content; doubting, and unacceptable impulses (Cooper, 1999).

Compulsions are defined as "repetitive behaviors (e.g., hand washing, ordering, checking) or mental acts (e.g., praying, counting, repeating words silently) that the person feels driven to perform in response to an obsession, or according to rules that must be applied rigidly" (American

Psychiatric Association, 2000, p. 462). The reason for this behavior is rooted in the need to exert constant efforts to avoid anxiety; performing routine and patterned behaviors provides some relief from the anxiety caused by the mental obsessions.

Obsessions (thoughts) and the resulting compulsive behaviors are inextricably linked. Yet there is little realistic connection between performing the compulsions and any relief from the obsessive thoughts (Eddy & Walbroehl, 1998). When "recurrent obsessions or compulsions . . . are severe enough to be time-consuming or cause marked distress or significant impairment," the diagnosis of *obsessive–compulsive disorder* (OCD) may be given (American Psychiatric Association, 2000, p. 456). In this disorder there is clear disruption of an individual's ability to perform daily activities and routines, including occupational and academic functioning, and related social activities or relationships (American Psychiatric Association, 2000). It is possible, however, for an individual to suffer from obsessions and not compulsions, or vice versa, but this occurrence is rare (Pato, Zohar-Kadouch, Zohar, & Murphy, 1988).

In this same area there are associated disorders, often referred to as *obsessive–compulsive spectrum disorders.* These include major depressive disorder, anxiety disorders, eating disorders, and personality disorders. In children, OCD is often associated with learning disorders and disruptive behavior disorders (American Psychiatric Association, 2000). According to Cooper (1999), alcohol abuse, Tourette's syndrome, epilepsy, and sydenhams chorea have frequently been found to be comorbid with OCD.

Extreme Stress Reactions

Extreme stress reactions occur when an individual experiences repeated episodes of intense fear, helplessness, or horror, and the resulting discomfort creates difficulty with sleep and temper control (e.g., irritability or outbursts of anger). When this extreme stress reaction is related to a stressful event that is either experienced or witnessed, the individual may develop *posttraumatic stress disorder* (PTSD) or *acute stress disorder* (ASD). PTSD is considered the more serious of the two, and the person generally has either directly experienced or witnessed a traumatic event.

To be regarded as PTSD, the symptoms must last more than a month. Individuals who suffer from PTSD frequently experience difficulty falling asleep, exhibit temper control problems such as irritability or angry outbursts, and want to avoid those thoughts, feelings, or conversations associated with the stressful event (American Psychiatric Association, 2000). Generally, the medications often used as the first line of treatment for this disorder are the SSRIs (see Chapter 4). ASD is similar to PTSD; indeed this new category was added to address acute reactions to extreme stress that occur during the first month excluded by PTSD criteria (see Table 6.3). These acute stress reactions are expected to occur within 4 weeks of exposure to the stressor and generally last from 2 days to 4 weeks. Although research is not conclusive, many professionals believe that the development of this condition can provide a foundation for the later heightened symptoms present in the emergence of PTSD (Dziegielewski, 2002a).

TABLE 6.3
Criteria for PTSD and ASD

Posttraumatic Stress Disorder
The individual experiences some type of extreme stressful event.

- *Frequency*: The individual experiences repeated (almost daily) and relentless feelings of fear, shock, horror, and disbelief, and the reported discomfort often persists, creating difficulties in falling asleep and temper control (e.g., irritability or outbursts of anger). The individual who suffers from this condition often wants to avoid thoughts, feelings, or conversations that remind him or her of the stressful event.
- *Intensity*: All symptoms experienced must be outside the range of usual experience; consumers report mentally reliving the stressful situation.
- *Duration*: Symptoms of extreme distress must last more than 1 month; and if the symptoms emerge more than 6 months after the event, it is referred to as delayed onset.

Acute Stress Disorder
The individual experiences some type of extreme stressful event.

- *Frequency*: The individual experiences repeated (almost daily) and relentless feelings of fear, shock, horror, and disbelief.

continued

TABLE 6.3 (*continued*)

- *Intensity*: The feelings must be severe enough to disturb ADLs and social and occupational functioning.
- *Duration*: The stress reaction occurs within days to weeks after the stressful event and lasts from 2 days to 4 weeks after the stressful event occurred.

Note: Adapted from *DSM-IV-TR* (American Psychiatric Association, 2000) and *DMS-IV-TR in Action* (Dziegielewski, 2002a).

Persistent Worry and Depression

Many individuals who suffer from anxiety complain of *persistent feelings of worry*. These concerns are so significant that they impair the individual's ability to function and to complete ADLs. Feelings of worry can be so varied and subjective that it is difficult to delineate categories for them. The fears could center on anything from worrying about daily activities and responsibilities to national or international events—where the individual can have no direct influence. Often the persistent feelings of worry and the resulting anxiety can be linked to feelings of *depression*. Barlow, Esler, and Vitali (1998) believe that the fewer coping mechanisms a consumer has when faced with an extreme stressor, the more likely the consumer is to develop depression along with anxiety. This interrelationship between anxiety and depression helps to explain why many of the medications used to treat anxiety can also be used as antidepressants, and vice versa (Marshall, 1994). The NMTP's observation of, or the consumer's report of, both feelings to intertwine in presentation, thereby influencing intervention efforts.

When the anxiety involves undue persistent worry about two or more life circumstances and extends for at least 6 months, it is referred to as *generalized anxiety disorder* (GAD; American Psychiatric Association, 2000). GAD is considered especially difficult to treat because consumers frequently report marked fluctuations in symptoms that last most of their adult life (McLellarn & Rosenzweig, 1998); because the course of the illness is so long, some professionals believe it would be better categorized as a personality disorder (Beck et al., 1985).

In summary, it appears that regardless of which anxiety disorder is being experienced, there is one element that all the anxiety conditions share: a misinterpretation of reality that results in unrealistic fear(s) or a dread of common life situations or both. The diagnostic criteria in the *DSM-IV-TR* delineate the different types of disorders, with their specific symptoms and varying ranges of discomfort, that fall in this category.

QUICK TIPS:
Functional Behavioral Assessment Factors in Anxiety

- Gather clear and concise information on the problem the consumer is experiencing.

- Identify whether, and in what ways, the anxiety-related symptoms are severe enough to disrupt daily functioning.

- Clearly record the frequency, intensity, and duration of the recurrences, highlighting the pervasiveness and persistence of the symptoms, and what events (relative to the recurrences) happened before and after the anxiety-provoking situation.

- Identify factors relevant to the consumer's environment (e.g., problems at work or home) that may provoke anxious responses.

- Once the symptoms to be addressed are identified, give careful attention to establishing a clear plan to help address and alleviate them.

- Identify the consumer's preexisting strengths and coping skills for handling the anxiety-provoking situations.

- Identify the nature and success of previous intervention efforts.

- Identify resources, such as family and community sources of support, that can help the individual. When medication is used, help the consumer to identify and monitor any side effects that emerge.

- Educate the consumer and the members of his or her support system to increase their understanding of the symptoms being experienced.

MEDICATION INTERVENTIONS FOR ANXIETY DISORDERS

Regardless of the type of anxiety a consumer is experiencing, medication can reduce levels of anxiety and panic-like symptoms (Maxmen & Ward, 2002). However, many professionals believe that psychopharmacological agents appear to be most effective when accompanied by some type of psychosocial intervention (Cohen & Steketee, 1998). Because the exact cause of anxiety is unknown and it remains an integral part of the human response (Marshall, 1994), it makes sense that the exact mechanism of action for these medications is also not clear. When anxiety is problematic, the biological mechanism that is considered natural to human functioning becomes disturbed and the consumer's anxiety becomes so intense that it overwhelms the usual patterns of coping. Therefore, utilizing a medication can initially help to get the consumer to agree to engage in psychosocial intervention efforts (Dziegielewski, 2004).

The primary drug categories utilized in treating anxiety disorders include the benzodiazepines; the atypical anxiety medications (i.e., nonbenzodiazepine, such as BuSpar [buspirone]; and the other classes of medications such as the SSRIs and several other antidepressants (e.g., Paxil [paroxetine], as described in Chapter 4. When working with consumers who have been prescribed medication for their anxiety, consider the following suggestions.

Benzodiazepines: The Typical Antianxiety Medications

Following their introduction in the 1960s, benzodiazepines became the most commonly prescribed drugs for the symptoms of anxiety, insomnia, panic disorder, and neuromuscular and seizure disorders, as well as for preoperative use and to manage alcohol withdrawal (Barker, Greenwood, Jackson, & Crowe, 2004; Gutierrez, Roper, & Hahn, 2001). Although considered addictive, this class of medications is also considered relatively safe. Nevertheless, most of these medications can be very seductive to the consumer, because they take effect fairly quickly, within an hour after they are taken. Although less common, benzodiazepines can also be used for social phobia, OCD, depression, drug withdrawal, and for the adverse effects related to antidepressant and antipsychotic medications (Barker et al., 2004). Several of the medications in this class have also been used to promote sleep. The sleep-related mechanism of action in benzodiazepines is the activation of gamma-aminobutyric acid (GABA), a neurotransmitter. GABA, a substance that is produced in the brain, inhibits i.e., slows down transmissions of nerves and many of the activities of the brain. Because benzodiazepines enhance the effects of GABA, they thereby

QUICK TIPS:
Beginning the Treatment Process

- Be sure the consumer has had a complete physical exam and medical workup. Because the symptoms of anxiety are multifactored (i.e., cognitive, behavioral, and somatic), a proper medical assessment is needed to rule out physical causes or medical complications caused by the disorder.

- If medication is being considered, take a comprehensive medication history to help save time for the medication prescriber in determining the need and continuance of medications. Be sure to include prescribed medications, OTC medications, and alternate therapies (e.g., herbal preparations) that may be used to control the anxiety and share this information with the prescriber as well.

- Screen the consumer for current or previous substance abuse and for the potential for substance-abusing activities to occur.

- Help the consumer to realize that medication is only one part of the therapeutic approach to the anxiety. A concrete plan needs to be created to continue other supportive interventions after the medication has been implemented.

reduce activity in the brain and promote sleep. Benzodiazepines are available in tablet, capsule, liquid, or injectable forms.

Three of the most well-known of these medications are Xanax (alprazolam), Valium (diazepam), and Ativan (lorazepam). Most professionals would agree that Xanax (alprazolam) is the most familiar to the public. Generally Xanax is used for the treatment of anxiety disorders and can be particularly helpful when the consumer experiences panic attacks. Because panic attacks often occur unexpectedly or in identifiable situations (e.g., driving), higher doses than those used for non-panic-related anxiety are usually recommended by the MTP. This medication is metabolized by the liver and excreted mainly by the kidneys, so dosages may need to be lower if a consumer has abnormal kidney function.

Very similar to Xanax (and probably second in name recognition among most consumers) is Valium (diazepam). This medication is often used for the short-term relief of symptoms related to anxiety disorders. One additional usage is in the area of alcohol withdrawal; this medication can be used to treat some of the symptoms related to withdrawal, such as agitation, tremors, delirium, seizures, and hallucinations. Also, like Xanax, this medication is metabolized by the liver and excreted by the kidneys, so dosages may need to be lowered in patients with abnormal kidney function.

Ativan (lorazepam) is often used for the management of anxiety disorders and provides short-term relief of the symptoms of anxiety, especially when it is associated with depression. In addition, Ativan has often been used for sleep disturbances such as insomnia. This medication has grown in popularity; it is now administered, along with other medications, to prevent nausea and vomiting during chemotherapy treatments for cancer.

Benzodiazepines seem to work best for somatic symptoms such as sweating, trembling, and insomnia; less success is noted when dealing with psychological symptoms such as worry and apprehension (Hendrick & Gitlin, 2004). Most of these medications are generally considered for short-term use (1–2 weeks) and for use during crisis periods or for extreme stress (Diamond, 2002). Although long-term use is possible, it is rarely recommended. Long-term use at low doses is most appropriate for individuals who have a long history of chronic anxiety (Diamond, 2002). Long-term use, however, should always be avoided with anyone who has a history of substance addiction.

Some of these medications act very quickly whereas others take longer. See Table 6.4 for a list of these medications and the rapidity of their effects. Take special note of the half-lives of these medications. As explained in Chapter 1, knowing the half-life of a medication is very important because it is pertinent information when determining whether the consumer should take a missed dose. Also, the half-life can affect the dosage routine and whether a consumer should take the medication once daily or in multiple doses.

Side-Effect Profiles

The use of any benzodiazepine can result in some degree of *drowsiness*. After a few uses of the medication, however, the drowsiness may seem less pronounced. When a long-acting medication such as Dalmane (flurazepam) is used to promote sleep, consumers may complain that they feel as if they have a hangover that could last several days. The shorter-acting medications are less likely to have this effect, although they can

> ## QUICK TIPS:
> ### Merging Medication Treatment with Other Supportive Interventions
>
> - Because many of these medications are addictive, start the intervention process with a behaviorally based contract (ideally, before the medication is prescribed). By contracting to participate in some type of psychosocial treatment prior to the medication, the consumer remains aware that the pill is only one facet of a multidimensional approach to the treatment of his or her anxiety.
>
> - Be sure to identify the stressor; help to gain some consensus on what is causing the anxiety, and how it can best be addressed.
>
> - Formulate goals and objectives; this process can help both the practitioner and the consumer to stay on task (Plaud & Vavrovsky, 1998). The consumer knows what to expect from treatment, and the practitioner has as a road map for interventions.
>
> - Identify significant stressors in the consumer's environmental and family systems (i.e., exogenous factors) that can be changed.
>
> - Recognize and plan for the potential for addiction that exists when using these medications, especially the benzodiazepines (Stein, 1998). This addictive reliance and false sense of security may dampen the consumer's desire to explore other therapies designed to address the exogenous factors.

cause the individual to wake up partway through the night with what is sometimes called *rebound insomnia*. The fact that a medication is short-acting causes the body to react to the rapid decrease of the substance in the system. Table 6.5 summarizes benzodiazepine side effects.

Whenever a medication can create symptoms of drowsiness, the standard warning not to use machinery or drive a car applies. This warning is especially important with this class of medications, because even with low doses, some degree of impairment in driving ability has been noted (Diamond, 2002). Other side effects reported, similar to those in alcohol use, are impaired judgment, lightheadedness, and decreased coordination. The use of these drugs can also unleash otherwise inhibited violent behavior. This effect was found to be particularly relevant for Restoril (temazepam) and Halcion (triazolam) (Gutierrez et al., 2001). Sexual disinterest and dysfunction have also been associated with all of the benzodiazepines. This effect should be noted with caution, however, (Seagraves

TABLE 6.4
Typical Anxiety Medications

Generic (Trade Name)	Rapidity of Effect	Half-Life	Usual Daily Dosage Range[a] (mg)
Xanax (alprazolam)	Intermediate	Intermediate	0.5–4
Librium (chlordiazepoxide)	Intermediate	Long	10–100
Klonopin (clonazepam)	Intermediate	Intermediate/long	0.5–3
Tranxene (clorazepate)	Rapid	Long	7.5–60
Valium (diazepam)	Rapid	Long	5–40
ProSom (estazolam)	Rapid	Intermediate	1–2
Dalmane (flurazepam)[b]	Intermediate	Long	15–30
Paxipam (halazepam)	Slow	Long	40–160
Ativan (lorazepam)	Intermediate	Intermediate	1–6
Serax (oxazepam)	Intermediate-slow	Intermediate	15–90
Doral (quazepam)	Rapid	Long	7.5–15
Restoril (temazepam)	Intermediate	Intermediate	15–30
Halcion (triazolam)	Intermediate	Short	0.125–0.5

[a]Ideal dosage ranges may vary.
[b]This medication is usually used to treat sleep problems.
Note: Dosage ranges and general information from the *Physicians' Desk Reference*, 2004, and Hendrick & Gitlin, 2004.

& Balon, 2003) because many individuals who suffer from an anxiety disorder also had difficulties with sexual dysfunction prior to taking any of these medications. Furthermore, all these medications can interfere with long-term memory (Barker et al., 2004), with the greatest effects experienced by those with preexisting memory problems (Diamond, 2002). General and serious side effects are listed in Table 6.5.

To be on the safe side, all benzodiazepines should be avoided during pregnancy and throughout breastfeeding. This is especially true for medications such as Valium (diazepam), which could possibly be linked to fetal problems and should not be used in pregnancy.

When looking specifically at Xanax (alprazolam) should never be taken with antifungal medications such as ketoconazole or itraconazole. Furthermore, as with all benzodiazepines, alcohol must be avoided. Because of the high potential for addiction and dependency, it is recommended that Xanax not be taken at high dosages over a prolonged period of time. Consumers should be warned against abrupt discontinuation of Xanax because it can lead to symptoms of withdrawal such as insomnia, headaches, nausea, vomiting, lightheadedness, sweating, anxiety, and fatigue. There is also a serious potential for the development of seizures when this medicine is discontinued abruptly. Consumers should be warned not to discontinue taking Xanax without the supervision of an MTP; generally, a slow taper of the medication is considered ideal for discontinuance.

TABLE 6.5
Benzodiazepine Side Effects

General	Serious
• Hypotension, dizziness, light-headedness	• Shuffling walk, tremors
• Dry mouth, decreased appetite, nausea	• Fever, difficulty breathing or swallowing
• Upset stomach, urinary retention or frequency	• Severe skin rash, yellowing of the skin or eyes
• Decreased sexual desire, impotence	• Irregular heartbeat
• Blurred vision, rash, nightmares, and depression	• Confusion/forgetfulness
	• Depression, mood changes
	• Muscle cramps
	• Difficulty sleeping, speaking, or passing urine

Special Considerations

Addiction potential is strong with the benzodiazepines, and when these *central nervous system* (CNS) depressants are combined with other CNS depressants, they can become lethal. For example, mixing the benzodiazepines with alcohol (a depressant) can result in significant physical depression or even a lethal effect (Diamond, 2002; Dulcan, 1999). Taking an overdose of benzodiazepines can also cause unconsciousness and possibly death. Anyone who shows signs of an overdose or of the effects of combining benzodiazepines with alcohol or other drugs should get immediate emergency help. Warning signs include slurred speech or confusion, severe drowsiness, staggering, and profound weakness.

Historically, 70–90% of all suicides involve benzodiazepines as the drugs of choice, particularly Valium (diazepam). The benzodiazepines that have a rapid onset of action (see Table 6.3), sometimes referred to as the "best kick," are the most likely to be abused. The most susceptible age group for potential abuse includes individuals between the ages of 18 and 25. Because of the high potential for abuse, it is illegal for anyone to give or sell these medications to a person for whom the medication has not been prescribed (Dulcan, 1999). Illegal benzodiazepine use has become a much bigger problem than one might expect, as individuals cross the border to countries such as Mexico and come back with large supplies; or they may use the Internet to secure medications, if the right site is found, without a prescription or even a physician's recommendation. The potential for abuse and addiction makes it essential for NMTPs to be aware of the dangers and to advise other professionals against prescribing these medications for a consumer who has a history of substance abuse.

Atypical Antianxiety Medications

Atypical medications for the treatment of anxiety have grown in popularity. These medications, primarily BuSpar (buspirone), Catapres (clonidine), and Tenex (guanfacine), are different from benzodiazepines in three ways: (1) they cause less sedation, (2) they have less abuse potential (so they are not regulated by the Controlled Substance Act), and (3) they are associated with fewer problems when combined with other CNS depressants. BuSpar (buspirone) has become the focus of attention because it is the medication of choice, when compared to the benzodiazepines, for people with a history of substance abuse or drug-seeking behavior. BuSpar (buspirone) has a different chemical composition from the benzodiazepines and does not have the same hypnotic, muscle relaxant, and anticonvulsant actions (Dulcan, 1999).

Although the SSRIs (described in Chapter 4), especially Paxil, are generally considered the first line of treatment for PTSD, there are two other medications that have grown in favor for the treatment of PTSD and the symptoms of anxiety or panic, among other anxiety-related conditions. Catapres (clonidine) and Tenex (guanfacine; Dulcan, 1999), originally manufactured for the treatment of high blood pressure, have become a

QUICK TIPS:
Working with Consumers Taking Benzodiazepines

- Always encourage the consumer to see the prescriber regularly while taking a benzodiazepine, especially during the first few months of treatment, to be assessed for unwanted side effects.

- Because many of these medications are not recommended for long-term use, it is important to advise the consumer to check with the MTP every 2–3 months to see if the medication should be continued.

- Clarify possible side effects with the consumer, noting that these medications can make him or her feel drowsy, dizzy, lightheaded, or less alert. These medications may also cause clumsiness or unsteadiness. Consumers should be warned about driving, using machines, or doing anything else that might be dangerous until they have found out how the drug affects them.

- Remind consumers of the great danger of mixing benzodiazepines with alcohol.

- Consumers who are taking benzodiazepines to promote sleep should check with their MTP if sleep patterns have not improved in approximately 7–10 days. If sleep problems last longer than this range, than they may be related to another medical problem or to a mental health problem such as depression.

- Warn consumers who are taking these medications to promote sleep that they may have trouble sleeping when the medications are stopped; but this effect should last only a short time (a few nights).

potential treatment for a variety of disorders. Both of these medications act by stimulating alpha-adrenergic receptors in the brain that decrease sympathetic outflow to distal arterioles and cause vasodilation, resulting in a subsequent reduction in blood pressure. Generally both of these medicines can help decrease symptoms of hyperactivity, impulsivity, anxiety, irritability, temper tantrums, explosive anger, conduct problems, and tics (Dulcan, 1999). There appears to be supportive evidence that these medications, when used in adults, can help improve self-control as well as increase cooperation with treatment regimens.

Side-Effects of BuSpar (Buspirone)

The most common side effects for BuSpar (buspirone) include dizziness, nausea, headache, nervousness, lightheadedness, and excitement. Less common side effects include decreased concentration, trouble sleeping, and nightmares or vivid dreams. Individuals may also report tired or weak, diarrhea, dryness of mouth, muscle pain, spasms, cramps, stiffness, or fatigue. Rare symptoms include ringing in the ears, blurred vision, and clamminess or sweating. If a consumer experiences these rare and serious side effects—chest pain; confusion; fast or pounding heartbeat; fever; numbness, tingling, pain, or weakness in hands or feet; skin rash or hives; stiffness of arms or legs—a physician should be contacted (Sifton, 2001).

This medication is not considered to have a high potential for abuse; however, the full effect may not appear for 1–2 weeks (Sifton, 2001), or may take as long as 3–4 weeks (Dulcan, 1999). BuSpar also appears to have fewer sexual side effects than the benzodiazepines, and does not seem to affect orgasm or erection. In fact, individuals suffering from GAD reported a decrease in, or alleviation of, their sexual problems (Segraves & Balon, 2003). BuSpar should not be used with MAOI such as Nardil and Parnate (discussed in Chapter 4). Furthermore, if BuSpar is taken with certain other drugs, the effects of either can be increased, decreased, or altered. For example, some medications that should be monitored carefully when combined with BuSpar are the blood-thinning drug Coumadin, the antipsychotic medication Haldol (haloperidol), and the antidepressant drug Desyrel (trazodone). Because the effects of BuSpar have not been adequately studied in pregnancy or with breastfeeding, it is best to recommend that consumers avoid this combination (i.e., pregnancy/breastfeeding and BuSpar).

Side-Effects of Catapres (Clonidine) and Tenex (Guanfacine)

According to Dulcan (1999), common side effects from the use of Catapres (clonidine) and Tenex (guanfacine) when first prescribed include a slow pulse rate, trouble sleeping (may be due to the medicine wearing off), ringing in the ears, and skin redness. When using the Catapres skin patch, the medicine releases its ingredients slowly for 5 days. Other side effects that may surface as the dose increases include sleepiness, fatigue or tiredness, low blood pressure, headache, mild dizziness or lightheadedness, and stomachache. When the following more serious side effects occur, they should be reported to a physician immediately: fainting, irregular heartbeat, trouble breathing, kidney failure and decreased frequency of urination, rapid swelling of the feet, or sudden headaches with nausea and vomiting. Tolerance for alcohol and other CNS depressants may be diminished when using these medications. Because these medication can induce drowsiness, caution should always be used when operating dangerous machinery or driving motor vehicles until it has been determined for certain that these medications do not make the individual drowsy or dizzy.

Before utilizing these medications, a physician may decide to order blood tests or obtain an electrocardiogram (EKG) to measure heart rhythm. Similar to other antihypertensive agents, Catapres and Tenex should be used with caution in patients with severe coronary insufficiency, recent myocardial infarction, cerebrovascular disease, or chronic renal or hepatic failure. Since it is not known whether these medications affect pregnancy or whether these drugs are excreted in human milk, it is best to avoid them during pregnancy or consult a MTP before use.

The Use of Antidepressants in the Treatment of Anxiety

As discussed in Chapter 4, antidepressants, particularly selective serotonin reuptake inhibitors (SSRIs), are often used as the sole modality for the treatment of anxiety or to supplement that treatment. These medications help block the signs of panic that are experienced by consumers who are distressed from anxiety (Internal Medicine Review, 1999). Most of the antidepressant medications have demonstrated antianxiety properties, independent of their antidepressant properties; however, the tricyclic and MAOI antidepressants have more pronounced side effects. It is not uncommon for SSRIs to be considered the drugs of choice for panic disorder and OCD (Ballenger, Lydiard, & Turner, 1995; Dopheide & Park, 2002). In the treatment of OCD, the most frequently prescribed SSRIs include Prozac (fluoxetine), Zoloft (sertraline), Paxil (paroxetine), and Luvox (fluvoxamine) (Cohen & Steketee, 1998). Luvox has also been approved for treating OCD in children. Unfortunately, many of these medications take up to 6 weeks to have significant antianxiety effects (Reid, 1997), so quicker-acting benzodiazepine "anxiolytics" (antianxiety agents) may be used instead. Consumers should be reminded and warned that these medications should never be stopped suddenly; and when planning to discontinue a medication, consultation should be sought (Dulcan, 1999). Almost always, tapering off these medications will be indicated. Furthermore, recent research indicates that the relapse rates are as high as 90% when withdrawing consumers from some of the antidepressant medications used to treat anxiety (Pato et al., 1988).

COUNSELING AND OTHER SUPPORTIVE INTERVENTIONS

Efficient and effective practice requires that medications should not be the sole treatment modality for the anxiety disorders; rather, supportive psychosocial interventions should be utilized concurrently. Previous research has shown that low-potency benzodiazepines have no greater efficacy than placebos (success rates are reported to range from 30 to 45%; Craske & Waikar, 1994; Roth & Fonagy, 1996), whereas psychosocial interventions such as cognitive therapy were significantly more effective than Tofranil (imipramine), a tricyclic antidepressant (Clark et al., 1994).

NMTP can provide important services to those who suffer from anxiety conditions by creating an environment for improved communication and service coordination, linking the consumer with other health care professionals, as well as mental health and community-based programs. In terms of direct intervention efforts, many of the techniques described in this chapter to assist with anxiety can also be used to help consumers suffering from depression because the symptoms of anxiety and depression frequently overlap.

Because anxiety is considered a normal part of life, it must be clear that the level of anxiety warrants psychosocial or supportive intervention. For example, a consumer who is diagnosed with a disabling medical condition is expected to experience some degree of anxiety; indeed, anxiety can even be beneficial by prompting the consumer to prepare for action and/or acceptance. Therefore, supportive interventions, whether medication- or counseling-related, generally are not considered essential unless the anxiety is so pronounced that occupational or social functioning problems have occurred (Dziegielewski, 2002, 2004).

Because individuals suffering from anxiety are often given medications that initially bring improvement, they may express resistance to the need for further intervention. Feeling better is attributed only to the medication taken, which leaves consumers with a false sense of security because they are still vulnerable to continued or new *exogenous* pressures (life problems such as financial stress, job loss, relationship issues). To help avoid discontinuance of the counseling and other supportive efforts, early completion of a formalized contract for the continuation of psychosocial counseling is recommended. The supportive and skill-building interventions of psychosocial counseling can help the consumer prepare for future anxiety-provoking situations. Examples of counseling and supportive interventions in this area include relaxation training, cognitive–behavioral interventions, and exposure intervention (e.g., systematic desensitization).

Relaxation Training and Stress Reduction

Relaxation training can provide support to individuals who spend a great deal of time worrying about life events or bodily sensations that rest within the early symptoms of their attacks. Teaching consumers how to relax can lead to them learning how to direct their energy in a more productive way, thereby reducing anxiety levels. *Applied relaxation* techniques require consumers to learn progressive relaxation skills and apply these in anxiety-producing situations (Ost, 1987). These techniques teach consumers to direct their energy in a more productive way toward reducing anxiety levels (Ost, Salkovskis, & Hellstrom, 1991) and gaining some semblance of control. Consumers suffering from anxiety need to learn that it can lead to physiological indicators of stress that raise their pulse, or result in bradycardia—slow heart action—and a decrease in blood pressure, which can result in fainting (Ost, Lindahl, Sterner, & Jerremalm, 1984; Ost, Sterner, & Fellenius, 1989).

Dziegielewski and MacNeil (1999) recommend that a type of autogenic (self-generating) training be emphasized with anxious consumers. Modeled after Seaward (1997a), the consumer is instructed to assume a restful position. The practitioner then educates the consumer about diaphragmatic breathing (see Seaward, 1997b, for a more comprehensive description) and models the use of the technique for the consumer. The consumer is instructed to practice the technique at home to reinforce the learning process.

Next, very general instructions are given to the individual, suggesting that he or she become aware of the following phenomena in his or her body: a feeling of heaviness, a feeling of warmth and tingling, a calmness of the heart, a calmness of breathing. About a minute is spent on each sensation, helping the consumer to recognize the sensation in him- or herself. When the consumer begins to feel relaxed, the state of mind is anchored by asking the consumer to think of an affirmative phrase, such as "My body is calm, my body is relaxed, and I can handle these anxious feelings."

As homework, the consumer is asked to repeat the diaphragmatic breathing and affirmative phrases. Repeated practice of these relaxation exercises is recommended. Because consumers sometimes weaken the effectiveness of the affirmative phrase by engaging in negative "self-talk," additional reinforcement may be helpful, such as stress-reduction tapes or even helping the consumer to make a personalized relaxation tape. Relaxation and stress reduction tapes can be used to supplement "in session" therapeutic exercises. Successfully learning and practicing this technique is particularly useful because the consumer can then use it with each type of supportive intervention, including medication management and the cognitive restructuring process.

Cognitive–Behavioral Interventions

Cognitive–behavioral techniques are considered a primary supportive intervention for those who suffer from anxiety-related conditions and may include cognitive restructuring, deep breathing exercises, and in-vivo exposure therapy (Craske & Waikar, 1994; Reid, 1997). Although variation exists in exactly how these techniques should be implemented, most professionals agree that they are best used in combination as a "treatment package."

Cognitive restructuring is based on the concept that cognitions (thoughts) precede (or trigger) the distress caused by feelings of anxiety and panic. Consumers are taught to identify the misinterpretations or misappraisals of bodily sensations (e.g., feeling threatened) and to challenge them through reasoning and experience, thereby helping to eliminate the anxiety. Teaching the consumer to identify the indicators of stress and how to reduce their physiological manifestations serves as an important precursor when exposing the consumer to the target of his or her anxiety. Often relaxation training and deep breathing exercises are used, along with cognitive restructuring, to help the consumer practice more affirmative statements in a relaxed state. Basically, the consumer is helped to identify stressful cues and to address them while in a relaxed state.

One concern with utilizing antianxiety medications (particularly the benzodiazepines) in the treatment of anxiety is that they can interfere with the cognitive–behavioral interventions because they may lessen the physical symptoms that are experienced. This conflation of approaches could lead the consumer to attribute gains resulting from behaviorally based attempts at overcoming fears to the medication alone. Such an attribution would detract from the primary purpose of implementing psychosocial interventions, which is to empower consumers to develop the confidence to cognitively overcome their fears and eventually be able to do so without the use of medication. Special attention should be given to the fact that the consumer may start to question the validity of psychological interventions, and this questioning could lead to an unnecessary dependence on the medication to prevent the return of anxiety symptoms.

Exposure therapy has many forms, but the most common method of implementation involves establishing a plan whereby sessions or exercises are conducted on a daily basis. Research suggests that exposure-based interventions can be administered by the practitioner or by the consumer him- or herself (Alfonzo & Dziegielewski, 2001; Dziegielewski & MacNeil, 1999); clearly there are cost benefits for the consumer who self-directs the intervention in this regard.

Developing a supportive intervention plan from a cognitive–behavioral approach requires that the consumer and practitioner identify cognitive, behavioral, and somatic (bodily) responses and document each in regard to the consumer's subjective interpretation. Mutually negotiated long-term and short-term goals are developed next, starting from a cognitive perspective and identifying what causes the consumer to worry excessively about certain circumstances in his or her life. It is particularly useful to find specific examples of how these anxious thoughts lead to the unwanted behaviors; later the thoughts (as they manifest through the behaviors) can be addressed in the contract and the intervention plan. In addition to the cognitive–behavioral responses, a connection to the bodily (somatic) responses is made by having the consumer identify concrete examples of symptoms of motor tension (restlessness, tiredness, shakiness, or muscle tension), autonomic hyperactivity (palpitations, shortness of breath, dry mouth, trouble swallowing, nausea or diarrhea), or symptoms of hypervigilance.

Once this behavior is identified and outlined clearly, a plan can be established to address it. Cognitive restructuring can be used to teach the consumer that he or she has control, and when feeling anxious, to start deep breathing exercises in order to initiate relaxation. A preplanned contract can be negotiated to provide a plan of action when the anxiety begins to get aroused. In addition, anxious individuals may have trouble with eating and sleeping (similarly to those who are depressed). They may have no appetite, or they may have trouble falling asleep, because of excessive worry. These behaviors should be documented and identified as part of the treatment component. Table 6.6 illustrates a sample treatment plan. Note that an individualized time frame should be established for each consumer.

In conclusion, all consumers need to receive a complete and accurate assessment and referral process. The confounding nature of the presentation of anxiety symptoms requires that practitioners become aware of, and address, the cognitive, behavioral, and somatic practice implications when treating anxiety disorders. This does not mean that they must become experts in all these areas; however, they do need to acquire the knowledge and information that can help consumers to obtain and maintain the most therapeutically productive treatment possible. Practitioners must be able to recognize potential problem areas related to medication use and misuse, and effective psychosocial interventions, in order to recommend changes, when needed, in the consumer's course of treatment.

TABLE 6.6
Sample Treatment Plan: Long- and Short-term Goals and Objectives

Long-Term Goals

1. Stabilize anxiety level while increasing ability to complete activities of daily living.
2. Reduce overall frequency, intensity, and duration of anxiety symptoms.

Short-Term Objectives	Plan or Intervention
1. Take medications responsibly, as prescribed by the physician, and report any side effects experienced from the medications.	Assess need for antianxiety medications and arrange for prescription, if needed.
	Monitor and evaluate medication compliance and the effectiveness of the medication in regard to level of functioning. Carefully monitor for potential abuse or suicidal tendencies.
	Contract at beginning of medication treatment to continue full treatment regimen while taking medication.
2. Verbally identify the source of the anxiety.	Consumer is asked to make a list of what he or she is anxious about in past and present. (Complete in session with worker.)
	Encourage consumer to share feelings of anxiety and to develop healthy self-talk as a means of handling it. Assign participation in recreational activities and reinforce social activities and verbalizations.
	Train consumer in deep breathing as means of stress reduction.
	Write at least one positive, affirmative statement each day. Identify at least one irrational thought and one way to address it.
3. Identify cognitive self-talk that supports irrational thoughts.	Educate about the condition of anxiety Assist in developing awareness of cognitive messages and fears that reinforce control, and address irrational fears.
4. Complete assessments of functioning (scales for ADLs and suicide potential)	Arrange or complete administration of the tests. Assess and monitor the need for suicide intervention.

Note: Modified from Dziegielewski & Leon, 2001.

7

Schizophrenia and the Psychotic Disorders

T he conditions that are characteristic of psychotic disorders, such as schizophrenia, can disrupt an individual's life and alienate the individual from his or her family and support systems (Stomwall & Robinson, 1998). These disorders can also cause tremendous stress and frustration for helping professionals because of the consumer's unpredictable and uncertain behavior. Because complete or total remission for consumers suffering from these conditions is rare, a chronic yet variable course of illness is expected.

OVERVIEW OF SCHIZOPHRENIA AND THE PSYCHOTIC DISORDERS

A general understanding of psychotic disorders and the resulting signs and symptoms is necessary for the NMTP to accurately facilitate and assist affected individuals. The most commonly recognized of the psychotic disorders is schizophrenia, followed by schizophreniform disorder, schizoaffective disorder, delusional disorder, brief psychotic disorder, shared psychotic disorder, psychotic disorder due to a general medical condition, substance-induced psychotic disorder, and psychotic disorder NOS (American Psychiatric Association, 2000). See Table 7.1 for a list and brief description of the schizophrenic (or primary) psychotic disorders.

TABLE 7.1
Schizophrenic Psychotic Disorders

Schizophrenia and its five subtypes:

- *Disorganized type*: marked incoherence; lack of systematized delusions; blunted, disturbed, or silly affect
- *Catatonic type*: stupor, negativism, rigidity, bizarre posturing, and excessive motor activity
- *Paranoid type*: one or more systematized delusions or auditory hallucinations with a similar theme
- *Undifferentiated type*: contains aspects of the other prominent types
- *Residual type*: symptoms of schizophrenia not currently displayed but have been in the past

Brief reactive psychosis: This condition has historically been called "3-day schizophrenia" because symptoms generally last at least a few hours but no longer than a month, and sudden onset is generally linked to some type of psychosocial stressor.

Schizophreniform disorder: This is usually considered a provisional diagnosis that is generally related to the first episode of psychosis. When the episode lasts longer than 6 months, the diagnosis should be changed to schizophrenia.

Schizoaffective disorder: Individuals who suffer from this disorder experience the signs and symptoms prevalent in both the schizophrenic disorder and the mood disorder. However, positive symptoms continue to exist (for at least 2 weeks) even when the mood disorder symptoms are not prominent.

Delusional disorder: The essential feature of this disorder is the presence of one or more non-bizarre delusions that persist for at least 1 month. Individuals often adhere to a delusional belief (e.g., that others are recording their phone messages) that cannot be shaken, even when presented with information that disproves the belief.

Shared psychotic disorder: In this disorder, often referred to as the *folie à deux*, two or more individuals share the same delusional belief system. Generally, one individual is considered the primary case and the other follows his or her lead.

Psychotic disorder due to a general medical condition: In this disorder the positive symptoms that exist are related directly to a general medical condition, and the general medical condition must be clearly identified. For example, a consumer may suffer from a metabolic disease (e.g., electrolyte imbalance) or an endocrine disease (e.g., hypothyroidism).

Substance-induced psychotic disorder: This condition is manifested by positive symptoms related to the direct physiological effects of a substance. For example, methamphetamines have an extremely long half-life, and it is possible an individual could experience positive symptoms up to 24 hours after ingesting the substance.

Psychotic disorder not otherwise specified (NOS): This diagnosis indicates the presence of psychotic symptomatology about which there is inadequate or contradicting information to make a more specific diagnosis.

Note: Adapted from American Psychiatric Association, 1994, 2000.

Because schizophrenia is probably not a single disorder, as is so often assumed (Flaum, 1995; McGrath, 1999b), the practitioner must be prepared to address problems that require multifaceted intervention efforts. Many of the behaviors exhibited can overlap with other mental health conditions, such as the mood disorders (bipolar and depression) and the dementia- or delirium-based disorders, so a general understanding of these related conditions is also needed. Taking this overlap of symptoms into account, it makes sense that antipsychotic medications are also used as adjunctive treatments for mood disorders without psychosis and in the management of agitation associated with other types of mental disorders (e.g., disruptive behavior disorders and attention deficit disorder; Segraves & Balon, 2003).

Although the exact cause of schizophrenia is unknown, what is clear is that it involves more than environmental stress. Some researchers believe that genetics plays a significant role (Brzustowicz, Hodgkinson, Chow, Honer, & Bassett, 2000); others make the argument that schizophrenia involves certain focal abnormalities in the brain tissues that have an effect on the frontal lobes, temporal lobes, limbic system, and basal ganglia within the brain (American Psychiatric Association, 2000; Farmer & Pandurangi, 1997); yet others believe that schizophrenia is related directly to neurotransmitter activity, particularly that of dopamine. This position referred to as the *dopamine hypothesis* (Buchanan, Brandes, & Breier, 1996; Karper & Krystal, 1996). According to this perspective, there is a functional excess of dopamine in the central nervous system of the person with schizophrenia, and antipsychotic medications achieve their beneficial action by blocking dopamine receptors in the brain (Farmer & Pandurangi, 1997). The simplicity of this explanation, however, has been tainted as many researchers warn that the involvement of dopamine alone is not comprehensive enough to explain the complex changes that occur in schizophrenia (Carpenter, Conley, & Buchanan, 1998; Karper & Krystal, 1996). The controversy continues as to what actually causes schizophrenia, and efforts to predict the potential occurrence and recurrence abound.

The first psychosis or break with reality usually occurs between the ages of 17 and 30 in males and between 20 and 40 in females (Carpenter et al., 1998). If this disorder occurs after the age of 45, it is considered to be of late onset (Sadavoy, 2004). Once onset has occurred, the course remains extremely variable; indeed, some individuals may not become psychotic again after a first episode. A majority of those affected improve after the first episode but continue to manifest symptoms, with future occurrences of the symptoms remaining unpredictable.

RECOGNIZING THE SIGNS AND SYMPTOMS

Individuals who suffer from a psychotic disorder generally experience a characteristic deterioration in adaptive functioning. Both *negative* (less severe) and *positive* symptoms are displayed. When referring to the psychotic disorders, the term *negative symptoms* refers to symptoms that interfere with an individual's functioning and impair the completion of normal activities of daily living (ADLs). One easy way to remember this symptom cluster is to use the *six A's* (see Table 7.2).

TABLE 7.2
The Six A's of Psychosis

- *Associative disturbances* affect how the consumer responds and relates to others and completes ADLs.
- *Affective disturbances* distort the way in which a consumer expresses his or her mood.
- *Autism* increases the individual's isolation; others may question whether the person is able to understand his or her environment and respond to external cues in a socially acceptable manner.
- *Ambivalence* hampers the person's ability to make decisions or complete follow-up.
- *Avolition* is a lack of goal-directed behavior.
- *Alogia* refers to poverty of speech or an inability to express the self.

Associative disturbances are characterized by perceptual difficulties; often these individuals are not sure how to relate with others. For example, a person may invade another person's social or personal space because his or her sense of personal boundaries is disturbed. When speaking, the person might get so close to another individual that he or she walks into the person before stopping. On the other hand, just the opposite may happen if the individual is touched, perhaps in an effort to reassure, and he or she withdraws, frightened by the contact. Taken together, these behaviors might seem disturbing to family, friends, and the unaware professional who is simply trying to express concern. Associative disturbances that are characteristic of this disorder impair social functioning and result in isolation from the supportive environmental context.

Affective disturbances are a prevalent feature of the disorder and may be particularly unsettling to everyone involved, because the affected person often exhibits unpredictable moods and emotions. Traditionally this symptom cluster has been referred to as a *splitting of mood*, where the person exhibits polarities in emotions that can result in anger being displayed one minute and laughter the next. These persons may feel depressed and exhibit the classic signs of depression yet show it by crying (which is consistent with depressed mood) and then almost immediately laughing loudly (which is inconsistent). The lack of relevance to what is actually happening may be alarming to family and friends, as well as to mental health professionals. It may be difficult for many to understand that the individual is suffering from something beyond his or her control because often he or she appears to be in control of his or her behaviors.

The term *autism* used to be used interchangeably with *childhood schizophrenia*. Today, however, this association is rarely made. Autism refers to a separation from, or lack of responsiveness to, usual daily environmental stimuli. This lack of connection makes it difficult to communicate with the person or to determine exactly how much he or she is able to comprehend. The condition can be particularly difficult or frustrating for family members and professionals, because it limits the person's ability to follow intervention efforts and participate in counseling.

Ambivalence is clearly reflected in the indecisive behavior that impedes the person's ability to make decisions or adhere to an intervention plan. Furthermore, when ambivalence is accompanied by autism, it is difficult to be sure the person can comprehend and focus on what is being expected. He or she may express willingness to do something but change his or her mind within moments and refuse to do so. Completing simple actions (e.g., dressing, deciding whether to go outside) may become daunting for some.

Avolition, a lack of goal-directed behavior, is most evident when an individual wants to do something but simply cannot. This type of behavior is common in conditions such as depression and anxiety as well. This lack of goal-directed behavior can block the completion of daily activities such as bathing, taking medications, or going to work.

With *alogia*, a poverty of speech, an individual wants to report what he or she is feeling but simply cannot find the words. Attempts at expressing the self often lead to frustration because the individual (and those around him or her) cannot understand why he or she cannot find the right words.

Malhotra, Pinsky, and Breier (1996) warn that these negative symptoms, which are often subtle (compared to positive symptoms) can be real stumbling blocks for consumers who are trying to lead fruitful and productive lives. In addition, these negative features can overlap with other disorders. For example, depression and its symptoms occur in 25% of people in whom there is clear documentation of schizophrenia (Siris, 2000). In order to provide the best care, NMTPs must realize that negative symptoms can overlap with other symptoms not typically related to the psychotic disorders.

In addition to negative symptoms, consumers who suffer from a psychotic disorder such as schizophrenia often report experiencing *psychotic* or *positive* symptoms: that is delusions, hallucinations, or thought disturbances (Kaplan & Sadock, 1990). Delusions are the most common of these symptoms. A delusion is a belief that a person holds despite evidence to the contrary (e.g., "Aliens control my thoughts"). In schizophrenia there may be numerous delusions so disturbing that functioning is impaired. Often these delusions are systematized (e.g. "Everyone and everything is out to get me") and may involve family and friends (referred to as *delusions of reference*). These unshakable distortions of reality may be difficult for loved ones to tolerate, because they cannot see any real or external basis for such beliefs or understand why they are so difficult to control.

In the psychotic disorders it is important to differentiate between the delusions of reference so common in schizophrenic conditions and the *ideas of reference* as experienced in some of the personality disorders. In schizotypal personality disorder, for example, social withdrawal from family and friends is common; and this forced separation is often accompanied by ideas of reference. An idea of reference is much more individualized than a delusion of reference. An idea of reference often refers to a specific individual, event, or item that may encompass magical thinking or involve a certain degree of exaggerated importance. An example is a person who believes he or she is so useless and worthless that a physician would come into his or her home and offer to assist in ending his or her life. This is different from delusions of reference because the fear is focused and not generalized to other areas. The specific or limited idea of reference is very different from the more extensive delusions of reference exhibited in the condition of schizophrenia. An example of a delusion of reference would be a person who believes that everyone who wears green is sending messages to take over the world. Delusions of reference are much more obvious and affect almost every aspect of the person's ADLs.

Hallucinations, the second positive symptom, involve a misperception of sensory stimuli that causes a break with reality. The most common form of hallucination is auditory; almost 70% of all reported hallucinatory symptoms are auditory (Hoffman, 2000). Generally, auditory hallucinations involve the hearing of voices, usually voices that are negative, controlling, and considered to be commanding in nature. Visual hallucinations are less common, and when experienced, careful assessment of the cause is warranted. Because this symptom is rare in schizophrenia, other causes (e.g., brain damage, closed head injury, substance withdrawal, another type of medical condition) should always be ruled out first. Less common forms of hallucinations in schizophrenia include tactile and olfactory sensations. These may also be indicative of an organic problem. In some cases, consumers may report feeling that bugs are crawling on them—a phenomenon often related to substance use and abuse. Therefore, the NMTP should first rule out a substance-related cause. The consumer should be referred immediately for a drug screen or physical examination to determine if the psychosis is related to substance abuse or another type of delirium. Table 7.3 summarizes the negative and positive symptoms of psychotic disorders.

TABLE 7.3
Identification of Negative and Positive Symptoms

Negative symptoms

- Occur more commonly than positive symptoms and are harder to detect.
- Often include avolition (lack of goal-directed behavior), blunted affect, emotional withdrawal, poor rapport, passivity, apathy, social withdrawal, difficulty in abstract thinking, lack of spontaneity, and stereotyped thinking patterns.

Positive symptoms

- Generally include delusions, conceptual disorganization, hallucinations, excitement, grandiosity, suspiciousness, feelings of persecution, and hostility.
- Are often obvious and easy to detect in the assessment process.

When working with consumers who have chronic types of schizophrenia, it is important to realize that they may experience disturbances in motor behavior, such as waxy flexibility and catalepsy (a state of stupor). In waxy flexibility, the person may appear somewhat rigid and may seem to get stuck in certain positions or stay frozen in these positions for a long period of time. Often times these individuals are said to be mannequin-like. Waxy flexibility and catalepsy are both characterized by a state of continual and unusual muscle tension (Moore & Jefferson, 1997). In catalepsy, however, the person appears to hold persistent and unusual postures, soldered in place and nonresponsive to outside stimuli. To the inexperienced practitioner, family member, or friend, this type of behavior can be very frightening. Therefore, it is essential to educate the consumer, his or her family, and unaware professionals about the signs and symptoms of schizophrenia, and the interventions that work best to address them.

Table 7.4 lists possible problematic behaviors for this population.

TABLE 7.4
Assessment of Problematic Behavior

The NMTP needs to assess the consumer for the following problem behaviors:

- Ambivalent feelings that impair general task completion related to independent living skills.

continued

TABLE 7.4 (*continued*)

- Affect disturbances such as feelings of depression or a difficulty in controlling anger.
- Poor concentration or an inability to stay on task.
- Autistic behaviors (an inability to socialize, isolated or detached from others).
- Associative disturbances (particularly being touched or approached by others).
- Auditory hallucinations (hearing voices that berate, torture, or degrade the consumer).
- Avolition evidenced by an inability, or lack of desire, to complete ADLs such as taking a shower or completing mundane tasks.
- Alogia, evidenced by an inability to say what is wrong or what is needed.
- Paranoid ideation (the consumer's belief that someone is trying to harm him or her).

OVERVIEW OF TYPICAL ANTIPSYCHOTIC MEDICATIONS

Medications for the treatment of schizophrenia date back to the early 1800s and have included drugs such as opium, bromide derivatives, chloral hydrate, and barbiturates (Bentley, 1998). Traditionally these drugs were used to calm down the violent or combative consumer but did little to control the symptoms that go along with the mental disorder. Known as *chemical restraints*, the calming effect these medications produced provided a more humane form of intervention. These earlier medications were so calming that they were often referred to as the *major tranquilizers*. The use of these *neuroleptic medications* (another name for this class of medications) assisted in preventing long-term institutionalization. The development of antipsychotic medications and the better control these medications afforded encouraged deinstitutionalization and the current emphasis on community-based outpatient care (Breier & Buchanan, 1996; Empfield, 2000).

Because many of these medications and their resultant effects were discovered serendipitously, the science that supports their use remains tenuous. For example, in the early 1950s the first medication introduced to treat the hallucinations, delusions, and psychotic depression of schizophrenia—chlorpromazine (the chemical name) or Thorazine (the brand name)—was discovered accidentally. Originally this medication was used to lower body temperature and serve as a type of cold pack; in the 1950s cold packs were thought to calm the agitated patient. The co-occurring sedative effect from the medication was also beneficial in reducing agitation. Although it did not decrease body temperature, as originally suspected, it did appear to lessen many of the psychotic symptoms of schizophrenia. Soon thereafter, it was marketed as a wonder drug for the treatment of this condition (Berstein, 1995; Bentley, 1998). Numerous other drugs followed (see Table 7.5), and these *typical* antipsychotics were recognized for treating mental health disorders. All of these older medications work by blocking dopamine in the brain (Diamond, 2002).

TABLE 7.5
Typical Antipsychotic Agents

Medication	Side Effect/Benefit Profile	Daily Dosage Range and Forms
Thorazine (chlorpromazine)	Highly sedating	400–500 mg
Mellaril (thioridazine)	Highly sedating, high anticholinergic effects	40–800 mg
Stelazine (trifluoperazine)	Low sedating, moderate EPS	2–80 mg
Prolixin (fluphenazine)	Minimal sedation	2–40 mg
Prolixin decanoate (fluphenazine decanoate)	High EPS	Oral: short-acting (lasts 6–8 hours) and long-acting (lasts over 2 weeks); injectable
Haldol (haloperidol)	Moderately sedating	1–40 mg
Haldol decanoate (haloperidol decanoate)	High EPS	Long-acting injection (given once a month)
Loxitane (loxapine)	Moderate EPS	30–250 mg
Navane (thiothixene)	Lower EPS for a high-potency medication	5–60 mg
Moban (molindone)	Less weight gain than other typical medications	20–225 mg

Note: EPS/*extrapyramidal side effects* (e.g., hand tremor, motor restlessness); dosages suggested by Diamond, 2002.

Side-Effect Profiles and Special Considerations

Understnading and helping the consumer to recognize and address medication side effects is extremely important. In schizophrenia and the psychotic disorders, the separation or distortion of reality characteristic of the condition can make symptom recognition a complicated process for the consumer, the MTP, the NMTP, and the family support system.

Medication Potency

All typical antipsychotic medications affect the neurotransmitter dopamine, and all are considered equally effective for the treatment of psychotic disorders and other mental health conditions with related symptoms. What is different to the NMTP about these medications is the dosing regimen, which is based on medication potency. *Potency* is the amount of medication needed to be equally effective for the symptoms when compared to other related medications. For example, Thorazine is prescribed in higher numbers (100 mg dose), whereas Haldol is equally effective as Thorazine when prescribed at the 2 mg dose. Haldol is considered high potency because less of it is needed. The side-effect profiles for the typical medications are similar; however, some differences do exist. For example, high-potency medications (Prolixin, Haldol, Navane) are considered easier to tolerate when compared to low-potency medications (Diamond, 2002). The high-potency medications are less sedating, have fewer anticholinergic effects (dry mouth, constipation, blurred vision) and have fewer problems with postural hypotension (the dropping of blood pressure when standing or sitting too quickly). However, these medications are more likely to cause extrapyramidal side effects (EPS), such as hand tremor and motor restlessness (Diamond, 2002).

Extrapyramidal Symptoms

Typical antipsychotics are dopamine inhibitors that block other neurotransmitters such as acetylcholine, histamine, and norepinephrine. *Extrapyramidal symptoms* (EPS), also referred to as parkinsonism, are a common side effect with these medications, and the practitioner must be able to recognize them. Parkinsonism is similar to the symptoms that are seen in Parkinson's disease (hence, its name). One major difference between the two, however, can be seen in the type of tremors the person exhibits. In Parkinson's disease the tremor is slow, rhythmic, and rotational (looks like pill rolling), whereas in EPS or parkinsonism the hands, fingers, and wrists move faster as a unit (Maxmen & Ward, 2002).

Dystonia is one of the movement problems that may occur; acute dystonic reactions may present as grimacing, difficulty with speech or swallowing, a crisis involving the upward rotation of the eyeballs (oculogyric), muscle spasms of the neck and throat, or extensor rigidity of the back muscles (Carpenter et al., 1998). Very often these Parkinson's-like reactions will occur within the first few days of treatment. It is not uncommon for the consumer to approach the practitioner complaining of a thick or stiff tongue that impairs his or her ability to speak. Once given a medication to control this side effect, such as Cogentin (benztrophine), the symptoms of dystonia will subside within minutes to hours (Maxmen & Ward, 2002).

Akathisia is the most common form of EPS. Less obvious than dystonia, akathisia is an extreme form of motor restlessness and may be mistaken for agitation. With this side effect the consumer feels compelled to be in a constant state of movement and may report inner restlessness that is evidenced by a shaking leg or constant pacing. During assessment these consumers often cannot sit still; restless legs or uncontrollable foot tapping are apparent. Although akathisia generally appears early in the course of treatment and can be related to other EPS, it can also occur independently (Carpenter et al., 1998). When given medicine to control this side effect, the symptoms, unlike dystonia, do not subside quickly; it can take 3–10 days to get a significant response (Maxmen & Ward, 20002).

Tardive Dyskinesia

Another form of EPS that involves involuntary movements of any group of muscles is *tardive dyskinesia* (TD). The most common involuntary movements involve the face, including both the mouth and tongue; the trunk, involving both the neck and shoulders and dramatic hip jerks; and limb movements, with tremors that are repetitive and rhythmic (Maxmen & Ward, 2002). Awareness of this side effect is particularly important because if it occurs, it is generally considered an irreversible consequence of long-term usage of typical antipsychotic medications (Carpenter et al., 1998).

Sometimes TD is confused with *rabbit syndrome*, known as *perioral tremor*. With this side effect there is a rapid lip tremor and buccal masticatory (chewing) movements that are said to mimic a rabbit. One major difference between this symptom and TD is that rabbit syndrome does not involve the tongue and often continues when the individual sleeps. Generally, this side effect will subside when the antipsychotic medication is stopped (Maxmen & Ward, 2002).

One way to address TD is to prescribe the medication in lower doses, but for chronic schizophrenia this may not be an option. The newer or atypical antipsychotics may offer a more hopeful course of treatment for consumers with this disorder, because these medications seem to have fewer EPS side effects, especially when given in low doses (Lambert, 1998).

Neuroleptic Malignant Syndrome

A rarer side effect associated with the more traditional antipsychotic medications is *neuroleptic malignant syndrome* (NMS). Although it occurs in only 0.2–0.5% of cases, it is considered a serious concern because 15–20% of those affected could die (*Physicians' Desk Reference*, 2004). The symptoms include severe rigidity of the muscles, a high fever, confusion, pallor and sweating, altered mental states, and evidence of autonomic instability (irregular pulse or blood pressure, tachycardia [rapid heart rate], diaphoresis [heavy sweating], and cardiac dysrhythmia [irregular heart rate]).

NMS occurs more frequently in males, and problematic symptoms often begin as early as 10 days after starting the medication. Once the problematic symptoms develop, consumers taking these medications are at significant risk for the development of further problems in this area. Because of the extreme severity of this condition, it is imperative that practitioners who work with consumers who have schizophrenia are aware of the symptoms and the potentially lethal consequences.

Reduction of Parkinsonian Effects

Medications prescribed to decrease or control movement-related side effects are referred to as antiparkinsonian medications. When a consumer is receiving a typical antipsychotic medicine, it is essential to determine if something has been prescribed to counter the EPS side effects that might result. The medications that are often used to address the side-effect profiles just described are listed in Table 7.6.

TABLE 7.6
Common Antiparkinsonian Medications

Drug	Dosage Range (mg/day)
Cogentin (benztrophine)	0.5–6
Akineton (biperiden)	2–8
Benadryl (diphenhydramine)	50–300
Artane (trihexyphenidyl)	1–15

Some factors to consider when consumers are taking these antiparkinsonian medications include noting whether the consumer has a history of substance abuse or might be involved in trying to sell these drugs on the street. This is particularly true for Cogentin and Artane, which consumers report make a person feel good—a quality that increases the potential for abuse. When the potential for abuse is suspected, it might be best for the treatment team or the prescriber to consider an OTC medication (such as Benadryl) to help control the symptoms of EPS.

OVERVIEW OF ATYPICAL ANTIPSYCHOTIC MEDICATIONS

Atypical antipsychotic drugs are often referred to as front-line medications for the treatment of schizophrenia and the other psychotic disorders. Examples of these medications include Clozaril (clozapine), Risperdal (risperidone), Zyprexa (olanzapine), Seroquel (quetiapine), Geodon (ziprasidone), and Abilify (aripiprazole) (see Table 7.7). These medications help to manage the positive symptoms (e.g., hallucinations, delusions, thought disturbances) along with the negative symptoms (e.g., social withdrawal, apathy, lack of motivation, inability to experience pleasure) associated with these disorders. These medications can also help delay relapses while assisting with the short-term management of behavioral disturbances such as verbal aggression (e.g., screaming, cursing) or physical aggression (e.g., kicking, hitting, biting, scratching, throwing things).

These medications have gained popularity because they appear to have lower EPS profiles. Atypical medications also help individuals to think more clearly, learn new information, master skills better, and follow directions better (Lambert, 1998). When working with these medications, however, dosing should always be cautiously monitored because the clinical trials used to support usage remain limited, and more research in this area is needed (Rogers, 2002).

Table 7.7
Atypical Antipsychotic Medications

Brand name	Generic name	Adult Dosage (mg/day)
Clozaril	clozapine	300–600
Risperdal	risperidone	4–6
Serlect	sertindole	12–24
Zyprexa	olanzapine	5–10
Seroquel	quetiapine	300–400
Geodon	ziprasidone	120–160
Abilify	aripiprazole	10–30

Note: Different sources may report slightly different dosages. These dosage recommendations are taken from the *Physicians' Desk Reference,* 2004, except for Serlect, which was obtained directly from supplemental product information.

Clozaril (Clozapine)

The oldest of the medications in this group is clozapine, known by the brand name Clozaril. As the first in its class, it is sometimes listed as both a typical and an atypical antipsychotic medication. The brand-name medication Clozaril was originally synthesized in 1957. In 1960 it was one of the first antipsychotics released on the European market and was considered more successful because it did not seem to have the same negative side-effect profiles as its predecessors (Hippius, 1989). Unfortunately, years after its introduction, eight documented cases of death were attributed to infections secondary to clozapine-induced agranulocytosis (also known as Shultz syndrome), and the product was withdrawn from unrestricted use (Davis & Casper, 1997).

Agranulocytosis occurs when there is a severe reduction in the number of granulocytes, a particular type of white blood cell. Without these granulocytes, the body is unable to fight life-threatening infections. Although the percentage of the Clozaril-consuming population that develops this side effect is small (only 1–2% of all consumers), the seriousness of this complication warrants strict monitoring. Once a system allowing for this monitoring was in place, the FDA approved use of this medication, and it was reintroduced in 1990 (Barnes & McEvedy, 1996).

When consumers are on Clozaril, two factors should be considered: (1) Because this medication is usually dosed 1 week at a time to ensure consumer compliance with the medical regimen, convenience for acquiring the medication needs to be considered; (2) consumers must have a blood count done every week or 2 to ensure that the potentially fatal condition of agranulocytosis does not start to develop. The potential for this side effect must be monitored because once this side effect occurs, the drug must be promptly discontinued and cannot be used again. Because of its effectiveness and minimal general side-effect profile, Clozaril remains a possible choice for intervention. The expense and inconvenience for consumers who take it, however, remains very limiting and may be related to its relative decrease in popularity.

Based on the side-effect profile and the monitoring required, a trial of at least two other standard antipsychotic drugs is recommended prior to using Clozaril (McGrath, 1999b; *Physicians' Desk Reference*, 2004). Sandoz Pharmaceuticals, the manufacturer of Clozaril, has suggested new guidelines requiring that weekly monitoring be done for the first 6 months and every 2 weeks thereafter if the white blood count remains stable (*Physicians' Desk Reference*, 2004).

Weekly monitoring can be very inconvenient for consumers who cannot get to the medical provider, pharmacy, or lab regularly, especially those who live in rural areas. Assistance may be needed to help the consumer gain weekly access to the drug. Caution is warranted with use of this medication, as several individuals have died despite weekly hematological monitoring.

Early signs of infection that need to be reported immediately to health care providers include fever, sore throat, fatigue, and mucous membrane ulcerations. The two most common side effects of Clozaril are sedation and weight gain (Diamond, 2002). Other side effects include seizures, tonic and clonic convulsions, drowsiness, dizziness, increased saliva production, increased heartbeat, lowered blood pressure, fever, and postural hypotension. Also, similar to other atypical antipsychotic medications, Clozaril can cause intestinal problems such as constipation, impaction, or blockage. Clozaril has also been linked to more serious side effects, such as hyperglycemia in consumers with no history of diabetes or blood glucose at baseline (Maxmen & Ward, 2002). Clozaril should never be used with drugs that can suppress bone marrow, such as anticancer drugs (*Physicians' Desk Reference*, 2004).

As with any prescription medication, Clozaril should be taken only as directed by the MTP who prescribes and monitors it. Clozaril can be taken with or without food; if a dose is missed, the missed dose should be taken as soon as remembered, unless it is very close to the time for the next scheduled dose.

Risperdal (Risperidone)

Another atypical medication, Risperdal (risperidone), was introduced as the first official atypical antipsychotic medication in 1992. This drug is the most frequently prescribed antipsychotic and is currently used by more than 10 million people worldwide. Today, use of long-acting risperidone (Risperdal Consta), an intramuscular formulation, appears to be increasing. This form is attractive to many because it offers a sustained and steady release of the drug (Harrison & Goa, 2004).

The exact mechanism of action of risperidone, in either the regular or long-acting version, is not yet fully understood, although it appears to block the action of two neurotransmitters in the brain: serotonin and dopamine. Risperdal (risperidone) is used for acute and maintenance treatment of schizophrenia and the related psychotic disorders. Labeled uses for Risperdal include bipolar disorder (Ghaemi, Sachs, Baldassano, & Truman, 1997), psychosis associated with a medical condition, and schizophrenia. The only off-labeled use noted is for infantile autism. In addition, risperidone has been used to treat the psychotic-like or positive

175

symptoms of schizotypal personality disorder, as well as its negative symptoms such as cognitive impairment (Saklad, 2000). Furthermore, risperidone studies suggest that this medication may be effective in the treatment of adolescents with schizophrenia at the doses typically used with adults (Findling & Pastor, 2000).

When compared to Haldol, a typical antipsychotic medicine, risperidone is reported to reduce more positive and negative symptoms (Armenteros, 1997) as well as being more effective for reducing relapse rates and keeping consumers free of symptoms longer (Manisses Communications Group, 2002). Hotujac and Sagud (2002) reported that, within the limits of naturalistic studies, it can be concluded that Risperdal is an effective and safe drug for long-term treatment in most consumers.

The most common side effects reported with this medication are sedation and weight gain. When using Risperdal with children, it is recommended that, in addition to a careful monitoring of weight, baseline liver function tests and periodic monitoring of liver function during the maintenance phase of treatment needs to be conducted (Walsh, 1998).

Zyprexa (Olanzapine)

Zyprexa (olanzapine), a benzodiazepene drug, was marketed after Risperdal and approved by the FDA in 1996. Given orally, Zyprexa works by preventing the binding of dopamine, serotonin, histamine, and other neurotransmitters to their receptors. Zyprexa is generally used to help reduce or eliminate the symptoms of schizophrenia. In 1999 the FDA approved bipolar disorder as a labeled use. Since its approval, it has been prescribed to more that 11 million people in 84 countries (Eli Lilly, 2003).

Zyprexa appears to be well tolerated and readily accepted by consumers, especially because of its low incidence of EPS and its ability to address the negative symptoms of schizophrenia (Harvard Mental Health Letter, 1999). Caution should be exercised, however, because Zyprexa may increase blood glucose levels in individuals with diabetes (APA Studies, 2000; Doraiswamy & Koller, 2002; *Physicians' Desk Reference*, 2004; Saklad, 2000). With a half-life of 21–54 hours, it is best not to take a missed dose. Also, adequate liver functioning in consumers of this drug is very important because 40% of it is metabolized in the liver.

Seroquel (Quetiapine)

In the fall of 1997 Seroquel (quetiapine) was introduced. This medication is primarily used to treat schizophrenia and involves the action of two neurotransmitters in the brain: serotonin and dopamine. Seroquel appears to produce less weight gain than other atypicals; however, side effects related to the movement disorders have been noted (*Physicians' Desk Reference*, 2004; Schulz, 2000). Drowsiness has also been reported, so this medication should not be taken when operating machinery, driving, or when expected to complete more complex tasks.

Geodon (Ziprasidone)

Geodon (ziprasidone) which was approved for use in 2001. This medication is primarily used to treat schizophrenia; like Seroquel, it is believed to work by utilizing the same two neurochemicals: serotonin and dopamine. In addition to tablet and capsule form, this medication is also available in intramuscular injection form (usually reserved for consumers who exhibit severe agitation).

Because of its newness to the market, the side effect profile of Geodon is not established; however, this is the first medication in this category to appear to be weight neutral and to have less sedating effects (Diamond, 2002). However, it appears that people who take this medication may have trouble sleeping and may become agitated. The most serious concern is its effect on the heart, specifically, the way it can affect the QT interval, causing the heart to quiver instead of contract fully. This occurrence is very dangerous because the heart can suddenly stop beating and the individual can die (Diamond, 2002).

Abilify (Aripiprazole)

Abilify (aripiprazole) was introduced and approved by the FDA in 2003. This medication is primarily used in the short-term treatment of schizophrenia. It appears to work by utilizing several neurotransmitters in the brain: serotonin, dopamine, as well as the alpha-adrenergic, and histamine receptors (*Physicians' Desk Reference*, 2004). More time is needed to delineate its side-effect profile, but to date, it appears to cause little weight gain or sedation, and has little effect on heart function (Diamond, 2002).

Side-Effect Profiles and Special Considerations

Levinthal (2002) reports that atypical antipsychotic medications, unlike earlier medications used for treating schizophrenia, do not put an individual at significant risk of developing Parkinson-like side effects; in other words, all of these medications have lower EPS profiles (Tandon, 2002). In addition, convenient and flexible dosing schedules allow these medications to be more easily prescribed at different strengths and formulations. One common problem that all the antipsychotic medications share, however, involves adverse effects on libido (sex drive). Because of reporting problems and the lack of precise definitions of libido, the exact influences—and which drugs have the greatest influence—are unknown (Segraves & Balon, 2003). Another shared side effect is that of weight gain, and this effect is associated with an increased risk of diabetes mellitus. Tandon (2002) warns, however, that it is too early to say conclusively that these medications can actually cause diabetes. Nevertheless, attention to potential complications is warranted.

The most common side effects for many atypical medications include sleepiness, restlessness, tremors, muscle stiffness, dizziness, constipation, nausea, indigestion, runny nose, rash, and rapid heartbeat. Furthermore, consumers may feel lightheaded or dizzy when they stand up or sit up too quickly (orthostasis).

EPS are limited but have been seen in consumers receiving high doses. Uncontrollable or jerky facial movements (a symptom of TD) are rare, as is NMS (both described earlier in this chapter). Table 7.8 summarizes the side effects common to atypical antipsychotic medications.

TABLE 7.8
General Side Effects of Atypical Antipsychotic Medications

- Drowsiness, somnolence
- Rapid heart rate
- Dizziness in changing position (orthostasis)
- Anxiety
- Dyspepsia (disorder of digestion, with pain or discomfort in the lower chest area)
- Constipation

continued

TABLE 7.8 *(continued)*

- Urinary retention
- Decreased sexual ability or interest
- Weight gain
- Problems with menstrual cycle
- More prone to sunburn or skin rashes

Note: The side effects listed in this table are a summary of the most common. For a complete listing of potential side effects for each of the drugs in this class, see *Physicians' Desk Reference*, 2004 which has the most updated information in relation to initial drug trials.

Drug interactions with this new classification of atypical medications are multiple. Because atypical antipsychotic medications are fairly new to the market, taking a medication history is essential. Potential drug interactions need to be recorded and monitored closely for changes in efficacy, toxicity levels, and, if applicable, drug concentration (Lam, 2000). For exact interaction and synergistic prospects, see the *Physicians' Desk Reference* (2004).

Adjunctive Medication

NMTPs are challenged to provide the best possible help to consumers who suffer from psychotic disorders. Most agree that medication treatment for the active symptomology of schizophrenia and other psychotic disorders is an absolute necessity. No type of verbal therapy is productive until the consumer has been stabilized, the psychotic symptoms reduced, and some semblance of reality is restored. Once the consumer is stabilized, supportive interventions that emphasize problem-solving methods may be used to address the significant problems that affect the daily lives of these consumers. Behavioral intervention strategies may also be employed to help consumers become aware of their actions and the consequences on their levels of daily functioning (Sensky et al., 2000).

Complex symptoms may require medication intervention that goes beyond antipsychotic medicines. It is not unusual for additional medications to be utilized in the management of the variety of psychotic symptoms. Supportive medications include lithium, the mood stabilizers and anticonvulsants (e.g., valproic acid), beta-blockers, and benzodiazepines (see Table 7.9). For more specific information on these medications, see the chapters in which they are discussed.

TABLE 7.9
Adjunctive Medications in the Treatment of Schizophrenia

Drug Category	Use in Psychotic Disorders
Lithium	Used in treatment-resistant schizophrenia
Mood stabilizers/anticonvulsants, carbamazepine, valproic acid	Used primarily for treatment of bipolar disorder with psychosis
Benzodiazepines	Used in treatment-resistant schizophrenia
Antidepressants	Used to address the depressive episodes often found in schizophrenia

Note: Information summarized from Carpenter, Conley, & Buchanan, 1998.

But the use of a medication, or supplementation with additional medications, is often not enough to achieve symptom relief; only a *partial response* occurs. For those who partially respond to intervention, the prognosis appears dim; only 15% attain optimal symptom relief or functional restoration (Breier, 1996). Therefore, medication can fall short for many individuals (although helpful for some individuals when used as a sole modality) and is not recommended without other supportive approaches.

Special Considerations

Women and Pregnancy
One major concern for women of childbearing age is that atypical antipsychotic medications can create disturbances in the menstrual cycle, and because of irregular menstrual cycles, these women could become pregnant and not know it. This unawareness could lead to a neglect of early prenatal care and a failure to obtain professional advice about whether to continue their medication. According to Empfield (2000), pregnancy rates appear to be rising among women with schizophrenia. Informed decisions can be made concerning whether to discontinue the medication to avoid endangering the fetus. Unfortunately, however, the chance of clinical decompensation increases by two-thirds when medication is dis-

continued. Current literature reports that maintaining the mother on low doses of an atypical antipsychotic medication reduces the probability of harm to the fetus (Empfield, 2000). Immediate hospitalization is always advised if a consumer becomes acutely psychotic during pregnancy.

Children with Autism

Atypical medications such as Risperdal have gained in popularity in the treatment of children, particularly children with autism who exhibit aggressive behaviors. Although not approved for this purpose by the FDA, some researchers believe the results are promising (Hollander, Phillips, & Yeh, 2003; Zepf, 2003). Use of this atypical medication was highlighted for treatment of children with autism in a study conducted by the *National Institute of Mental Health* (NIMH). This study involved 101 children with autism (from 5 to 17 years old, including 82 boys and 19 girls) and was designed to determine the effectiveness of Risperdal as a treatment option. The results revealed that 69% of the children receiving Risperdal showed improvements in aggressive behaviors, as opposed to only 12% of the placebo group. Reported side effects were minimal, with the exception of weight gain in some children (Hollander et al., 2003).

The treatment of aggressive behaviors in children with autism was reviewed in the *American Family Physician*. It was reported that 68% of the children using Risperdal for the treatment of aggressive behaviors associated with autism had good results, and no children had to be removed due to adverse drug effects (Zepf, 2003). Both studies mentioned here support the use of the atypical antipsychotic medication Risperdal as an effective short-term treatment for the aggressive behaviors of autism.

Older Adults

Special consideration should be given to older adults using any antipsychotic drug. According to Katona and Livingston (2003), the intolerability of all antipsychotic drugs is exacerbated by the higher rates of comorbidity found in older people, the interaction with other drugs prescribed for these other conditions, and the increased susceptibility of older adults to experiencing side effects. Particular attention should be given when these individuals suffer debilitation related to severe renal (kidney) or hepatic (liver) impairment, and when they are predisposed to, or at risk of, hypotension (low blood pressure). Renal impairment results in a diminished ability to eliminate the drug from the system. These consumers need to be given low dosages of the drug and to be monitored closely (Janssen Pharmaceutica Products, 2003).

Medications, especially Risperdal, have been used to combat the symptoms associated with dementia in older adults. Katona and Livingston (2003) warned, however, that these individuals are more vulnerable to side effects and at higher risk of developing EPS with antipsychotic medications. Furthermore, a study in the *Canadian Medical Journal* reported that when using Risperdal, consumers with Alzheimer's disease or vascular dementia were more likely to experience adverse cerebrovascular events such as strokes and transient ischemic attacks (Wooltorton, 2002).

It is here that the NMTP can serve as a catalyst in helping consumers increase their level of functioning while establishing or reestablishing a strained support system. Supportive intervention includes providing advice and recommendations on those medications that will complement the current therapy being provided (Dziegielewski & Leon, 1998; 2001). Those with schizophrenia are more likely to harm themselves than someone else (Ferriman, 2000).

COUNSELING AND OTHER SUPPORTIVE INTERVENTIONS

The unpredictable course of the illness, the varied responses to medication and intervention efforts, and the severe level of impairment experienced make individuals who suffer from psychotic disorders difficult to treat. One reason for this reluctance is that these consumers can be difficult to handle on an outpatient basis. In most cases the consumer suffering from a psychotic disorder cannot be given a prescription and sent home without continued supervision. Once assessed, all the subsequent intervention efforts require extensive monitoring and support. There is no standard intervention strategy that fits all consumers; intervention generally involves the use of medication, consistent medication management and monitoring, family support, and other supportive interventions such as the provision of training in problem solving, skill building, and vocational rehabilitation.

Family Education and Support Building

Because people with schizophrenia or other psychotic disorders alienate their family and friends unknowingly, interventions that involve the family or other support system are considered essential. Aspects of the disease itself can be isolating as well, such as the splitting of mood response, which may frighten family and friends. Family or friends may shy away from demonstrating the affection and support that are so desperately needed. The strained relationships that typically occur in this population are based on a lack of understanding and an inability to control the symptoms of the disease. Education, therefore, becomes a critical component of any intervention strategy. With adequate education, families may become more tolerant of the eccentricities that are common with this condition. Education includes learning about the condition and what to expect from a loved one who is afflicted; becoming aware of medication regimen and the side effects that can result; and learning the best ways to handle the consumer's resistance and possible rejection of helping efforts.

> **QUICK TIPS:**
> **Steps in Developing an Intervention Plan to Help the Consumer's Family**
>
> - Identify the behaviors that are creating problems for the consumer and his or her family system.
>
> - Encourage family and friends to participate in the planning process by sharing their valuable perceptions and insights.

Problem Solving, Skill Building, and Vocational Rehabilitation

The emphasis for problem solving and skill building is to identify clear, concise goals and objectives (Dziegielewski, 2004). Skill building involves helping consumers develop the social and vocational skills necessary to live independently. With the help of the practitioner, consumers can learn independent living skills (e.g., good hygiene, cooking, traveling, coping skills) that help them find and keep jobs. With fewer consumers requiring long-term hospitalization, more active support networks in the community are needed.

Treatment plan formulation and execution can be difficult when working with the consumer who has schizophrenia or a related psychotic disorder, because he or she may resist the helping efforts or have difficulty participating. Individualized intervention efforts need to reflect the general as well as the unique symptoms and needs of the consumer. The importance of a formal treatment plan cannot be overestimated because it will help to determine, structure, and provide focus for any type of supportive intervention. When the intervention plan is clearly delineated, family and friends of the consumer may feel more at ease and may agree to participate in any behavioral interventions that will be applied.

The development of an individualized intervention plan always begins with clear identification of the problem behaviors that interfere with functioning. The assessment data that led to the diagnostic impression, as well as the specific problems experienced by the consumer with schizophrenia need to be considered. The identified problems are then prioritized so that goals, objectives, and action tasks can be developed. Goals must be broken down clearly into objectives that reflect the target behaviors and that can be clearly measured. Each objective is then broken down into action tasks or steps to be taken by the consumer and the worker to ensure successful completion. Tables 7.10 and 7.11 present sample individualized treatment plans.

TABLE 7.10
Sample Individualized Intervention Plan: Short Form

- **Identified problem:** The consumer is experiencing ambivalent feelings that impair general completion of ADLs.
- **Goal:** The main goal is to help the consumer decrease feelings of ambivalence about ADLs.
- **Objective:** The consumer takes a shower daily
- **Action tasks:**
  —Consumer: Will lay out clothes and supplies the night before.
  —Practitioner: Will ask consumer if he or she has taken a shower and if he or she followed the routine planned.

TABLE 7.11
Sample Individualized Intervention Plan: Long Form

Objective	Intervention	Responsibility
Identify task that needs to be completed	Assist consumer in planning how and when task can be completed	Team, consumer/support system representative
Help consumer to develop trust in the support/care role of providers and family system	Develop a list of support/ issues to be addressed Probe possible causes for outbursts or noncomplaint behaviors	Practitioner, team, consumer
Consumer will take antipsychotic medications consistently, with or without supervision	Assist in arranging follow-up medication regimens Monitor side-effect profiles that might decrease compliance	Practitioner, team, consumer
Help consumer to understand necessity of taking medication	Educate consumer about importance of taking medications and their side effects and benefits Help consumer establish a plan or routine for taking medications (identify rewards)	Practitioner, team
Report diminishment in, or absence of, hallucinations	Monitor medication effects and need for readjustment Explore consumer's feelings or events that might trigger episodes Assist consumer in restructuring irrational beliefs using reality-based approach	Practitioner

continued

185

TABLE 7.11 *(continued)*

Increase family or system support for consumer's needs	Help support system to become aware of consumer's needs	Practitioner
	Refer for family therapy	
	Conduct formal problem-solving session prior to discharge	

Work with consumers that suffer from schizophrenia or the psychotic disorders can be facilitated with a strong team effort supported by a clear individualized treatment plan. With this disorder, it is easy for consumers to become confused and frustrated with the identified plan, making the role of the NMTP essential for intervention success.

8

Herbal Preparations, Essential Oils, and Flower Essences

A s a means of achieving increased levels of mental health, consumers are utilizing alternative approaches and medicinal preparations to supplement or replace traditional prescription medications (Dziegielewski, 2003). To promote effective, efficient and comprehensive helping relationships, NMTPs need to know about these products and how they may affect supportive interventions. Whether out of cultural preferences or due to dissatisfaction with the increasingly impersonal treatment from health care providers, more and more individuals are using complementary approaches such as acupuncture, massage, homeopathic remedies, nutrition, herbs, essential oils, and flower essences, and a host of other nonallopathic treatments. Many consumers take combinations of herbal preparations offered by manufacturers in one concoction or easy-to-take capsule. Because herbal preparations have a great deal in common with prescription medications (Sanderoff, 2001), some consumers choose to take herbal preparations instead of their prescription medication or along with it. For safety's sake, one medicine at a time is always the best choice with all medicinal substances (Russo, 2001). Consumers often believe that "natural is safe" and therefore may not realize that many of these preparations have the potential to interfere with or intensify the actions of traditional medications and supportive interventions (Dziegielewski, 2002; Dziegielewski & Sherman, 2004). Indeed, some traditional herbs have been shown to contain toxic alkaloids and can only be used with extreme caution. The role of the NMTP is pivotal in helping consumers make effective choices, one caveat: I recognize that herbal and other natural medicines may be considered the most "traditional" forms of therapeutic agents in the sense that they have been used for hundreds or thousands of years; everyday usage, however, suggests that most people call the conventional modern medicine with which they grew up "traditional."

BEYOND MAINSTREAM MEDICINE

Medical treatments in North America remain varied, and can range from home remedies shared among family and friends to medications prescribed by a physician. The most traditional and widely used form of mainstream medicine in this country involves standard drug therapies and surgical interventions. Mainstream medicine is often supplemented with *complementary* or *integrative* approaches (Gottlieb, 1995). According to Stehlin (1995), *alternative medicine* involves any medical practice or intervention utilized instead of conventional treatment. Unfortunately, these practices often lack sufficient standard documentation on safety and efficacy. See Table 8.1 for a summary of some of the available alternative approaches. Consumers who express interest in these types of therapy should be cautioned to choose licensed or certified practitioners.

TABLE 8.1
Overview of Alternative Therapies

Alternative Medicine Systems

• *Traditional Chinese Medicine* (TCM)—uses herbs, acupuncture, acupressure (shiatsu, tsabu, jin shin, jujitsu), and physical exercise like tai chi chuan or qigong.

• *Ayurveda*—ancient Hindu art of medicine that uses *pranayama* (alternate nostril breathing), *abhyanga* (rubbing skin with oil, usually sesame), *rasayana* (herbs and mantras during meditation), yoga, *panchakarma* (intense cleansing therapy, including diaphoretics, diuretics, cathartics, and emetics), and herbal remedies.

• *Naturopathy*—holistic approach that uses homeopathy, vitamin and mineral supplements, physiotherapy, TCM, stress management, and herbs.

continued

TABLE 8.1 (*continued*)

• *Nomeopathy*—uses homeopathic (minute doses of herb, mineral, or animal products) remedies as catalysts to aid the body's inherent healing mechanism; correct remedy treats the physical, emotional, and mental symptoms.

• *Osteopathy*—uses diagnostic and treatment techniques similar to medical practitioners, but also treats the musculoskeletal system with adjustive maneuvers.

• *Chiropractic*—diagnoses and treats illnesses that affect the nerves, muscles, bones, and joints by relieving pressure through manipulation.

• *Environmental Medicine*—focuses on the effect of chemicals such as pesticides, food preservatives, car exhaust fumes, and formaldehyde on the immune system; uses nutritional supplements, immunotherapy, and desensitization techniques.

Dietary Supplements

• *Nutritional Supplements*—determines deficiencies through blood, stool, urine, and hair analyses.

• *Orthomolecular*—uses mega doses of supplements; found useful for hypercholesterolemia and AIDS.

• *Botanical Medicine*—prescribes herbs for specific symptoms.

Note: Information modified from Dziegielewski & Sherman, 2004.

Interest has increased so dramatically in alternative approached that in 1992 the National Institutes of Health established the Office of Alternative Medicine (OAM), with a budget of $2 million. In 1997 alone, 42% of Americans spent over $27 billion on some type of alternative therapy (Eisenberg, David, Ettner, et al., 1998). In the year 2000 the National Center for Complementary and Alternative Medicine (NCCAM), established by Congress as a replacement for OAM, had a budget of $68.7 million. In addition, more than 60% of physicians from a wide range of specialties have recommended alternative therapies to their consumers (or for themselves) at least once (Borken, Neher, Anson & Smoker, 1994). This movement toward alternative practices is becoming so prominent that many United States medical schools are now offering elective courses in complementary/alternative medicine (Wetzel, Eisenberg, & Kaptchuk, 1998). Even with this increased interest, however, many MTPs frown upon the use of alternative therapies. This lack of support, even scorn from some, can cause consumers using these products to fear mentioning to their MTPs that they are using these products.

Furthermore, lack of professional education in this area remains a concern, as evidenced by a University of Mississippi study, in which 60% of retail pharmacists stated that they had learned about herbal medicines from their patients (Kroll, 1997).

HERBAL PREPARATIONS FOR MENTAL WELL-BEING

The fascination with herbs involves multiple interests, from potpourri and crafts utilizing herbs as dried arrangements, to aromatherapy, to the use of herbs as a culinary art, to the landscaping of herbs, to their medicinal applications (Hoffman & Manning, 2002). Originally most popular in Asia and Europe, particularly Germany, France, and Italy, these products constitute a blossoming market that continues to spread across the United States. Indeed, herbal preparations as medicines are the primary choice for over 70% of the world's population (Goeddeke-Merickel, 1998a; 1998b; 1998c) and about 50% of the U.S. population (Vazquez & Aguera-Ortiz, 2002).

The terms most often used in the lay community when referring to these natural preparations are *herbs* and *botanicals*. The exact difference between an herb and a botanical has become less clear because these terms are often used interchangeably. Traditionally, the definition of an herb was limited to nonwoody plants that had either a culinary or medicinal purpose (Russo, 2001). Herbal medications, considered dietary supplements, have become a popular alternative to Western medicinal therapies. In the professional community these all-natural products are commonly referred to as *botanicals, nutraceuticals,* and *phytomedicines* (National Institutes of Health, 2004). Generally, manufacturers typically refer to herbal products by using the name and the part of the plant used to make the supplement, which is often the root, stem, or leaf. If the common name is not listed in the American Herbal Products Association's *Herbs of Commerce,* then the Latin name is used.

Herbal substances can be prepared and used in numerous ways. The most common form is the *extract*, which can be liquid or powdered or viscous. Often the concentrations are derived from plant parts that have been either *macerated* (softening a solid by soaking it in a liquid) or *per-*

colated (passing a liquid through the solid plant matter and dissolving the active principles). Herbal remedies are often processed as *volatile oils* whereby the concentrates of active plant parts are extracted by a distillation process. Another type of herbal remedy is the *tincture*, wherein alcohol and hydroalcohol solutions are derived from the botanicals, resulting in low concentrations of the active ingredients. When an extract is labeled *standardized*, a process has been implemented whereby the unwanted components have been removed and the more concentrated active ingredients remain at a consistent percentage.

Any herb that is capable of infusion can be used as a tea. The term *infusion* means to steep or soak an herb in (usually hot or boiled) water, then strain out the solids and use the liquid. A second way to prepare teas is called *decoction*. In this method, the tea mixture is prepared by adding it to cold water; then it is covered, brought to a boil, simmered, and finally strained for optimum use. (Typically, infusions are made of leaves or flowers, whereas decoctions are made of barks or roots—though there are a few exceptions.) Generally, herbs are infused (when boiled, care should be taken; the active ingredients can be destroyed by the heat. Typically, leaves and flowers are steeped, and barks and roots are simmered. In the cold maceration process the tea is mixed with room-temperature water, covered, and left to stand for 6–8 hours; thereafter the mixture is strained and ready for use (Dziegielewski & Sherman, 2004).

There are well over 600 medicinal herbs available to the consumer in the United States (*Physicians' Desk Reference for Herbal Medications*, 2000), with little government oversight or regulation, and with limited standardized testing to clearly establish their effectiveness (Foster & Tyler, 2000; Russo, 2001; National Institute for Health, 2004). The FDA remains concerned that these preparations continue to lack formal regulation, which in turn leads to the lack of adequate controls (LaPuma, 1999). In the United States the Dietary Supplement Health and Education Act (DSHEA) of 1994 legislated the legal sale of herbal preparations as long as manufacturers did not make claims for disease treatment on the label (Kroll, 1997). This regulation allowed for the development of a loophole that encouraged ambiguous and misleading information. For example, labels of popular products primarily used for a specific pur-

TABLE 8.2
Herbal Preparations

Herbal Preparation	Description	Other Names	Indications/Usage	General Precautions	Drug Interactions	Dosage/Types
Cascara or cascara sagrada	Dried bark	Yellow bark dogwood bark	Constipation	Electrolyte imbalance gastrointestinal complaints, carcinogenesis	Thiazide, diuretics, antiarrythmics	425–850 mg; oral, capsule, or liquid
Capsicum (cayenne)	Dried ripe fruit flower	Cayenne herbal cayenne pepper	Pain relief, muscular tensions, arthritis, gastrointestinal disorders	Hematological hyper-sensitivity, gastroin-testinal complaints	Aspirin and salicylic acid	400–500 mg; external usage
Chaste tree berry	Dried ripe fruit	Chasteberry vitex	Premenstral and menopausal symptoms	Formation of rashes	Dopamine receptor antagonists	30–40 mg; oral, capsule, or liquid
Cohosh (black)	Fresh and dried root	Remifemin	Menopause		Antihypertensive medications	60–545 mg; oral or external
Echinacea	Roots, leaves, or whole plant parts	*Echinacea purpurea,* black Sampson, purple conefower	Immuno-stimulant	Nausea, hypersensitivity, reactions with anaphylaxis, formation of rashes	Cyclosporine, corticosteroids	6–9 ml; oral or external use
Evening primrose	Oil from ripe seeds	Mega primrose oil	Premenstral or menopausal symptoms, anti-inflammatory	Possible seizures in patients with schizophrenia	Drugs used to lower seizure threshold	500 mg orally

continued

TABLE 8.2 (*continued*)

Herbal Preparation	Description	Other Names	Indications/Usage	General Precautions	Drug Interactions	Dosage/Types
Feverfew	Dried leaves	Featherfew, feather foil	Migraine	Gastrointestinal irritation, dermatitis impairment of muscle contractibility; do not take if you have allergy to ragweed or hypersensitivity to chamomile	Thrombolytics, anticoagulants, platelet aggregation	200–250 mg for migraine; oral
Garlic	Fresh dried bulb	Garlicin, poor man's treacle	Arteriosclerosis, hypertension, cholesterol reducer	Allergic reactions, gastrointestinal discomfort, hematological effects	Anticoagulants, aspirin	4 gm fresh daily or 8 mg oil form
Ginger	Fresh dried root (rhizome)	Ginger root, ginger kid	Stimulate appetite, motion sickness, dyspepsia	Hypersensitivity dermatitis	Anticoagulants, antithrombolytic agents	100–1000 mg; oral, tea, powder
Ginkgo	Dried leaves	Ginkgo biloba, ginkgold	Short-term memory, concentration, vertigo	Blood pressure problems, adversly affects fertility, hematological effects	Antrithrombolytic agents, inhibitory effect on platelet-activating factor	40–80 mg; three times daily; oral
Ginseng	Fresh dried root	Ginsana, Chinese red, Panax	Lack of stamina, fatigue, stress	Cardiovascular effects, diabetes, hypertension, breast nodularity, vaginal bleeding	Insulin, hypoglycemic effects, coumaden antiplatelet agents, MAOIs	1–2 gm root tea, powder, tablet

continued

TABLE 8.2 (*continued*)

Herbal Preparation	Description	Other Names	Indications/Usage	General Precautions	Drug Interactions	Dosage/Types
Goldenseal	Dried root (rhizome)	*Hydrastis canadensis*	Irregular menstruation, bronchitis, herpes, immuno-stimulant	Pregnancy precautions, digestive disorders	Berberine, Heparin, decreased Vitamin B absorbtion	250–500 mg; oral
Gotu kola	Fresh and dried leaves and stem	*Centella asiatica*, Indian pennywort	Memory "brain food," skin diseases, depression	Allergic contact dermatitis		400–500 mg; oral
Grape or grape seed	Leaves and seeds	Vitis, Vinifera, Activin	Headache, as anti-oxidant, skin diseases	Inhibition of intestinal enzyme activity		150–600 mg; oral
Green tea	Dried fresh leaves	Chinese tea, green tea extract	Cancer, hypertension, dental caries	Gastric irritation, cardiov-vascular vulnerabities; precaution in pregnancy, children	Reabsorption of alkaline medications can be delayed	300–400 mg; pill or tea form
Guarana or guarana seed	Dried crushed seed paste	*Paullinia cupana*	Headache, as cerebral stimulant	Precautions with cardiac disorders and panic and anxiety disorders	Diuretic action of guarana may lead to hypokalemia	800–1000 mg; oral
Saw palmetto	Dried ripe fruit	*Serenoa repens*, Sabal palm	Prostate complaints, irritable bladder	Antiestrogenic effects hormonal effects	Hormonal drugs, preg-nancy and breastfeeding, precautions; secondary to hormonal effects effects	1–2 gm or 320 mg extract

Note: Table modified from Dziegielewski, 2003. Information and abbreviated descriptions taken from the *Physicians' Desk Reference for Herbal Medicines* (2000), *Physicians' Desk Reference for Prescription Medications*, 2004, and Dziegielewski & Leon, 2001. Only some of the most common uses and dosage ranges for these sub-stances are listed. Be advised that guidelines for dosing and the actual purpose of the herbal preparation vary tremendously based on source and how and why a herbal preparation is being taken.

pose (e.g., St. John's wort, for depression) use ambiguous phrases for product use, such as "promotes mental well-being" or "to improve mental health." To avoid legal penalties, many manufacturers of herbal and natural products continue to use vague terminology, such as "supports body function" or "safely balances emotions." This questionable practice is allowed to continue because, as dietary supplements, these products remain shielded from government oversight.

Considering how long herbal preparations have been in use as medicinal remedies, it remains a mystery why uniform testing is so limited. One possible reason is that drug companies have little incentive to do so because whole herbs cannot be patented. What is even more disturbing is the fact that, even if controlled in a drug trial, once on the market the same active ingredients that were found in the fresh herb might not be present in the manufactured product. When using herbal preparations, how will consumers know the product has active ingredients? And without a professional's verification, how can they determine whether they actually have the problem for which the herbal remedy is seen as an antidote? One reality remains clear: In the United States, more controlled studies in this area are needed (Bender, 1996; Rhodes-Kropf & Lantz, 2001). Table 8.2 highlights lists types of herbal preparations and what are often considered the reasons for general use.

What is crucial to remember is that when herbal preparations act like medicines in the body, problems can arise if too much is taken, if they are used for too long, or if taken with certain medicines. For example, Taxol, a medication used in cancer treatment, comes directly from the Pacific Yew tree. Ginseng, often used to reduce stress and increase energy, can cause problems if taken with Coumadin (warfarin), a medication designed to prevent blood clotting; when ginseng is taken at the same time, the antiplatelet properties of ginseng can promote increased or uncontrolled bleeding if injury should occur (*Physicians' Desk Reference*, 2004). Another example is the interaction effects that can result from drinking grapefruit juice while using medication (Rosch, 2000). For example, the drinking of grapefruit juice can inhibit the absorption of medications used in dialysis (Goeddeke-Merickel, 1998a). In addition, grapefruit juice reportedly blocks the effects of medications used to treat cancer, hypertension, heart disease, and allergies (Mitchell, 1999; Rosch, 2000). Preparations used to treat depression, such as St. John's wort, have been found to raise the risk of organ rejection in transplant patients (Walsh, 2001).

Mixing herbal remedies and prescription medicine does not always have a negative outcome. Regardless of whether there are positive or negative effects, when dealing with any type of medication (herbal and natural included), it is essential to remember that every remedy that is strong enough to create an action can also cause a reaction (Dziegielewski, 2003).

TREATMENT OF ANXIETY AND DEPRESSION WITH HERBAL PREPARATIONS

With all the undesirable side effects that can occur with many of the prescription antianxiety and antidepressant medications (benzodiazepines, TCAs, MAOIs, SSRIs, and others), many consumers are seeking safer alternatives. It is beyond the scope of this chapter to discuss all herbal preparations in detail. Three common herbal preparations that have gained increased interest in the United States are kava-kava (*Piper methysticum*) for anxiety, St. John's wort (*Hypericum perforatum*) for depression, and ginseng (*Panax ginseng*) to relieve stress and increase energy. Table 8.3 summarizes the properties and interactions of these herbs.

Kava-Kava

There are over 200 varieties of the leafy green kava-kava plant, which that is often considered to have a mildly intoxicating effect. Kava-kava is a bitter herb derived from the rhizome fibers of the *Piper methysticum* plant, which is a member of the black pepper family (Bilia, Gallori, & Vincieri, 2002). The plant root is washed and then cut into pieces and chopped or finely grated into a pulp-like mass. The mass is then placed in cold water and left to steep until a strong tea or infusion is created (Humberson, Akhtar & Krenzelok, 2003). Once ingested, kava-kava exerts a relaxing effect, reportedly reducing anxiety and tension and promoting restful sleep. Other diverse purposes include treating rheumatism, asthma, worms, obesity, headaches, fungal infections, leprosy, vaginal infections and diseases, urinary infections, menstrual problems, and insomnia

TABLE 8.3
Antianxiety/Antidepressant Herbal Preparations

Herbal Preparation	Description	Other Names	Indications/ Usages	Side-Effects/ Precautions	Drug Interactions	Dosage/ Types
Kava-kava	Dried root (rhizome)	*Piper Methysticum,* ava pepper	Nervousness, insomnia, gastritis	Dyskinesia, mouth inflammation or ulcers	Alcohol, Xanax, CBNS depressants Dopamine	60 mg– 200 mg twice a day, oral
St. John's wort	Fresh flowers, plant parts dried above ground	*Hypericum perforatum,* amber, goatweed	Anxiety, depression, skin inflammation, blunt injuries, wounds, burns	Restlessness, fertility effects, gastrointestinal effects photosensitivity	MAOIs and SSRIs; may inhibit iron absorption; cyclosporine, indinavir, ethinylocstradiol	500– 900 mg/ day for depression; capsule, tea, external topical

(Wurges & Frey, 2002). It is used as a diuretic and an aphrodisiac. The most common uses, however, are anxiety reduction and sleep promotions. Kava-kava affects the brain differently from the benzodiazepines and therefore has been used to assist with benzodiazepine withdrawal (Bilia, Gallori, & Vincieri, 2002).

What is most attractive about this substance is that most individuals do not report developing tolerance or problems with mental alertness or clarity. There are multiple ways in which kava-kava can be taken, including the raw root form, as an emulsified powder, an alcohol-based tincture, or in powder-containing capsules or liquid-filled gel capsules. After taking this substance, whether in liquid or solid form, consumers often report that the tongue and inner mouth become numb (Zal, 2000).

Potential side effects include dermatitis, shortness of breath, and visual disturbances. High-dose effects include loss of appetite, difficulty breathing, blurred vision, bloodshot eyes, and gait difficulties (Wong, Smith & Boone, 1998). Prescription medications that should be avoided when taking this herb include barbiturates, antidepressants, and tranquilizers such as BuSpar (Zal, 2000). Although some studies have found kava-kava to be extremely dangerous or even deadly in some cases, most side effects are relatively mild and can be avoided by taking recommended doses. Serious side effects may include liver cirrhosis, hepatitis, skin reactions, tremors, depression, increased anxiety and insomnia, yellowing of the skin, weight changes, confusion, and death. Habitual users often report eye irritation, puffy face, shortness of breath, changes in blood pressure, and significant changes in certain blood and urine test values. It has been also shown that chronic abuse of this herb can lead to malnutrition, weight loss, liver toxicity, and depression of certain plasma protein levels, lymphocytes, and platelets (Bilia, Gallori, & Vincieri, 2002).

St. John's Wort

St. John's wort (*Hypericum perforatum*) is a popular herbal preparation that is commonly known to treat the symptoms of mild to moderate depression (St. John's Wort: The Sunshine Herb; 2000). This flowering herb is often found in meadows and along roadsides, reaching a plant size of 1–3 feet (McCabe, 2002). This plant, which often grows in the wild, is harvested for its active ingredients, usually referred to as *hypericins* (Becket, 2000). The attractive yellow blossoms have been used for centuries as a medicinal herb for "anti-inflammatory, sedative, analgesic, diuretic, anti-malarial, antidepressant and vulnerary action" (Nathan, 1999, p. 333). St. John's wort, when prepared as an infusion, also makes herbal tea and can be used to treat fevers and "nervous conditions including depression" (Henderson, Yue, Bergquist, Gerden & Arlett, 2002, p. 349).

This herbal preparation, like so many others, is not free from side effects. Some of the most commonly reported side effects include gastrointestinal upset, fatigue, photosensitivity, and itching. Less commonly reported side effects include sedation, decreased muscle tone, neuropathies, reduced body weight, and serotonin syndrome (McCabe, 2002). This syndrome generally involves an adverse combination of serotonin-related agents that may produce changes in mental status, such as agitation, confusion, hypomania, restlessness, disorientation, and in severe cases, coma. Symptoms of this syndrome include headache, nausea, anxiety, diarrhea, and shivering. Treatment requires "prompt recognition, removal of the offending agent(s), close observation until resolution, and the use of various supportive measures such as hydration, attention to electrolyte and acid-base balances, cooling baths and antipyretics" (Parker, Wong, Boon, & Seeman, 2001, p. 78).

In addition, drug interaction effects have been cited with St. John's wort when mixed with other nonprescription substances (e.g., caffeine) and prescription medications (e.g., MAOIs, SSRIs, or TCAs). Symptoms from these drug–drug interactions include increased anxiety, especially when taken with caffeine or theophylline derivatives (i.e., antiasthmatics, bronchodilators). Furthermore, St. John's wort appears to increase liver enzymatic induction. The liver metabolizes drugs, and liver imbalances can lead to lower concentrations of these medications in the bloodstream, thereby reducing the medications' effectiveness. McIntyre (2000) emphasizes that St. John's wort can have significant MAOI-type effects and warns that the same dietary cautions should be used with this herb as would be used with any of the MAOIs; similarly to the MAOIs this herb can give "rise to potentially serious side-effects when combined with tyramine-rich foods such as red wine or cheese" (2000, p. 116). Because St. John's wort is a complex agent "where the whole is considered different from and more potent than any single ingredient" (McIntyre, p. 100), the synergistic effect that can occur when mixing this substance with other active substances must always be considered.

Ginseng

The plant known as ginseng (*Panax ginseng*) is derived from the roots of several different plants within the Araliaceous family, Panax genus. The specific types and names for this herb include American ginseng (*Panax quinquefolius*), Korean or Asian ginseng (*Panax ginseng*), and Siberian ginseng (*Eleutherococcus senticosus*) (Court, 2000). (Although Siberian ginseng is botanically unrelated to the Panax species, it has similar adaptogenic and tonic qualities.) Panax is one of the oldest plant families in the world; it is believed to have evolved 65–100 million years ago. In general, typical ginseng roots are "persistent, thick, flaky, fusiform and cream to pale yellowish buff in color" (Court, 2000, p. 16). For the most part, the use of ginseng with depressed consumers mitigates the side effects of depression such as decreased libido or lack of sexual desire. Unlike St. John's wort, this plant is not as hardy, and optimal growing conditions are crucial. For example, the plant cannot tolerate direct sunlight, frost, snow, heavy rain, high winds, and other extreme conditions. It is also slow-growing and needs to be harvested in September or October when the roots are firm, which allows the herb to be cleaned and prepared by hand.

Keifer and Pantuso report that the active ingredients of ginseng are "ginsenosides, which have been shown to have a variety of beneficial effects, including anti-inflammatory, anti-oxidant and anticancer effects" (2003, p. 1,539). The benefits of this herb are many; ginseng is said to "enhance the immune system, improve psychological function, relieve stress, increase energy and improve sexual performance." Vuksan, Sievenpiper, and associates noted that, according to Chinese tradition, "it is used as a tonic with prophylactic, restorative and aphrodisiac properties" (2000, p. 1,009).

Several studies have tested the efficacy of ginseng for diabetes, sexual function, immune system function, psychological function, and other areas. For example, in the area of sexual function, ginseng has been associated with "an increase in lubrication, clitoral sensitivity, frequency of orgasm and an accompanying increase in sexual desire" (Ito, Trant, & Polan, 2001, p. 546). Keifer and Pantuso reported that "use of ginseng improved erectile dysfunction, sexual desire and intercourse satisfaction" (2003, p. 1,541). In the treatment of diabetes, "American ginseng attenuated postprandial glycemia" (Vuksan et al., 2000, p. 1,009) and "improved fasting blood glucose levels" (Keifer & Pantuso, 2003, p. 1,541).

For the most part, ginseng is considered a stimulant. According to Schwartz, "It is a stimulant like caffeine, but its effect is more subtle than that from drinking coffee" (2001, p. 32). Where the plant is grown and how it is cultivated are important because the potency of ginseng depends on growing conditions. Asian ginseng is believed to "affect blood flow and have antistress, memory increasing, and antifatigue activities" (Vuksan et al., 2000, p. 1,009), whereas American ginseng is credited with "improving sex drive, memory and learning, decreas[ing] aging, and possess[ing] both digestion regulating and liver protective activities" (Vuksan et al., 2000, p. 1,009). (Many therapeutic qualities are attributed to both species; reputable herbal books are recommended for more in-depth information.)

Side effects for this herb are difficult to outline because the product is usually not standardized. Nevertheless, some adverse effects that users may experience include "nausea, diarrhea, euphoria, insomnia, headaches, hypertension, hypotension, mastalgia [breast pain] and vaginal bleeding" (Keifer & Pantuso, 2003, p. 1,541). Synergistic effects that can actually decrease its effectiveness have been noted when ginseng is used in combination with certain blood pressure medications such as warfarin (Coumadin) and when using caffeine.

For the most part, special consideration should be given to individuals who use this product and have "high blood pressure, acute asthma, acute infections and nose bleeds or excessive menstruation" (Keifer & Pantuso, 2003, p. 1,541). Furthermore, it is recommended that ginseng not be used by anyone taking insulin for the treatment of diabetes, because of possible interactions. Like so many other herbs and prescription medications, this herb is not recommended for use by children or by pregnant or lactating women until more research to ascertain its effects on these populations has been conducted.

Ginseng should not be used by consumers who are also taking MAOIs, such as Nardil. As Keifer and Pantuso (2003) warned, taking ginseng along with an MAOI could lead to the development of manic-like symptoms. Ginseng is considered an aphrodisiac and can be used to assist in the treatment of sexual dysfunctions. It has been shown to improve psychological function and relieve stress. It can be recommended for those individuals who do not want to take prescribed medications.

A Nutritional Note

Many nutritional supplements have also been used to improve psychological well-being. This work cannot go into these substances in detail, but they should be mentioned because some consumers will be found to be using them. They include, but are not limited to, SAMe, DLPA, and nutritional supplements such as vitamin C, calcium, magnesium, and B-complex (*PDR for Nutritional Supplements*, 2001). There are also nutrients purported to improve brain function, such as *phosphatidylserine*. Many health professionals recommend a high-potency multiple vitamin and mineral supplement daily, to cover possible deficiencies that could be direct or indirect causes of physical and mental health disorders. The same warnings apply to nutritional supplements as to herbal ones, though: Consumers are well advised not to pick nutrients casually from store shelves without informing themselves about the nutrients first and carefully reading the labels (Foster & Tyler, 2000). Consultation with a professional nutritionist would be appropriate, especially given that so many health care professionals have limited knowledge in this area. There are also excellent nutritional manuals available for more in-depth information.

ESSENTIAL OILS FOR MENTAL WELL-BEING

For thousands of years essential oils have been used to enhance the environment and improve psychological and physiological well-being (Stevensen, 1996). Enjoyable aromas or scents can vary from burning a scented candle or rubbing oils on the skin to enhance mood to simply walking in a rose garden after a refreshing rain. Reports of the power of essential oils in healing date back to the early 1900s with the work of Maurice-Rene Cattefosse, who accidentally discovered the healing benefits of oils when he treated a third-degree burn with lavender oil and experienced immediate relief. He continued the treatment for several weeks and healed without the expected scarring (Maxwell-Hudson, 1994). This documented experience was influential in the development of a branch of herbal medicine known as aromatherapy, in which essential oils are vaporized by applying heat, and the resulting scents are used individually or in combination (Gattefosse, 1938; Russo, 2001).

Essential oils generally have been used to treat conditions ranging from infections and skin disorders to immune deficiencies and stress. Through a process of *steam distillation*, essential oils are extracted from plant flowers, leaves, branches, or roots. After the flower is dried, it is processed for herbal use or distilled to be utilized as part of an essential oil (Russo, 2003). The concentrated essence of aromatic plants is then used alone or in combination, through inhalation, topical application, or ingestion. Some of these oils are very concentrated and require only a few drops to achieve the desired therapeutic effect. These oils work by stimulating the olfactory system and are reported to affect memory, breathing, and circulation (McIntyre, 1995).

Massage is the most common method of application; it allows the oil to penetrate the skin and underlying tissues. Different oils vary in their absorption rates and reach peak effectiveness at varying times following treatment. People with sensitive skin or allergies should be cautious about the use of essential oils. Some desired effects are mood enhancement with calming and sedative properties, as well as digestive, diuretic, decongestant, and pain-relieving effects.

Although oils are considered natural, they can be powerful and should not be used during pregnancy or with certain chronic health problems without the approval of a health care professional. For example, it has been advised that lavender (with its calming effect and sedative properties) should not be used during early pregnancy or in cases of low blood pressure (McIntyre, 1995).

There is a difference between essential oils and perfume or fragrance oils. Essential oils are derived from plants, whereas perfume oils are artificially created fragrances and may not offer the same therapeutic benefits. Because essential oils are very potent, they should never be applied directly to the skin because they may be toxic in that form or burn the skin. For this reason, prior to their use on the skin, all essential oils need to be diluted with carrier oil (usually sweet almond oil, apricot kernel oil, or grape seed oil). The therapeutic benefit of inhaled aromas may occur in two ways: when the oil molecules enter the lungs and are absorbed into the bloodstream, and when they stimulate the olfactory system and thereafter the brain. Individuals with sensitivities or allergies to a particular substance may sneeze in response.

Essential oils are usually sold in very small dark bottles that vary greatly in quality and price. Factors that can affect the quality and price of the oil include the rarity of the plant, the country and conditions where the plant is grown, the quality standards of the distiller, and how much oil the plant produces. Essential oils can be purchased as a blended product. The advantage of the blend is the cost-savings from not having to buy each essential oil individually. The disadvantage is that the consumer has no control over the blend, because he or she does not directly mix it.

Essential oils have been used for bacterial and viral infections, skin disorders, immune deficiencies, muscular disorders, arthritis, and cold scores. Aromatherapy remains an option as part of the varied spectrum of alternative therapies (Healthwell, 2001; McIntyre, 1995). Table 8.4 below gives an overview of oils and their properties.

TABLE 8.4
Selected Essential Oils

Common Name	Latin Name	Comments
Chamomile	*Anthemis nobilis*	Fresh, sweet, herbaceous aroma; relaxing and soothing
Cypress	*Cupressus sempervirens*	Pale yellow-green oil with a smoky, sweet, balsamic aroma; very astringent; soothing and refreshing
Eucalyptus	*Eucalyptus citriodora*	Has a penetrating, camphoric woody-sweet scent; stimulating, antiseptic, and antiviral
Frankincense	*Boswellia thurfera/carterii*	Has a rich, tenacious aroma; comforting, used for relaxation
Geranium	*Pelagonium graveolens*	Pale yellow-green oil with a delicate, sweet, rose-like aroma; appetite stimulant
Ginger	*Zingiber officinale*	Has a warm, woody scent; preventative for stomach upset and sea-sickness
Jasmine	*Jasminum officinale*	Dark orange-brown oil with a sweet, warm, floral aroma; antidepressant and aphrodisiac
Juniper	*Juniperus communis*	Distilled from juniper berries; refreshing and invigorating; antiseptic, astringent, and diuretic
Lavender (French)	*Lavandula augustifolia*	A deep, soothing floral aroma; analgesic, antiseptic, antidepressant, antibacterial, decongestant, and sedative
Peppermint	*Mentha piperita*	Pale yellow color with a strong, penetrating mint aroma; cooling and invigorating

continued

TABLE 8.4 (*continued*)

Sandalwood	*Santalum album*	Pale yellow oil with a smooth, tenacious, sweet-woody aroma; sedative

Note: Information compiled from McIntyre, 1995.

FLOWER ESSENCES FOR MENTAL WELL-BEING

McIntyre (1995) believes that the use of the scent of flowers to address emotional problems and foster feelings of well-being has led some professionals to contend that these methods can be advantageous as a supplement to brief psychotherapy, with less potential for negative drug interactions than ingested herbal preparations. Deriving the flower essences requires that blossoms be placed in water and in the sun for several hours, allowing the sun to draw out the essence. The resulting solutions are then preserved with brandy and utilized in a diluted form. For example, a consumer might use a prescription medication in conjunction with Cassandra (a flower essence) to enhance a calming feeling. See Table 8.5 for a selected sample of flower essences.

It is a matter of good health care education to caution the consumer about potential allergic reactions and to identify known allergies. Serious investigation into the sources of flower essences should be conducted before incorporating them into any treatment regimen. Furthermore, once therapy has begun, monitoring for adverse reactions should be a part of the evaluation of therapeutic effects.

Flower essences do not interfere with most medications, including homeopathic and herbal remedies, and there are no known side effects; but as with any alternative therapy, caution should always be exercised (Mendola, 1997a; 1997b). When a consumer expresses interest in this type of treatment, the NMTP should encourage him or her to investigate the desired remedy and methods of administration before trying it.

TABLE 8.5
Flower Essences for Stressful Situations

- **Bleeding heart**: Used to assist with moving beyond a relationship or to cope with the death of a loved one.
- **Chamomile**: Used for calming.
- **Impatiens**: Used to calm an individual who is quick to anger and is impulsive.
- **Morning glory**: Used to wake up in the morning without the use of stimulants.
- **Shasta daisy**: Used to clarify thinking.
- **Zinnia**: Used to lift mood.
- **Elm**: Used for everyday stress or feelings of being overwhelmed by responsibility.
- **Hornbeam**: Used for fatigue due to chronic stress.
- **Mimulus**: Used to address anxiety.
- **Star of Bethlehem**: Used to relax.
- **White chestnut**: Used for everyday stress and to promote sleep.
- **Wild oat**: Used for stress.

Note: Information modified from Dziegielewski & Sherman, 2004. These are reported uses; specific effects on individuals may vary.

THE USE OF SELF-HELP TREATMENTS

As the use of herbal preparations increases, so does the prevalence of self-diagnosis and self-treatment. Poor communication (or none at all) can make it very difficult for health care practitioners to assess the needs of the consumer. Furthermore, this total lack of supervised care can clearly complicate ongoing treatment regimens. Not knowing what a consumer is taking can put the consumer at significant risk for problematic interactions and synergistic effects. Many NMTPs regard learning about alternative mental health preparations as a sign of the times and an important step for gaining a better understanding of various disorders (Kroll, 1997). Knowledge in this area is limited because of the lack of controlled research and the conflicting, ambiguous information that is available. The resultant lack of standardized testing and evidence-based interventions often leaves the consumer responsible for educating the professional about the herbal preparations, nutrients, oils, or flower essences they are using and why. The movement is growing to integrate alternative and conventional health care as a means of increasing therapeutic speed and effectiveness.

Once informed about what the consumer is taking, the NMTP can use his or her professional expertise to help the consumer determine if this is the best remedy available. Be sure to encourage consumers to inform their other NMTPs and MTPs of all the natural remedies they are taking. This information will allow the NMTP to better prepare for the potential effects that these natural remedies can have on intervention outcomes.

Increasing numbers of consumers are using natural types of medicinal preparations and are not automatically accepting the traditional approach to medical care (Seligson, 1998). By understanding that their patients may be reluctant to discuss the use of natural remedies with the mainstream medical community, NMTPs can help consumers prepare for such discussions. To provide the best possible care for consumers, practitioners must keep abreast of all forms of intervention and discourage the use of medications and herbal preparations as the only form of intervention when other therapeutic alternatives could prove to be supplemental or just as effective.

**QUICK TIPS:
When Using Complementary
Practices . . .**

- Always encourage consumers to share information about the substances they are taking.

- Remind consumers that "any substance strong enough to create an action is strong enough to create a reaction."

- Ask consumers to write down all the herbs, oils, flower essences, and other supplements that they are taking regularly.

- Always encourage informed self-determination whereby consumers make their own informed decisions of what is best for them.

- Encourage the utilization of other supportive interventions, such as stress management, relaxation techniques, or counseling, to address the problem.

9

Special Populations

wo populations that frequently receive psychotropic medications—
children and older adults—exhibit unique characteristics that merit
special attention. Although medication concerns and considerations
identified throughout this book apply to all consumer populations, the
distinctive biological and physiological processes of children and older
adults warrant a closer examination of the impact that these medications
can have. Because these two groups represent opposite ends of the developmental continuum, each presents unique challenges. This chapter provides an overview of the issues that NMTPs should be aware of when
working with children and older adults who are taking mental health
medications.

SPECIAL CONSIDERATIONS WHEN WORKING WITH CHILDREN

Further research is needed on the effects that medications can have on
children and adolescents. The National Institute of Mental Health (2004)
clearly emphasized this point, especially in relation to very young children. More than half of the prescription drugs that are likely to be prescribed to children have not been adequately tested or labeled for the use
for which they are prescribed (Nordenberg, 1999a). Children and adolescents often present with behaviors reflective of a complex and evolving

biopsychosocial picture that requires special care and attention (McAdoo, 1997; Dziegielewski & Leon, 2001). Aggression, shyness, low self-esteem and poor concentration are just some of the behaviors and feelings that are often exhibited (Harper-Dorton & Herbert, 1999).

To facilitate their development, youngsters need to experience events that foster the coping skills necessary to adapt to their changing roles and expectations. Because children and adolescents often test the limits in terms of conflict, control, and opposition, it is crucial not to confuse what could be considered normal development with psychopathology (Maxmen & Ward, 1995). Whether these behaviors occur in the school setting or in the home environment, hasty misinterpretation could lead to an unwarranted prescription. If children are medicated too quickly, important life lessons could be denied them. Prematurely using medications can also give parents and professionals a false sense of control, which, in the long term, only further limits normal childhood development. Therefore, it is always best to tread cautiously during assessment and to identify the significant aspects of the child's presenting problems.

CHILDREN, ADOLESCENTS, AND MEDICATION

Because a child's emotional and physiological response to medication can vary so widely, many mental health providers who prescribe medications do so in a cautious and conservative manner. When working with children and adolescents, Rushton, Clark, and Reed (2000) found that the diagnostic evaluation and resulting interventions could be predicted based on the type of nonspecialist physician a child sees. Furthermore, because children can present such a unique picture, many physicians are more likely to refer them to a specialist. This method could lead to a matching of mental disorder and treatment to the provider, rather than having it individualized to the needs of the young consumer.

Kubiszyn (1994) expressed concern that in prescribing for children, there is little empirical research that confirms the efficacy of pediatric psychopharmacology. Others report that one of the biggest concerns in the prescribing patterns for children is that the majority of medication prescribers tend to be nonpsychiatric physicians (Baldessarini, 1990; Barkley,

> **QUICK TIPS:**
> **Assessment Procedure**
>
> - Identify specific problem behaviors that are being exhibited.
> - Record specific information (i.e., behavior-based) about the following:
>   — the problem presented by the child;
>   — behaviors that demonstrate the problem;
>   — the intensity, frequency, duration, and specific environmental circumstances that accompany or appear to be linked to the problem;
>   — areas that are affected by the problem;
>   — previous coping skills and problem-solving methods that have been used to address the problem and behaviors;
>   — any previous and current medication and counseling interventions prescribed.
> - Identify what appears to be causing the problem behaviors.
> - Identify possible mental health concerns as well as environmental or school-related difficulties.
> - Assess whether the identified problem is a reaction to an identifiable stressor.
> - Identify the factors in the child's daily living activities that are being affected or impaired by the problem behaviors.

1990). The debate centers around the issue that general practitioners are not specifically trained to deal with children and often have only limited knowledge of child development and child psychopharmacology. Supporting this trend, Ruston et al. (2000) found that 42% of family physicians had prescribed an antidepressant to at least one child in the last 6 months, compared to 25% of pediatricians. Clearly these prescribing patterns provide grounds for further investigation. Indeed, 80–90% of children in hospital or residential settings are on at least one medication, with almost 50% on two or more (Lyons, 2000).

One important factor in prescribing medications in this population is taking into account the interaction between the child, the family system, and additional components in the child's environment (e.g., the school system). Medication should not be prescribed without the ongoing support of various interventions that may include family therapy, parent–child work, behavioral interventions, and marital counseling

(Boyd-Webb, 1991). Even when medication is effective and alleviates the presenting symptoms, young consumers need to be equipped with new coping skills to address the same or similar difficulties that may arise in the future. The use of medications warrants an accurate diagnosis; these medications should never be given simply because it is what a specialist is most familiar with or knows the best; nor should it be prescribed merely to appease parents or school-related professionals.

All NMTPs need to be aware of medications that are appropriate for childhood disorders (Jensen, 2004), and they should also assist young consumers and their families in understanding the nature of the illness, the side effects of medications, and the improved efficacy of combining medication and psychosocial interventions. Dealing with young consumers and the medications they take is an ongoing process that will involve constant reassessment and evaluation (see Table 9.1).

TABLE 9.1
Medications Used in Pediatric Mental and Behavioral Disorders

Brand Name	Generic Name	Approved Age (years)
Stimulant Medications		
Adderall	amphetamines	3 and older
Concerta	methylphenidate	6 and older
Cylert[a]	pemoline	6 and older
Dexedrine	dextroamphetamine	3 and older
Dextrostat	dextroamphetamine	3 and older
Ritalin	methylphenidate	6 and older
Antidepressant and Antianxiety Medications		
Anafranil	clomipramine	10 and older
BuSpar	buspirone	18 and older
Effexor	venlafaxine	18 and older
Luvox (SSRI)	fluvoxamine	8 and older
Paxil (SSRI)	paroxetine	18 and older
Prozac (SSRI)	fluoxetine	18 and older
Serzone (SSRI)	nefazodone	18 and older
Sinequan	doxepin	12 and older
Tofranil	imipramine	6 and older

continued

TABLE 9.1 (continued)

Wellbutrin	bupropion	18 and older
Zoloft (SSRI)	sertraline	6 and older
Antipsychotic Medications		
Clozaril (atypical)	clozapine	18 and older
Haldol	haloperidol	3 and older
Risperdal (atypical)	risperidone	18 and older
Seroquel (atypical)	quetiapine	18 and older
(generic only)	thioridazine	2 and older
Zyprexa (atypical)	olanzapine	18 and older
Orap	pimozide	12 and older
Mood Stabilizing Medications		
Cibalith-S	lithium citrate	12 and older
Depakote	divalproex sodium	2 and older
Eskalith	lithium carbonate	12 and older
Lithobid	lithium carbonate	12 and older
Tegretol	carbamazepine	any age

[a]Because of its potential for serious side effects affecting the liver, Cylert should not ordinarily be considered as first-line drug therapy for ADHD.

Note: Information retrieved from the National Institute of Mental Health, Treatment of Children with Mental Disorders, July 29, 2005, *www.nimh.nih.gov/publicat/childqa.cfm#link3*

Attention-Deficit/Hyperactivity Disorder

According to the *DSM-IV-TR* (American Psychiatric Association, 2000), *attention-deficit/hyperactivity disorder* (*ADHD*) is a persistent pattern of inattention and/or hyperactivity–impulsivity that is more frequently displayed and more severe in individuals so diagnosed, than is typically observed in other individuals at a comparable level of development. ADHD is further distinguished by types of symptoms: the inattentive type, the hyperactive–impulsive type, and the combined type.

The inattentive type is characterized by symptoms of distractibility, forgetfulness, losing things, lack of attention to details, careless mistakes, poor listening, and poor organization—just to name a few. The hyperactive–impulsive type is characterized by signs of fidgeting and squirming, leaving the seat, inappropriate running and climbing, excessive talking, and difficulty coping with quiet activities. The combined type exhibits the symptoms of both the inattentive type and hyperactive–impulsive type (American Psychiatric Association, 2004).

Although many school-age children are referred to health and mental health facilities for ADHD-like symptoms, it is believed that only 5–9% of children are actually affected by the disorder (Barkley, Conners, Barclay, et al., 1990). In practice, children with ADHD present with many different types of symptoms, most of which are behavioral and cognitive in nature (Austin, 2003; Wimett & Lausten, 2003). According to Anastopoulos (1999), the clinical picture of what constitutes ADHD is blurred by (1) the wide range of assessment instruments with varying levels of reliability and validity; (2) the fluctuation of ADHD symptoms in relation to specific situations; (3) the amount of structure provided in each situation; (4) the existence of comorbid conditions such as conduct disorders and learning disabilities; and (5) changes in parenting methods and styles.

There are several types of medications that can be used in the treatment of this disorder. The types of medications most commonly used include stimulants, mood stabilizers, and antidepressants. It is believed that these medications address the neurochemical imbalances thought to precipitate the symptoms of ADHD (Anastopoulos, 1999). Amphetamines are stimulants, also referred to as psychostimulants. When used to treat ADHD, amphetamines increase attention and decrease restlessness in consumers who are overactive, unable to concentrate for very long or are easily distracted, and have unstable emotions.

Only the most common stimulants are discussed in this chapter: Ritalin, Ritalin S-R, Concerta (methylphenidate); Dexedrine (dextroamphetamine); Adderall (dextroamphetamine and amphetamine); Desoxyn (methamphetamine); and Provigil (modafinil) (see Table 9.2). A non-stimulant medication, Strattera (atomoxetine), is also discovered, as are the mood stabilizers and antidepressants that are used off-label for this condition.

TABLE 9.2
Stimulant Medications

Drug	General Use	Dosage Availability
Ritalin Metadate (methylphenidate)	Treatment of ADHD and sleep disorders such as narcolepsy	Tablets: 5, 10, 20 mg
Ritalin-SR (methylphenidate)		Sustained-release tablets: 20 mg Extended-release tablets: 20, 30, 40 mg
Concerta (methylphenidate extended release)		Extended-release tablets: 18, 27, 36, 54 mg
Dexedrine (dextro-amphetamine sulfate)	Treatment of ADHD; short-term treatment for weight reduction and sleep disorders such as narcolepsy	Tablets: 5 mg Capsules: 15 mg
Adderall (dextro-amphetamine and amphetamine)	Treatment of ADHD	Tablets: 5, 7.5, 10, 12.5, 15, 20, 30 mg
Adderall XR		Extended-release tablets: 5, 10, 15, 20, 25, 30 mg
Desoxyn (methamphetamine)	ADHD, narcolepsy, epilepsy, and certain depressive reactions	Tablets: 5 mg; long-acting tablets 5, 10, and 15 mg
Provigil (modafanil)	ADHD	Tablets: 100, 200 mg
Cylert (pemoline)	ADHD	Tablets: 18.75, 37.5, 75 mg

Note: Information summarized from Fernandez & Calix, 2003, and Valente, 2001.

Of the stimulants used to treat ADHD, Ritalin or Metadate (the generic methylphenidate) or Dexedrine (the generic dextroamphetamine) are the preferred drugs (Valente, 2001). Ritalin was patented in 1950 but was first introduced in the United States in 1956. Originally, Ritalin was intended to treat chronic fatigue, depression, psychosis associated with depression, and narcolepsy. In the 1970s, however, research indicated the benefits of treating symptoms associated with attention-deficit disorder (ADD). In the 1990s Ritalin became the drug of choice in the treatment of ADD and ADHD symptoms. It is not uncommon for these medications to be used with adult consumers who have a clear history of these problems in childhood (Diamond, 2002). The average dose is approximately 20–30 mg a day, divided into two or three doses. Caution on dosing is subjective because some children respond with 10–15 mg whereas others need 40–60 mg to get the maximum effect (Sifton, 2002).

One reason for the greater popularity of Ritalin is that it is a faster-acting medication than others in its class, taking effect within 30–45 minutes after being ingested; the effects last 3–7 hours (Anastopoulos, 1999). Some of the side effects most often related to this medication are appetite reduction, delay in falling asleep, headaches, weepiness, and increased heart rate.

A longer-acting form of methylphenidate, Ritalin-SR, has been developed that can be given twice a day. Although it is said to be the same as regular Ritalin, Diamond (2003) warned that anecdotal research supports the view that a higher dose may be needed to experience the same relief. Another form of sustained release, Concerta, was released in 2000. This extended-release tablet allows for a once-a-day dosing pattern, which can be very convenient for both the consumer and the support system. The beginning dose is generally 37.5 mg a day, with most children taking doses between 55 to 75 mg a day (Sifton, 2002). Many parents and professionals prefer these extended-release versions over the limited half-life of the traditional form of methylphenidate (Pelham, Gnagy, Burrows-Maclean, et al., 2001).

Adderall (dextroamphetamine and amphetamine), a psychostimulant used to treat ADHD, was approved by the FDA in 1996 (Adderall-XR is an extended release form). Some of the side effects most commonly related to this medication (and similar to the others in its class) include appetite loss, insomnia, depression, nervousness, headaches, and high blood pressure.

Desoxyn (methamphetamine), similar to the others in this category, is an addictive methamphetamine that strongly activates certain systems in the brain. Methamphetamine is chemically related to amphetamine; the main difference is that methamphetamine has greater effects on the central nervous system. The term *methamphetamine* may sound both familiar and illegal; indeed, it has a high potential for abuse and addiction. Street methamphetamine is referred to by many names such as "speed," "meth," and "chalk." Methamphetamine hydrochloride, often referred to as "ice" or "crystal," is generally inhaled by smoking. Desoxyn is used to treat conditions such as ADHD and narcolepsy; in rare cases this drug is used to treat depression.

Cylert (pemoline) is another Central Nervous System stimulant that has been used in the treatment of conditions such as ADHD, autism, and conduct disorder. It has also been used to treat adults with narcolepsy and to relieve certain types of fatigue in consumers who have multiple sclerosis. As directed by the FDA, Abbott Laboratories, the manufacturer of Cylert, has recommended baseline evaluation of liver function followed by biweekly liver function evaluations while the drug is being used. As noted in Table 9.1, it should no longer be used as a first-line medication in the treatment of ADHD because of its potential for toxicity to the liver. If the child develops any signs of liver damage, be sure to recommend that the parent call the MTP immediately. Warning signs include fatigue, loss of appetite, digestive problems, yellow skin or eyes, and pain in the upper right section of the abdomen.

Provigil (modafinil), the latest of the stimulant preparations used for ADHD, is believed to be chemically unrelated to the other stimulants (Rugino & Copley, 2001). What makes it different from conventional stimulants is that, although it is able to ramp up arousal and set off a flurry of activity throughout the brain, it appears to aim its effect at specific structures and chemicals. Those who have taken it report that it can help keep them awake, feeling refreshed and alert, but still able to go to bed when they are ready. Furthermore, because the side effects appear minimal (e.g., mild headaches, slight nausea), it is expected to continue to grow in popularity (O'Connor, 2004). The benefits are similar to the other psychostimulants; however, it appears to be less subject to abuse and less likely to cause psychotic symptoms because of the way it initiates action (Diamond, 2003). Although approved to treat ADHD, it is possible that sedative-like side effects could result.

QUICK TIPS:
Working with Consumers on Psychostimulants

- Encourage and foster education on potential side effects; sensitivity to individualized reactions is paramount.
- In assessment, explore any medications the child has taken in the past, including OTC drugs or herbal supplements.
- Conduct a family history to assess whether there are any genetic connections or family traits that would have required other family members to take a psychostimulant medication.
- Examine the possibility of using supportive interventions to address problematic behaviors.
- Make sure that the consumer knows that these medications need to be taken on a regular basis.
- Make sure that the consumer knows that the prescriber should always be contacted before the medication is self-adjusted.
- Be aware that, when a child is taking these medications, most physicians want to see him or her on a fairly regular basis.
- To ensure adequate monitoring, encourage following the treatment regimen and seeking ongoing follow-up.

Strattera (atomoxetine) is a norepinephrine reuptake inhibitor, a non-stimulant medication; it is the first new medication class in three decades to be used in the treatment of ADHD (Wimett & Laustsen, 2003). Strattera was approved by the FDA in November 2002. According to Stein (2004), the drug increases both norepinephrine and dopamine levels. Therefore, the long-lasting Strattera affects two mental-health-related neurotransmitters, as opposed to just dopamine (Ritalin). Research looks promising for the use of Strattera. For example, Lynch

(2003) described how Strattera was found to be more effective than placebo in reducing the symptoms of ADHD (measured on an ADHD rating scale) in children ages 6–18. Short-term use of Strattera appears positive for reducing symptoms associated with ADHD; however, the long-term effects still need to be considered.

Side-Effect Profiles
The side-effect profiles of all the psychostimulant medications used primarily to treat ADHD are similar, including Strattera. The most common side effects are insomnia, loss of appetite, nausea, dizziness, heart palpitations, headache, fast heart rate, and skin rash (*Physicians' Desk Reference*, 2004). Less common side effects include hallucinations; hepatitis and other liver problems; increased irritability; involuntary, fragmented movements of the face, eyes, lips, tongue, arms, and legs; uncontrolled vocal outbursts (e.g., grunts, shouts, obscene language; i.e., Tourette's disorder), mild depression, seizures, stomachache, suppressed growth, and weight loss. With Cylert, in particular, special attention should be given to yellowing of skin or eyes. Rare side effects may include an equally rare form of anemia, with symptoms of bleeding gums, bruising, chest pain, fatigue, headache, nosebleeds, and abnormal paleness. Psychostimulants should not be taken with MAOIs, including Nardil (phenelzine) and Parnate (tranylcypromine). Of special note: Consumers on Adderall as well as antihypertensive medications may experience problems maintaining blood pressure control. The use of all of these medications is discouraged during pregnancy and lactation; mothers taking amphetamines should refrain from nursing their infants, because these drugs are excreted in the milk and can have undesirable effects on the child.

Many professionals are becoming increasingly concerned with the use of Ritalin when it is not taken as prescribed. Ritalin can become addictive, and it is possible that it can be given or sold to other children and adolescents for the potential high that can result. Cases have been reported of children and adolescents crushing and then snorting or injecting the drug, so that the effects could be felt more quickly (Gottlieb, 2001).

Because Strattera is relatively new to the market, more studies are needed on its long-term side effects; however, there is some evidence that use may have negative effects on the cardiovascular system. For example, in a recent study that investigated the short-term cardiovascular safety of children, adolescents, and adults with ADHD on Strattera, results showed that Strattera treatment was associated with small but statistically significant increases in blood pressure in the participants—although once the drug was discontinued, the subjects' blood pressure returned to baseline (Wernicke, Faries, Girod, et al., 2003). On the positive side, Strattera may be helpful when treating children and adolescents who do not respond to stimulant medication, or those who have experienced intolerable side effects from the other psychostimulants tried in the past. This medication may provide one alternative when a parent or family member requests nonstimulant treatment (Stein, 2004).

Supportive, Alternative, Adjunctive Medications
Recognizing that stimulants may not be effective for all children who present with ADHD symptoms, and that there may be unwanted side effects, some medication prescribers have chosen to utilize other medications to assist with the problematic symptoms (see Table 9.3). Evidence to support the use of these medications is limited, and more research in this area is strongly recommended (Guevara, Lozana, Wickizer, et al., 2002).

Disruptive Behaviors in Young Consumers
Mental health professionals frequently get referrals of children with disruptive behavior problems. One diagnosis that generally involves such behaviors is *oppositional defiant disorder* (*ODD*). This disorder consists of negative, defiant, and hostile behavior directed at authority figures (Kronenberger & Meyer, 1996). When this diagnosis is combined with ADHD, the difficulties that result can be pronounced. In deciding whether there may be a co-occurring (in addition to ADHD) mental health condition, it is essential to make sure that the child or adolescent exhibits significant impairment in functioning, because some oppositional behaviors may be characteristic of normal developmental growth. For the diagnosis of ODD to be made, the *DSM-IV-TR* requires that symptoms persist for a period of 6 months or longer, and that children experience

significant impairment in academic, social, or occupational functioning is present.

These children and adolescents must also demonstrate behaviors that include loss of temper, arguing with adults, anger, deliberately annoying other individuals, and evidence of vindictive behaviors (American Psychiatric Association, 2000); they are often found to be disruptive in school or community settings and have academic as well as anger management problems (Myers, Burket, & Otto, 1993).

The literature on psychopharmacotherapy has identified a comorbid relationship between the disruptive disorders and ADHD; the psychostimulants are the most common class of medications used to treat ODD (Dulcan, 1990). The stimulants that are the most successful in reducing the impulsive and aggressive behaviors associated with these disorders, as discussed in this chapter, include Ritalin, Dexedrine, and Cylert. Other medications used to treat aggressive problems include lithium for aggressive behavior, Tegretol for ADHD symptoms, Catapres for low frustration tolerance and aggressive behaviors, and Tenex for overactivity and aggression (Kronenberger & Meyer, 1996). Another medication that can be used to assist with behavior problems is Wellbutrin. As discussed in Chapter 4, this medication is now being used to treat emotional and behavioral problems in children and adolescents, including depression and ADHD, as well as conduct disorder (Dulcan, 1999). The antidepressants Desyrel (trazodone) and Serzone (nefazodone) are also now being used in young consumers to address emotional and behavioral problems, including depression, insomnia, and disruptive behavior disorders, by helping to decrease depression, irritability, and aggression (Dulcan, 1999).

Like ADHD, these disruptive behaviors also require a multidimensional approach to treatment. Comprehensive approaches to ODD and conduct disorders include medication therapy, cognitive–behavioral techniques, parent management training, and family therapy. A multimodal approach is needed because although the drug will help to balance the brain chemistry, a behavioral treatment plan is also needed to facilitate skill building. Teaching problem solving and other coping behaviors will help provide a better foundation for ongoing solid personal adjustment.

TABLE 9.3
Common Pediatric Mental Health Medications

Brand Name	Generic Name	Type of Medication	Conditions Treated	Common Side Effects
BuSpar	buspirone	Antianxiety	Anxiety disorder, social phobia	Nausea, headache
Catapres	clonidine	Antihypertensive	ADHD, Tourette's syndrome	Sedation, headache, nausea, dry mouth, constipation
Depakene	valproic acid	Anticonvulsant	Bipolar disorder, conduct disorder	Upset stomach, nausea, vomiting, weight gain sedation, tremor
Elavil	amitriptyline	Tricyclic antidepressant	Depression	Same as Tofranil but less frequent
Eskalith	lithium	Salt	Bipolar disorder, conduct disorder	Nausea, vomiting, diarrhea, mild tremor, fatigue, acne, weight gain
Norpramin	desipramine	Tricyclic antidepressant	ADHD	Similar to Tofranil but less frequent
Pamelor	nortriptyline	Tricyclic antidepressant	ADHD, depression	Similar to Tofranil but less frequent
Paxil	paraxetine	SSRI	Depression, OCD, panic disorder, GAD, PTSD	Nausea, diarrhea, weight loss, insomnia, upset stomach, excess sweating, jitteriness
Tegretol	carbamazepine	Anticonvulsant	Bipolar disorder	Double vision, drowsiness, poor concentration, mild nausea
Tenex	guanfacine	Antihypertensive	ADHD, Tourette's syndrome	Similar to Catapres but less frequent
Tofranil	imipramine	Tricyclic antidepressant	ADHD, eating disorders, enuresis, depression	Sedation, dry mouth, changes in blood pressure, constipation
Wellbutrin	bupropion	Atypical antidepressant	ADHD	Similar to Ritalin and Dexedrine but less frequent

Note: Table modified from Dziegielewski & Leon, 2001.

A nutritional note: Not many kids with ADHD or other mental conditions will get better on good nutrition alone—but it is very fair to say that a terrible diet often makes treatment harder, whereas an optimal diet usually makes treatment and recovery easier. The NMTP may not be in a position to be a nutrition counselor, but he or she can help parents understand that how they feed their children can have a most beneficial effect on their behavior. It may often make sense to enlist the help of a good nutritionist or dietitian as part of a wellness team, especially when the MTP lacks the time or experience to monitor this important factor.

SUMMARY: WORKING WITH YOUNG CONSUMERS

Children and adolescents need to be monitored closely when taking medications. Of greatest concern is the increased use of these medications in young children (Rowland, Sandler, Umbach, et al., 2002). The literature has limited data on the long-term side effects of stimulants, (even Ritalin, which has been in use for over 30 years) so routine physical exams are important to monitor the child's growth and weight gain and to see if either is being affected by the drug(s).

Practitioners must be keenly aware that not all medications used for children have printed information available that directly relates to their

> **QUICK TIPS:**
> **Effective Management of Behavioral Disorders**
>
> - Consider using interviews and behavior scales to conduct a thorough assessment.
>
> - Directly observe and record the child's behaviors in those situations that appear to be the most problematic (e.g., in the classroom, or when interacting with the parent or teacher).
>
> - Implement parent training to help parents learn how to provide the structure needed by their ADHD child.
>
> - Coordinate with teachers and schools for classroom management plans.
>
> - Consider recommending individual and family counseling as well as marital counseling, so that all involved can better cope with the effects of the disorder.
>
> - Assess for nutritional factors and, if not previously handled by any MTP or NMTP, explore the dietary or nutritional intake of the child and the subsequent problem behaviors exhibited by the child.

use with children. Such information often is not available because the medications have not been approved by the FDA for use in children. The primary reasons for this lack of FDA approval are the time, expense, and difficulty involved in obtaining this type of approval. According to Meadows (2003), only 20–30% of the medications approved by the FDA are labeled for pediatric use. The absence of this pertinent information, however, does not mean that the medication is dangerous or does not work (Dulcan, 1999). It *does* mean, however, that particular attention must be given to assessment and reassessment and the side effects that are reported.

SPECIAL CONSIDERATIONS AND SERVICES FOR OLDER ADULTS

Similar to the child consumer, the older consumer is in a state of constant flux, but unlike the child's, the elder's changes are often characterized by a deterioration of biological, physical, and cognitive processes. He or she may be enduring ongoing medical problems and increasing reliance on others. These issues can become troublesome and often lead to feelings of loss. There are normal feelings of loss related to diminishing health, waning independence, retirement, changes in socioeconomic status, and the loss of spouse or friends. These normal feelings, however, can turn into serious depressive episodes that require treatment (Dziegielewski & Harrison, 1996).

The use and misuse of prescription medication can present particular problems for older consumers, and all NMTPs must stay informed on the subject. Whenever medication is given to older consumers, the well-known precaution "start low and go slow" should be applied (Cohen, 2000). When asked, many consumers reveal long histories of adverse drug reactions. In Some authorities assert that as many as half of all deaths in consumers age 60 or older are caused by some type of adverse drug reaction (Cohen, 2000; Larsen, 1999). It takes longer for medication to be metabolized by the liver and excreted by the kidneys, due to slower rates of metabolism, circulation, and elimination. Lower-than-recommended doses often can be effective for older consumers. NMTPs can encourage these consumers to remind their physicians to provide more individualized care and attention. Older consumers can also be educated to identify whether a medication is working, and when adverse reactions occur, they can inform their physician. This type of education can facilitate medication compliance, thereby assisting both the consumer and the MTP and NMTP alike.

Older consumers frequently take more than one medication and are often given complex dosing schedules (Kane, Ouslander, & Abrass, 1999). The number of side effects and contraindications increases dramatically when taking more than one medication. Older consumers may be seeing more than one physician, and one prescriber may not be aware of what another has prescribed. Furthermore, for all individuals taking multiple prescriptions, mistakes in dosing or in eating prohibited food or drinks can happen—and lead to a toxic drug reaction.

In the assessment process, before beginning any type of intervention, NMTPs should explore the possibility that the consumer's social or interpersonal problems might be side effects of medication or of drug interactions. Some complaints that are minimized as merely "signs of growing old" might really be side effects of medication. For example, researchers have begun to document cases of older individuals, given antipsychotic medications to control their symptoms of dementia (Magnuson, Roccaforte, Wengel, & Burke, 2000), developing symptoms of dystonia (slow, sustained muscular contraction or spasm).

Depression in Older Adults

According to Butler, Lewis, and Sunderland (1998), as many as 20% of those 65 years of age or older suffer from various mental health disorders. Depression in older people is sometimes difficult to diagnose and has traditionally been linked to phys-

> **QUICK TIPS:**
> **Assessing Older Adults**
> **The NMTP should always . . .**
>
> - Encourage older individuals to stay as active, independent, and psychologically stable as possible.
>
> - Keep assessment time and evaluation as brief as possible and determine the changes in behavior that have occurred over time.
>
> - Include the perceptions of family members or those in the immediate support system and recognize the effect that these individuals can have on the intervention regimen.

iological and medical changes resulting from the aging process. Difficulties in accurately assessing depressive symptoms can also stem from complications presented by other illnesses, which can mask or precipitate depression. Illnesses that are commonly associated with depression in the older population include hypertension, coronary problems, Alzheimer's disease, Parkinson's disease, diabetes, certain types of cancers, rheumatoid arthritis, chronic constipation, and sexual dysfunction (Butler et al., 1998). Depressed older consumers should always be referred for a medical exam to rule out any physical causes of depressive symptoms.

Although depression is considered a common problem among older people, there is little consensus among researchers regarding the prevalence of this condition and how best to recognize it in this age group (Ban, 1987; Reynolds, Frank, Perel & Miller, 1994). There is a disproportionately high suicide rate among older people (Ban, 1987), with the highest rate found among males 75 and older (Apfeldorf & Alexopoulous, 1999; Blazer, 1999). It is unfortunate that so many older individuals may avoid seeking treatment for a condition that is treatable or may minimize the symptoms they are experiencing for this or other mental health conditions (Belsky, 1988; Maldonado, 1987).

Common signs and symptoms in older adults are similar to those in younger ones and include feelings of sadness, loneliness, guilt, boredom, marked decrease or increase in appetite, lack of, or increase in, sleep behavior, and a sense of worthlessness (American Psychiatric Association, 2000; Kane, Ouslander, & Abrass, 1999). When the etiology of depression is related to life circumstances, it is generally considered situational in nature. Situational depression presents a particular problem for older people who are likely to have endured many tragic experiences, including the loss of loved ones, jobs, status, independence, and other personal disappointments. Perodeau and du Fort (2000) warned that, when dealing with situational depression in older adults, prescribing psychotropic drugs alone is not an adequate response. The addition of supportive intervention and counseling can improve life satisfaction for many of these individuals. Practitioners can assist by teaching those suffering from situational depression how to control the frequency of their depressive thoughts. Relaxation techniques such as imagery and deep muscle relaxation (as discussed in Chapter 6) can be used to help consumers calm down during times of anxiety. Concrete problem-solving techniques and behavioral contracting can be implemented to help older consumers change problem behaviors. Whenever possible, family members should be included in treatment contracting to provide support and to assist in recording and observing behaviors that the consumer seeks to change.

Psychopharmacotherapy for older people with depression usually involves some type of antidepressant medication. (See Chapter 4 for a list and clinical explanation of the antidepressant medications that are most frequently used.) When specifically addressing this type of medication use among older consumers, it is believed that at least 60% will respond with improvement of depressive symptoms; however, even among responders, many continue to have significant residual symptoms (Rabins, 1999). Side-effect profiles may be magnified, and these consumers may be more likely to develop delirium, constipation, urinary retention, dry mouth, and orthostatic hypotension. For this reason, the initial dose is generally lower than that used for younger adults; the medication should be titrated at a slower pace; and the treatment period should last longer (7 to 9 weeks) than that used for younger adults (Rabins, 1999).

All of the major antidepressant medications discussed in Chapter 4 can be used with older adults. According to Apfeldorf and Alexopoulos (1999), the antidepressant medications that are generally used with older individuals include tricyclics (e.g., nortriptyline or desipramine, because these have lower anticholinergic and sedative effects) and SSRIs (e.g., fluoxetine, sertraline, and paroxetine).

When working with older consumers who are believed to be suffering from depression, practitioners should always gather as detailed a medical and medication history as possible. It is also critical to remember that medications used with older consumers often have limited and not well-established safe and effective prescription doses (Sadavoy, 2004). It was not until August of 1997 that the FDA made it mandatory for drug manufacturers to include a separate section in the drug literature that addresses "geriatric use" directly (Nordenberg, 1999b).

A nutritional note: Sometimes the NMTP, with the time to ask and the experience to know, can see things that the prescribing physician, in his or her hurry, might miss. Nutrition often plays a very important role in mental health, and proper nourishment and nutrition are often more problematic for older consumers. Many elders live off cheap starches such as noodles and white rice and do not get enough vitamins, minerals, enzymes, and fiber from fresh fruits and vegetables and high-protein foods (e.g., meat, poultry, fish, eggs, dairy, beans, seeds). The addition of a broad-spectrum multiple vitamin and mineral supplement (in liquid form if necessary) and the assurance of getting at least one high-protein meal a day can sometimes provide the missing elements that could stave off depression, or at least reduce its severity. Including a nutritionist or dietitian in the wellness team can improve both the quality of life and the outcome of treatment for older adults.

Dementia in Older Adults

Dementia is acknowledged to be the most devastating and debilitating condition affecting older adults, and it has a multitude of possible causes (Kawas, 1999). Dementia remains the fourth leading cause of death for those ages 65 and older (American Association of Retired Persons, 1993). It is estimated that the number of older individuals in our society is increasing, with an expected increase in the number of cases of dementia (Kawas, 1999). As of 2001 there were an estimated 19 million people with dementia worldwide, and this number is expected to double by 2050 (Waldemar, 2001). This disease is particularly problematic because it can drastically affect an individual's functional independence, requiring that every need be met by others. The American Psychiatric Association (2000) described the essential feature of this condition as multiple cognitive deficits of a sufficient nature to interfere with social or occupational functioning, thus limiting an individual's judgment, abstract thought, intelligence, and orientation. The American Psychiatric Association (2000) has also warned that the diagnosis of depression in the elderly can be particularly problematic because the symptoms of dementia in the early stages are very similar to depression. Loss of interest and pleasure in one's usual activities, disorientation, and memory loss are common in both conditions. Although many of the same signs and symptoms can exist in both cases, the individual suffering from early stages of dementia usually does not improve with treatment.

Unfortunately, the term *dementia* has been used as a catchall phrase when discussing older people, and the professional community has not always attempted to diagnose or differentiate which type of dementia an individual is experiencing. There are different types of dementia with different etiology. The most common form of dementia is dementia of the Alzheimer's type (DAT), followed by either vascular dementia, previously referred to as multi-infarct dementia (MID), or Lewy body dementia (DLB). Although these types of dementia are frequently linked, their etiology is different (Roman, 2003). The possible reasons for this lack of attention to the precise type of dementia may be that the person is sometimes viewed as hopeless, helpless, and unworthy of careful evaluation and treatment; or that the general approach is to treat symptoms of dementia as they appear, because remedial treatments and cure are not available.

Another possible reason for this lack of attention is the difficulty of differentiating the subtypes. NMTPs should be aware of the different forms of dementia and the signs and symptoms this progressive disease presents. As members of the health care team, NMTPs have the unique opportunity to educate and provide counseling and support for individuals suffering from dementia, and to provide support and education to their families and caregivers, thereby increasing the reach of support networks for all involved (Dziegielewski, 1991). Furthermore, the medications now being used to assist individuals who are experiencing cognitive difficulties have improved. Although there is no known medication that can cure or completely reverse the devastating effects of dementia, there is some promising research that might indeed make it possible one day (Allian, Bentue-Ferrer, Gandon, et al., 1997; Nordberg, 1996).

Medications Designed to Enhance Cognitive Processing

The most commonly used prescription medications to assist with cognitive decline are Aricept (donepezil), Cognex (tacrine), Exelon (rivastigmine), and Reminyl (galantamine). All of these medications are approved by the FDA for use with individuals who have mild to moderate declines in cognitive functioning (Antai-Otong, 2003). The way these medications work is related to their influence on the neurotransmitter acetylcholine, one of several neurotransmitters in the brain that mediates communication among brain cells. Reduced levels of acetylcholine in the brain are believed to be responsible for some of the symptoms of Alzheimer's disease. By blocking the enzyme that destroys acetylcholine, these medications help to increase the concentration of acetylcholine in the brain; this increase is believed to be responsible for the improvement in cognitive processing (see Table 9.4).

TABLE 9.4
Cognitive Enhancers

Drug	Purpose and Actions
Aricept (donepezil)	May slow pace of disease progression; no known effect on underlying disease; reduced agitation.
Cognex (tacrine)	May slow pace of the disease progression; can have problematic side effects that require discontinuance.
Exelon (rivastigmine)	May slow progression of disease; helps to improve psychotic features.
Reminyl (galantamine)	May slow progression of dementia, particularly Alzheimer's disease, and moderately improve cognition; helps to prevent decline in ADLs.

Aricept (donepezil) is often prescribed for older adults who have mild to moderate dementia. There are numerous off-label uses for this medication, from addressing the symptoms that occur in the late stages of the disease to handling psychosis and other behavioral difficulties that occur as part of the disease process. Therapeutic gains with this medicine appear to be dose-dependent, with larger amounts of the medication producing the maximum effect (Sadavoy, 2004).

Cognex (tacrine) is also used to treat mild to moderate dementia. Some of the off-label uses include the treatment of apathy, anxiety, and hallucinations. The most serious side effect with this medication is the potential for liver toxicity. This side effect can be so serious that this medication should be considered as a last resort, now that the others are available (Sadavoy, 2004).

Exelon (rivastigmine), similar to the others, is generally used for mild to moderate forms of dementia. Off-label uses often involve trials with consumers in the advanced stages of the disease. It seems to work best with DLB and may improve psychotic features present in the illness without heightening depressive symptoms.

Reminyl (galantamine) is similar to Cognex, Aricept, and Exelon and is used to address the symptoms of mild to moderate cognitive decline. Off-label uses include the treatment of psychosis and cognitive decline related to DLB and the agitation and aggression often associated with Alzheimer's disease (Sadavoy, 2004).

Benefits of each of these medications include mild memory enhancement, increased capacity for social interaction, and heightened attention. One drawback of all of these medications: Some consumers demonstrate only modest clinical benefits.

Side-Effect Profiles

Because all four of these medications are cholinesterase inhibitors, their side-effect profiles are similar. All have some gastrointestinal side effects that may manifest in anorexia, nausea, vomiting, diarrhea, or hypersalivation (may be very disturbing and can be a common complaint). Neurological side effects may include tremor, dizziness, agitation, sleep disorders, and possibly disturbed dreaming, along with some EPS symptoms such as gait disturbances. Consumers may report fatigue, lack of energy or malaise, dizziness or headache. Psychological symptoms include agitation, behavioral disturbances, confusion, delusions, and paranoid reactions. Often these symptoms can be managed by discontinuing the medication. Some symptoms are highly unlikely, but if experienced, can have very serious side effects; these may include convulsions, black stool, bloody or "coffee-ground" vomit, and irregular heartbeat.

SUMMARY

This chapter has provided an overview of several considerations when addressing mental health problems for younger and older consumers. These populations have unique characteristics, challenges, and concerns, which this chapter only begins to identify. It is hoped that the information provided here will motivate readers to seek more information in this area. NMTPs need to be familiar with and sensitive to the unique attributes of all consumers in order to accurately develop intervention plans, participate in medication recommendations, and help consumers monitor the effects of prescribed drugs.

As health and mental health care continues to evolve, NMTPs will find that they can remain viable contributors in the field. Ethical professional practice requires having knowledge of medications. This knowledge adds a valuable skill to the repertoire of interventions used by practitioners, and may make NMTPs more appealing to health care companies who require continuous monitoring of consumer medications.

Conclusion and Future Considerations

In closing, I would like to stress the purpose of this handbook once again. It is not meant to provide exhaustive information related to the medications or preparations that may be used by all consumers, nor is it meant to include all psychosocial supportive techniques available. Rather it is written to assist NMTPs in developing an appreciation for the importance of acquiring and integrating knowledge of mental health medications into the psychosocial intervention process. A working knowledge of the different types of medications, their side effects, and their benefits can help NMTPs monitor such issues as medication compliance and medication-related problems. Furthermore, having knowledge about current therapies can help prepare NMTPs to educate consumers and their families about responsible use of mental health medications (Matorin & DeChillo, 1984; Bentley & Walsh, 1998). The overriding message in this handbook is that *knowledge of medications is essential for delivering and monitoring effective and efficient services.*

Lastly, many practitioners acknowledge the importance of being well-versed on prescription medications, yet they place little emphasis on the effects of nonprescription medications or herbal preparations. More nonprescription medications are being marketed to consumers every day, and for many a trip to the pharmacy is fast becoming a substitute for a trip to the physician (Colino, 2000). The numerous alternative medicines and treatment strategies available to consumers today reflect the fact that educated consumers are increasingly concerned about the long-term effects of standard medications, and that they want to rely less on traditional drugs and more on alternative or holistic means for their health and mental health wellness. Given the increasing numbers of consumers pursuing these alternative medications, NMTPs need to fully appreciate the medications, their potential toxic interactions with other drugs, their effects on mental disorders, and their impact on the treatment process.

References

Ables, A. Z., & Baughman, O. L. (2003). Antidepressants: Update on new agents and indications. *American Family Physician*, *67*(3), 547–560.

Airaksinen, M., Ahonen, R., & Enlund, H. (1993). Drug information for pharmacies: Desire for more spontaneous information. *Medical Care*, *31*(9), 846–850.

Alfonso, S., & Dziegielewski, S. F. (2001). Self-directed treatment for panic disorder: A holistic approach. *Journal of Research and Social Work Evaluation: An International Publication*, *2*(1), 5–18.

Allan, E. L., Barker, K. N., Malloy, M. J., & Heller, W. M. (1995). Dispensing errors and counseling in community practice. *American Pharmacy*, NS35, 25–33.

Allian, H., Bentue-Ferrer, D., Gandon, J. M., LeDoze, F., & Belliard, S. (1997). Drugs used in Alzheimer's disease and neuroplasticity. *Clinical Therapeutics*, *19*, 4–15.

American Association of Retired Persons (1993). *Coping and caring: Living with Alzheimer's disease* [Brochure]. Washington, DC: Author.

American Heritage Dictionary of the English Language, Fourth Edition (2004). New York: Houghton Mifflin.

American Psychiatric Association (1994). *Diagnostic and statistical manual of mental disorders* (4th ed.). Washington, DC: Author.

American Psychiatric Association (2000). *Diagnostic and statistical manual of mental disorders* (4th ed., text rev.). Washington, DC: Author.

Anastopoulos, A. D. (1999). Attention-deficit/hyperactivity disorder. In S. D. Netherton, D. Holmes, & E. C. Walker (Eds.), *Child adolescent psychological disorders: A comprehensive textbook* (pp. 98–117). New York: Oxford University Press.

Anderson, I. M., & Tomenson, B. M. (1995). Treatment discontinuation with selective serotonin reuptake inhibitors compared with tricyclic antidepressants: A meta-analysis. *British Medical Journal, 310,* 1433–1438.

Antai-Otong, D. (2003). Acetylcholinesterase inhibitors in dementia. *Perspectives in Psychiatric Care, 39*(2), 83–86.

APA studies focus on side effects, efficacy of antipsychotics. (2000). *Outcomes and Accountability Alert, 5*(1), 5–6.

Apfeldorf, W., & Alexopoulos, G. (1999). Psychopharmacology and psychotherapy. In W. R. Hazzard, J. P. Blass, W. H. Etinger, J. B. Halter, & J. G. Ouslander (Eds.), *Principles of geriatric medicine and gerontology* (4th ed., pp. 1369–1378). New York: McGraw-Hill.

Armenteros, J. L. (1997). Risperidone in adolescents with schizophrenia: An open pilot study. *Journal of the American Academy of Child and Adolescent Psychiatry, 36,* 694.

Arnold, L. M. (2003). Gender differences in bipolar disorder. *Psychiatric Clinics of North America, 26*(3), 595–620.

ASHP Report (1993). ASHP guidelines on preventing medication errors in hospitals. *American Journal of Hospital Pharmacy, 50,* 305–314.

Ashton, A. K. (2004). Reversal of fluoxetine-induced sexual dysfunction by switching to escitalopram. *Journal of Sex and Marital Therapy, 30,* 1–2.

Associated Press (1998, January 17). Drugs online—no doctor visit needed. *Orlando Sentinel,* p. A24.

Austin, V. (2003). Pharmacological interventions for students with ADD. *Intervention in School and Clinic, 38*(5), 289–297.

Austrian, S. G. (1995). *Mental disorders, medications, and clinical social work.* New York: Columbia University Press.

Ayd, F. J. (2001). Interactions between prescription drugs and natural remedies. *Psychiatric Times, 18*(8), 1–12.

Badger, L. W., & Rand, E. H. (1998). Mood disorders. In J. B. W. Williams & K. Ell (Eds.), *Mental health research: Implications for practice* (pp. 49–117). Washington, DC: NASW Press.

Baizabal, J. M., Furlan-Magaril, M., Santa-Olalla, J., & Covarkubias, L. (2003). Neural stem cell in development and degeneration medicine. *Archives of Medical Research, 34*(6), 572–588.

Baldessarini, R. J. (1990). Drugs and the treatment of psychiatric disorders. In A. Goodman Gilman, T. W. Rall, A. S. Nies, & P. Taylor (Eds.), *The pharmacological basis of therapeutics* (8th ed., pp. 383–435). New York: Pergamon Press.

Baldwin, D. S. (2000). Pharmacological provocation and prevention of suicidal behavior. *International Review of Psychiatry, 12*(1), 54–68.

Ballenger, J. C., Lydiard, R. B., & Turner, S. M. (1995). Panic disorder and agoraphobia. In G. O. Gabbard (Ed.), *Treatments of psychiatric disorders* (2nd ed.). Washington, DC: American Psychiatric Press.

Ban, T. A. (1987). Pharmacological perspectives in therapy of depression in the elderly. In G. L. Maddox & E. W. Busse (Eds.), *Aging: The universal experience* (pp. 127–131). New York: Springer.

Banta, D. (2000). Increase in global access to essential drugs sought (medical news and perspectives). *Journal of the American Medical Association, 283*(3), 321.

Barker, M. J., Greenwood, K. M., Jackson, M., & Crowe, S. F. (2004). Cognitive effects of long-term benzodiazepine use: A meta-analysis. *CNS Drugs, 18*(1), 37–48.

Barkley, R. A. (1990). *Attention-deficit/hyperactivity disorder: A handbook for diagnosis and treatment.* New York: Guilford Press.

Barkley, R. A., Conners, C. K., Barclay, A., Gadow, K., Gittelman, R., Sprague, R. L., & Swanson, J. (1990). Task force report: The appropriate role of clinical child psychologists in the prescribing of psychoactive medication for children. *Journal of Clinical Child Psychology, 19*(Suppl.), 1–38.

Barlow, D. H., Esler, J. L., & Vitali, A. E. (1998). Psychosocial treatments for panic disorders, phobias, and generalized anxiety disorder. In P. E. Nathan & J. M. Gorman (Eds.), *A guide to treatments that work* (pp. 288–318). New York: Oxford University Press.

Barnes, T. R., & McEvedy, C. J. (1996). Pharmacological treatments strategies in non-responsive schizophrenic patient. *International Clinical Psychopharmacology, 11,* 117–121.

Bassett, S. (2000). Herbal drugs: Medicines within food supplements? *Manufacturing Chemist, 16,* 27.

Beck, A. T. (1991). Cognitive therapy: A 30-year retrospective. *American Psychologist, 46,* 368–375.

Beck, A. T., & Emery, G., with Greenberg, R. L. (1985). *Anxiety disorders and phobias: A cognitive perspective.* New York: Basic Books.

Beck, A. T., & Freeman, A. (1990). *Cognitive therapy of personality disorders.* New York: Guilford Press.

Beck, A. T., Rush, A. J., Shaw, B. F., & Emery, G. (1979). *Cognitive therapy of depression.* New York: Guilford Press.

Beck, A. T., & Weishaar, M. E. (2000). Cognitive therapy. In R. J. Corisini & D. Wedding (Eds.), *Current psychotherapies* (6th ed., pp. 241–272). Itasca, IL: Peacock.

Beck, A. T., Wright, F. D., Newman, C. F., & Leise, B. S. (1993). *Cognitive therapy of substance abuse.* New York: Guilford Press.

Becket, H. (2000). Boosting the quality and potency of St. John's wort. *Agricultural Research, 48*(7), 12–14.

Beizer, J. L. (1994). Medications and the aging body: Alteration as a function of age. *Generations, 18*(2), 13–18.

Belsky, J. (1988). *Here tomorrow: Making the most of life after fifty.* Baltimore: Johns Hopkins University Press.

Bender, K. J. (1996, October). St. John's wort evaluated as an herbal antidepressant. *Psychiatric Times.* Retrieved July 6, 1999, from *www.mhsource.com/edu/psytimes/p964058.html.*

Bentley, K. J. (1997). Should clinical social workers seek psychotropic medication prescription privileges?: No. In B. A. Thyer (Ed.), *Controversial issues in social work practice* (pp. 152–165). Boston: Allyn & Bacon.

Bentley, K. J. (1998). Psychopharmacological treatment of schizophrenia: What social workers need to know. *Research on Social Work Practice, 8,* 384–405.

Bentley, K. J., & Walsh, J. (1998). Advances in psychopharmacology and medication management. In J. B. Williams & K. Ell (Eds.), *Advances in mental health research: Implications for practice* (pp. 309–342). Washington, DC: NASW Press.

Berstein, J. G. (Ed.) (1995). *Handbook of drug therapy in psychiatry* (3rd ed.). St Louis, MO: Mosby.

Bezchlibnyk-Butler, K. Z., & Jeffries, J. (1999). *Clinical handbook of psychotropic drugs.* Seattle: Hogrefe & Huber.

Bilia, A. R., Gallori, S., & Vincieri, F. F. (2002). Kava-kava and anxiety: Growing knowledge about the efficacy and safety. *Life Sciences, 70,* 2581–2597.

Blazèr, D. G. (1999). Depression. In W. R. Hazzard, J. P. Blass, W. H. Etinger, J. B. Halter, & J. G. Ouslander (Eds.), *Principles of geriatric medicine and gerontology* (4th ed., pp. 1331–1400). New York: McGraw-Hill.

Boerlin, H. L., Gitlin, M. J., Zoellner, L. A., & Hammen, C. L. (1998). Bipolar depression and antidepressant-induced mania: A naturalistic study. *Journal of Clinical Psychiatry, 59*(7), 374–379.

Borken, J., Neher, J. O., Anson, O., & Smoker, B. (1994). Referrals for alternative therapies. *Journal of Family Practice, 39*(6) 545–50.

Bowden, C. L. (2002). Diagnosis of bipolar disorders: Focus on bipolar I and bipolar II disorder. *Medscape Psychiatry and Mental Health eJournal, 7*(4), 1–7. Retrieved August 21, 2004, from *www.medscape.com/viewarticle/440094.*

Boyd-Webb, N. (1991). *Play therapy with children in crisis.* New York: Guilford Press.

Bradley, S. S. (2003). The psychology of the psychology triangle: The client, the clinicians, and the medication. In K. Bentley (Ed.), *Psychiatric medication issues for social workers, counselors, and psychologists* (pp. 29–50). Binghamton, NY: Haworth Press.

Brain–Body Connection (2000). *Exploring the brain.* Films for the Humanities and Sciences. Available from *www.films.com.*

Breier, A. (1996). Introduction and overview. In A. Breier (Ed.), *The new pharmacotherapy of schizophrenia* (pp. xix–xx). Washington, DC: American Psychiatric Association.

Breier, A., & Buchanan, R. W. (1996). Clozapine: Current status and clinical applications. In A. Breier (Ed.), *The new pharmacotherapy of schizophrenia* (pp. 1–14). Washington, DC: American Psychiatric Association.

Brennan, J. W. (1995). A short-term psychoeducational multiple-family group for bipolar patients and their families. *Social Work, 40*(6), 737–744.

Brewin, C. R. (2001, Summer). Cognitive and emotional reactions to traumatic events: Implications for short-term intervention. *Advances in Mind–Body Medicine, 17*(3), 1–7.

Brophy, J. J. (1991). Psychiatric disorders. In S. A. Schroeder, M. A. Krupp, L. M. Tierney, & S. J. McPhee (Eds.), *Current medical diagnosis and treatment* (pp. 731–786). Norwalk, CT: Appleton & Lange.

Brotter, B., Clarkin, J. F., & Carpenter, D. (1998). Bipolar disorder. In B. Thyer & J. Wodarski (Eds.), *Handbook of empirical social work practice: Mental disorders* (vol. 1, pp. 287–308). New York: Wiley.

Brower, A. M., & Nurius, P. S. (1993). *Social cognitions and individual change: Current theory and counseling guidelines.* Newbury Park, CA: Sage.

Brzustowicz, L., Hodgkinson, K., Chow, E., Honer, W., & Bassett, A. (2000). Location of major susceptibility locus for familial schizophrenia on chromosome 1q21-q22. *Science, 288*, 687–682.

Buchanan, R. W., Brandes, M., & Breier, A. (1996). Treating negative symptoms: Pharmacological strategies. In A. Breier (Ed.), *The new pharmacotherapy of schizophrenia* (pp. 179–204). Washington, DC: American Psychiatric Association.

Buppert, C. (2000). *Avoiding prescription errors.* Gold Sheet, 2(5), 1–3.

Butler, R. N., Lewis, M. I., & Sunderland, T. (1998). *Aging and mental health: Positive psychosocial and biomedical approaches.* Needham Heights, MA: Allyn & Bacon.

Cao, Q., Benton, R. L., & Whittemore, S. R. (2002). Stem cell repair of central nervous system injury. *Journal of Neuroscience Research 68*, 501–510.

Carey, J. (2000, February). A crackdown on e-druggists: Online pill pushers are in U.S. regulators' sights. *Business Week, 3667*, 104.

Carlson, G. A., Bromet, E. J., & Jandorf, L. (1998). Conduct disorder and mania: What does it mean in adults? *Journal of Affective Disorders, 48*(2–3), 199–205.

Carpenter, W. T. (1996). Foreword. In A. Breier (Ed.), *The new pharmacotherapy of schizophrenia* (pp. xvii–xviii). Washington, DC: American Psychiatric Association.

Carpenter, W. T., Conley, R. R., & Buchanan, R. W. (1998). Schizophrenia. In S. J. Enna & J. T. Coyle (Eds.), *Pharmacological management of neurological and psychiatric disorders.* New York: McGraw-Hill.

Cassano, G. B., Pini, S., Saettoni, M., & Dell'Osso, L. (1999). Multiple anxiety disorder comorbidity in patients with mood spectrum disorders with psychotic features. *American Journal of Psychiatry, 156*(3), 474–476.

Cassidy, F., Murry, E., Forest, K., & Carroll, B. J. (1998). Signs and symptoms of mania in pure and mixed episodes. *Journal of Affective Disorders, 50*(2–3), 187–201.

Cauchon, D. (2000, April). FDA moves to make more drugs Rx-free. *USA Today,* [01.A online]. Retrieved June 3, 2000, from *www.usatoday.com.*

Centers for Disease Control. (2004). Surgeon General's 2004 report: The health consequences of smoking on the human body. *National Center for Chronic Disease Prevention and Health Promotion.* Retrieved July 5, 2004, from *www.cdc.gov/tobacco/sgr/sgr_2004/sgranimation/flash/index.html.*

Chen, I. (1999, September). Worry box: Is it dangerous to buy drugs off the web? *Health, 13*(7), 1–2.

Clark, D. B., Salkovskis, P. M., Hackmann, A., Middleton, H., Anastasiades, P., & Gelder, M. (1994). A comparison of cognitive therapy, applied relaxation, and imipramine in the treatment of panic disorder. *British Journal of Psychiatry, 164,* 759–769.

Cohen, D. (2003). The psychiatric medication history: Context, purpose, and method. In K. Bentley (Ed.), *Psychiatric medication issues for social workers, counselors, and psychologists* (pp. 5–28). Binghamton, NY: Haworth Press.

Cohen, I., & Steketee, G. (1998). Obsessive–compulsive disorder. In B. Thyer & J. Wodarski (Eds.), *Handbook of empirical social work practice: Mental disorders* (vol. 1, pp. 343–363). New York: Wiley.

Cohen, M. R. (1994). Medication errors: Second-guessing and sound-alike generic names. *Nursing, 94,* 29.

Cohen, M. R. (2004). Writing a wrong. *Nursing, 34,* 21.

Cohen, S. J. (2000). Avoiding adverse reactions: Effective lower-dose drug therapies for older patients. *Geriatrics, 55*(2), 54–56.

Colby, I., & Dziegielewski, S. F. (2004). *Introduction to social work: The people's profession.* Chicago: Lyceum.

Colino, S. (2000, April). The pharmacist is in. *Good Housekeeping, 230*(4), 185.

Conference Report (2003). Medication may help prevent suicide in teens. *Brown University Child and Adolescent Psychopharmacology Update, 5*(3), 1–5.

Cooper, M. (1999). Treatment of persons and families with obsessive compulsive disorder: A review article. *Crisis Intervention, 5,* 25–36.

Corbin, L., Hanson, R., Happ, S., & Whitby, A. (1988). Somatoform disorders. *Journal of Psychosocial Nursing, 6,* 31–34.

Corcoran, K., & Vandiver, V. L. (2004). Implementing best practice and expert consensus procedures. In A. R. Roberts & K. R. Yeager (Eds.), *Evidence-based practice manual: Research and outcome measures in the health and human services* (pp. 15–19). New York: Oxford University Press.

Costello, P. (2000, April). Easy drugs online. *Glamour, 102,* 104.

Court, W. E. (2000). *Ginseng: The genus panax.* Amsterdam, The Netherlands: Harwood Academic Publishers.

Cowley, G. (1994, February 7). The culture of Prozac. *Newsweek, 123*(6), 41–42.

Coyle, J. T., & Enna, S. J. (1998). Overview of neuro-psychopharmacology. In S. J. Enna & J. T. Coyle (Eds.), *Pharmacological management of neurological and psychiatric disorders.* New York: McGraw Hill.

Craig, C. (1995). Teaching food–drug interactions. *Journal of Psychosocial Nursing Mental Health Services, 33*(2), 44–46.

Craske, M. G., & Waikar, S. V. (1994). Panic disorder. In M. Hersen & R. T. Ammerman (Eds.), *Handbook of prescriptive treatments for adults* (pp. 135–155). New York: Plenum Press.

Crone, C. C., & Gabriel, G. (2002). Herbal and nonherbal supplements in medical–psychiatric patient populations. *Psychiatry in the Medically Ill, 25,* 211–225.

Currie, J. (2005). The marketization of depression: Prescribing SSRI antidepressants to women. *Women and Health Protection.* Retrieved November 24, 2005, from *www.whp-apsf.ca/pdf/ssris.pdf.*

Danner, V., & Kipp, A. (2003). New help for PMDD sufferers. *Access 17*(9), 10.

Dattilio, F. M. (2001, Summer). Crisis intervention techniques for panic disorder. *American Journal of Psychotherapy, 55*(3), 1–12.

Davis, J. L. (2004). Talk, drug therapies have similar effect. *WebMD Medical News.* Retrieved August 5, 2004, from *http://aolsvc.health.webmd.aol.com/content/article/79/96082.htm.*

Davis, J. M., & Casper, R. (1997). Antipsychotic drugs: Clinical pharmacology and therapeutic use. *Drugs, 12,* 260–282.

DeAngelo, M. (2000). Internet solution reduces medical errors. *Health Management Technology, 21*(2), 20.

DeGrandpre, R. (2004). Trouble in Prozac nation. *Nation, 278*(1), 6–8.

DeLeon, P. H. (1994). Should non-prescription mental health professionals be allowed to prescribe medications? In S. A. Kirk & S. D. Einbinder (Eds.), *Controversial issues in mental health* (pp. 177—187). Boston: Allyn & Bacon.

DeLeon, P. H., Fox, R. F., & Graham, S. R. (1991). Prescription privileges: Psychology's next frontier. *American Psychologist, 46,* 384–393.

Department of Defense (1995). *Psychopharmacology demonstration project: Training military psychologists to prescribe.* Government Relations, Practice Directorate. Washington, DC: Author.

deVane, C. L. (1994). Pharmacogenetics and drug metabolism of the newer antidepressant agents. *Journal of Clinical Psychiatry, 55*(12), 38–45.

Deyo, R. A. (2004). Gaps, tensions, and conflicts in the FDA approval process: Implications for clinical practice. *Journal of the American Board of Family Practice, 17,* 142–149.

Diamond, R. J. (2002). *Instant psychopharmacology.* New York: Norton.

Diamond, S., Balm, T. K., & Freitag, F. G. (2000). Ibuprofen plus caffeine in the treatment of tension-type headache. *Clinical Pharmacology and Therapeutics 68*(3), 312–319.

Dopheide, J., & Park, S. (2002). The psychopharmacology of anxiety. *Psychiatric Times, 19*(3), 1–10.

Doraiswamy, M., & Koller, E. A. (2002, June). *Duke warning: Zyprexa–diabetes link.* Alliance for Human Research Protection. Retrieved August 3, 2004, from *www.ahrp.org/infomail/0702/12b.php.*

Dotinga, R. (2002, February 24). Ecstasy-Prozac a dangerous cocktail. *USA Today Health and Science.* Retrieved June 29, 2003, from *www.usatoday.com/news/health/addiction/2002-02-24-ecstasy.htm.*

Dulcan, M. K. (Ed.) (1999). *Helping parents, youth, and teachers understand medications for behavioral and emotional problems: A resource book of medication information handouts.* Washington, DC: American Psychiatric Association.

Dziegielewski, S. F. (1991). Social group work with family members of elderly nursing home residents with dementia: A controlled evaluation. *Research on Social Work Practice, 1,* 358–370.

Dziegielewski, S. F. (1996). Managed care principles: The need for social work in the health care environment. *Crisis Intervention, 3,* 97—111.

Dziegielewski, S. F. (1997). Should clinical social workers seek psychotropic medication prescription privileges?: Yes. In B. A. Thyer (Ed.), *Controversial issues in social work practice* (pp. 152–165). Boston: Allyn & Bacon.

Dziegielewski, S. F. (1998). Psychopharmacology and social work practice: Introduction. *Research on Social Work Practice, 8*(4), 371–383.

Dziegielewski, S. F. (2002a). *DSM-IV-TR in action.* New York: Wiley.

Dziegielewski, S. F. (2002b). Herbal preparations and social work practice. In A. Roberts & G. Green (Eds.), *Social workers' desk reference.* New York: Oxford University Press.

Dziegielewski, S. F. (2003). Complementary medications and herbal healing: A new frontier in counseling practice. *Social Work in Mental Health, 1*(4), 123–139.

Dziegielewski, S. F. (2004). *The changing face of health care social work: Professional practice in managed behavioral health care.* New York: Springer.

Dziegielewski, S. F. (2005). *Understanding substance addictions: Assessment and intervention.* Chicago: Lyceum.

Dziegielewski, S. F., & Harrison, D. F. (1996a). Counseling the aged. In D. F. Harrison, B. A. Thyer, & J. Wodarski (Eds.), *Cultural diversity in social work practice* (2nd ed.). Springfield, IL: Thomas.

Dziegielewski, S. F., & Harrison, D. F. (1996b). Social work practice with the aged. In D. F. Harrison, B. A. Thyer, & J. S. Wodarski (Eds.), *Cultural diversity and social work practice* (2nd ed., pp. 138–175). Springfield, IL: Thomas.

Dziegielewski, S. F., & Leon, A. M. (1998a). Psychopharmacological treatment of major depression. *Research on Social Work Practice, 8*(4), 475–490.

Dziegielewski, S. F., & Leon, A. M. (1998b). Psychopharmacology knowledge and use with social work professionals: A continuing education evaluation. *International Journal of Continuing Education, 1*(3), 31–40.

Dziegielewski, S. F., Leon, A. M., & Green, C. E. (1998). African American children: A culturally sensitive model for group practice. *Early Child Development and Care, 147*, 83–97.

Dziegielewski, S. F., & MacNeil, G. (1999). Time-limited treatment considerations and strategy for specific phobias. *Crisis Intervention and Time-Limited Treatment, 5*(1–2), 133–150.

Dziegielewski, S. F., & Powers, G. T. (2000). Procedures for evaluating time-limited crisis intervention. In A. Roberts (Ed.), *Crisis intervention handbook* (2nd ed., pp. 487–506). New York: Oxford University Press.

Dziegielewski, S. F., & Leon, A. M. (2001). *Social work practice and psychopharmacology.* New York: Springer.

Dziegielewski, S. F., & Sherman, P. (2004). Complementary therapies: Tips and techniques for health care social workers. In S. Dziegielewski & Contributors, *Changing face of health care practice: Professional practice in managed behavioral health care* (pp. 422–438). Springer: New York.

Dziegielewski, S. F., Turnage, B. F., & Roest-Marti, S. (2004). Handling stress and preventing burnout: A controlled evaluation. *Journal of Social Work Education, 40*(1), 105–119.

Eberhard-Gnon, M., Eskild, A., Opjordsmoen, S. (2005). Treating mood disorders during pregnancy: Safety considerations. *Drug Safety, 28*(8), 695–706.

Eddy, M. F., & Walbroehl, G. S. (1998, April). *Recognition and treatment of obsessive–compulsive disorder.* Retrieved March 14, 2005, from *www.aafp.org/afp/980401ap/eddy.html.*

Eggertson, L. (2005). Regulatory system: Drug approval system questioned in U.S. and Canada. *Canadian Medical Association Journal, 172*(3), 317–318.

Eisenberg, D. M., David, R. B., Ettner, S. L., Appel, S., Wilkey, S., Van Rompay, M., & Kessler, R. C. (1998). Trends in alternative medicine use in the United States: Results of a follow-up national survey. *Journal of the American Medical Association, 280*(18), 1569–1575.

Eisenhauer, L. A. (1998). Variations in patient responses to drug therapy: The role of pharmacodynamics and pharmacokinetics. In L. A. Eisenhauer & M. A. Murphy (Eds.), *Pharmacotherapeutics and advanced nursing practice* (pp. 53–66). New York: McGraw-Hill.

Eisner, R. (2000, May 24). *Falling off Prozac.* Retrieved June 29, 2003, from *www.abcnews.go.com/sections/living/DailyNews/ssri000524.html.*

Eli Lilly (2001). *Prozac makes history.* Retrieved June 29, 2003, from *www.prozac.com/HowProzacCanHelp/ProzacMakesHistory.jsp.*

Eli Lilly (2003). *Zyprexa (olanzapine) tablets.* Retrieved April 11, 2006, from *www.zyprexa.com/understanding/index_print.jsp.*

Ellicott, A., Hammen, C., Gitlin, M., & Brown, G. (1990). Life events and the course of bipolar disorder. *American Journal of Psychiatry, 147*(9), 1194–1198.

Empfield, M. (2000). Pregnancy and schizophrenia. *Psychiatric Annals, 30,* 13–17.

Encyclopedia of Drugs, Alcohol, and Addictive Behavior (2001). (2nd ed., vol. 2, E–Q). New York: Macmillan & Gale Group.

Escitalopram information from Medline Plus (2003a, July 1). Retrieved April 5, 2004, from *www.nlm.nih.gov/medlineplus/druginfo/medmaster/a603005.html.*

Escitalopram systemic information from Medline Plus (2003b, January 21). Retrieved April 5, 2004, from *www.nlm.nih.gov/medlineplus/druginfo/uspdi/500409.html.*

Fanger, M. T. (1994). Brief therapies. In R. Edwards (Ed.), *Encyclopedia of social work* (19th ed., pp. 323–334). Washington, DC: NASW Press.

Farmer, R. L., & Pandurangi, A. K. (1997). Diversity in schizophrenia: Toward a richer biopsychosocial understanding for social work practice. *Health and Social Work, 22,* 109–116.

Food and Drug Administration [FDA] (2003). New labels for over-the-counter medicines: Author receives plain language award. *FDA: Center for Drug Evaluation Research,* pamphlet (May, 2003). Retrieved November 19, 2005, from *www.fda.gov/cder/otc/default.htm.*

Food and Drug Administration (2005). Aspirin for reducing your risk of heart attached and stroke: Know the facts. FDA: Center for Drug Evaluation Research, pamphlet. Retrieved November 17, 2005, from *www.fda.gov/cder/consumer-info/dailyaspirin_brochure.htm.*

FDA, Consumer (1997). Plan will give consumers better prescription drug information. *FDA Consumer, 31*(3), 2.

FDA, Medwatch (2005). The FDA safety information and adverse event reporting program. Retrieved November 20, 2005, from *www.fda.gov/med-watch/index.html.*

FDA News (2004). *FDA launches a multi-pronged strategy to strengthen safeguards for children treated with antidepressant medications.* Department of Health and Human Services, (October 15, 2004). Retrieved June 12, 2005, from *www.fda.gov/bbs/topics/news/2004/NEW01124.html.*

FDA Public Health Advisory (October 15, 2004). Suicidality in children and adolescents being treated with antidepressant medication. Retrieved November 26, 2005, from *www.fda.gov/cder/drug/antidepressants/ SSRIPHA200410.htm.*

Fernandez, M., & Calix, L. (2003). *Modell's drugs in current use and new drugs* (49th ed.). New York: Springer.

Ferriman, A. (2000). The stigma of schizophrenia. *British Medical Journal, 320,* 522.

Fimerson, S. S. (1996). Individual therapy. In V. B. Carson & E. N. Nolan (Eds.), *Mental health nursing: The nurse patient journey* (pp. 367–384). Philadelphia: Saunders.

Findling, R., & Pastor, J. (2000). Atypical antipsychotics in pediatric populations. *Psychiatric Times, 27*(2), 1–5.

Flaum, M. (1995). In C. L. Shriqui & H. A. Nasrallah (Eds.), *Contemporary issues in the treatment of schizophrenia* (pp. 83–108). Washington, DC: American Psychiatric Association.

Foreman, J. (2000, March 25). Health sense: Treatments for manic depression are improving. *Boston Globe,* p. 4a.

Foster, S., & Tyler, V. E. (2000). *Tyler's honest herbal 4th ed.* New York: Haworth Press.

Frank, R. G., Conti, R. M., & Goldman, H. H. (2005). Mental health policy and psychotropic drugs. *The Milbank Quarterly, 83*(2), 271–298.

Friebert, E., & Greeley, A. (1999). Taking time to use medicines wisely. *FDA Consumer, 33*(5), 30–31.

Fugh-Bergman, A. (2000). Herbs–drug interactions. *Lancet, 355*(9198), 134–138.

Gambrill, E. (2004). Contributions of critical thinking and evidence-based practice to the fulfillment of the ethical obligations of professionals. In H. E. Briggs & T. L. Rzepnicki (Eds.), *Using evidence in social work practice: Behavioral perspectives* (pp. 3–19). Chicago: Lyceum.

Gattefosse, M. R. (1937). *Gattefosse's Aromatherapy.* England: C. W. Daniel Company, Ltd.

Ghaemi, N., Sachs, G., Baldassano, C., & Truman, C. (1997). Acute treatment of bipolar disorder with adjunctive risperidone in outpatients. *Canadian Journal of Psychiatry, 42,* 96–199.

Gitlin, M. J. (1996). *The psychotherapist's guide to psychopharmacology* (2nd ed.). New York: Free Press.

Goeddeke-Merickel, C. M. (1998a). Herbal medicine: Some dos and don'ts for dialysis patients. *For Patients Only*, March/April, 22–23.

Goeddeke-Merickel, C. M. (1998b). Alternative medicine and dialysis patients: Part II. *For Patients Only*, May/June, 19–20.

Golden, F. (1997, September 29). Who is to blame for Redux and Fenfluramine? *Time*, pp. 78–79.

Goode, E. (1991). Addiction and dependence. In E. Goode (Ed.), *Drugs, society, and behavior, 91/92* (pp. 40–44). Guilford, CT: Dushkin.

Gottlieb, B. (1995). *New choices in natural healing.* Emmaus, PN: Rodale Press.

Gottlieb, S. (2001). Methylphenidate works by increasing dopamine levels. *British Medical Journal, 322*(7281), 259–261.

Gruenwald, J. (1999). *Physicians' Desk Reference for herbal medications.* Montvale, NJ: Medical Economics.

Guevara, J., Lozano, P., Wickizer, T., Mell, L., & Gephart, H. (2002). Psychotropic medication use in a population of children who have attention-deficit/hyperactivity disorder. *Pediatrics, 109*(5), 733–742.

A guide to essential oils and their uses: Essential oils, names, and comments. Retrieved October 21, 2001, from *www3.sympatico.ca/derekwatts/Oilcom.htm.*

Gutierrez, M. A., Roper, J. M., & Hahn, P. (2001). Paradoxical reactions to benzodiazepines. *American Journal of Nursing, 101*(7), 34–38.

Hales, R. (1995). Anxiety disorders. In D. Hales & R. Hales (Eds.), *Caring for the mind* (pp. 119–153). New York: Bantam Books.

Hall, L. L. (1997). Fighting phobias: The things that go bump in the mind. *FDA Consumer, 31*(13), 13–15.

Hamilton, M. S., & Opler, L. A. (1992). Akathisia, suicidality, and fluoxetine. *Journal of Clinical Psychiatry, 53*, 401–406.

Harper-Dorton, K. V., & Herbert, M. (1999). Working with children and their families (rev. ed.). Chicago: Lyceum.

Harrison, T. S., & Goa, K. L. (2004). Long-acting risperidone: A review of its use in schizophrenia. *CNS Drugs, 18*(2), 113–132.

Harvard Mental Health Letter. (1999, January). In brief: Olanzapine preferred. *Harvard Mental Health Letter, 15, 7.*

Haynes, L. M., Patterson, A. A., & Wade, S. U. (1992). Drug information service for drug product procurement in Veterans' Affairs healthcare system: Preliminary experience. *American Journal of Hospital Pharmacy, 49*, 595–598.

Healthwell (n.d.). *Aromatherapy.* Retrieved October 21, 2001, from *www.healthwell.com/healthnotes/Info/Aromatherapy.cfm?path=hw.*

Heller, W. M. (1993). Initial responses to recommendations of the blue-ribbon committee on generic medicines. *American Journal of Hospital Pharmacy, 50*, 318–321.

Henderson, L., Yue, Q. Y., Bergquist, C., Gerden, B., & Arlett, P. (2002). St. John's wort (Hypericum perforatum): Drug interactions and clinical outcomes. *British Journal of Clinical Pharmacology, 54,* 349–356.

Hendrick, V., & Gitlin, M. (2004). *Psychotropic Drugs and Women: Fast Facts.* New York: Norton.

Henkel, J. (1998). Reporting adverse reactions and other product problems. *FDA Consumer, 32*(6), 7–15.

Henkel, J. (1999). Monitoring medical product safety. *Consumer's Research Magazine, 82*(2), 27–28.

Henkel, J. (2000). Buying drugs online: It's convenient and private but beware of "rogue sites." *FDA Consumer, 34*(1), 29.

Hickling, L. (2000, May 11). Questions persist concerning Prozac's role in suicide risk. *Health News,* 3.

Hilty, D. M., Brady, K. T., & Hales, R. E. (1999). A review of bipolar disorder among adults. *Psychiatric Services, 50*(2), 201–213.

Hippius, H. (1989). The history of clozapine. *Psychopharmacology, 99,* S3–S5.

Hoffman, F., & Manning, M. (2002). *Herbal medicine and botanical fads.* New York: Haworth Press.

Hoffman LaRoche, Inc. Product information. (2005). *Marglan.*

Hoffman, R. E. (2000). Transcranial magnetic stimulation and auditory hallucinations in schizophrenia. *Lancet, 355,* 1073–1076.

Hollander, E., Phillips, A., & Yeh, C. (2003). Targeted treatment for symptom domains in child and adolescent autism. *Lancet, 362,* 732–734.

Hotujac, L., & Sagud, M. (2002). Efficacy and safety of long-term risperidone treatment. *International Journal of Psychiatry in Clinical Practice, 6,* 193–197.

Hughes, C. M. (2004). Medication non-adherence in the elderly: How big is the problem? *Drugs Aging, 21*(12), 793–811.

Humberston, C. L., Akhtar, J., & Krenzelok, E. P. (2003). Acute hepatitis induced by kava-kava. *Journal of Toxicology: Clinical Toxicology, 41*(2), 109–114.

IMS Health (2005). Dollar growth in 2003 US prescription sales. *IMS Report.* Retrieved March 3, 2005, from *www.imshealth.com/ims/portal/front/articlec/0,2777,6599--_41382706_44771558,00.html.*

Internal Medicine Review. (1999, November). Antidepressants for general anxiety disorder. *Internal Medicine Alert, 21*(21), 164.

Ito, T. Y., Trant, A. S., & Polan, M. L. (2001). A double-blind placebo controlled study of Argin-Max, a nutritional supplement for enhancement of female function. *Journal of Sex and Marital Therapy, 27,* 541–549.

Jacobson, N. S., Wilson, L., & Tupper, C. (1988). The clinical significance of treatment gains resulting from exposure-based interventions for agoraphobia: A re-analysis of outcome data. *Behavior Therapy, 19,* 539–554.

James, R. K., & Gilliland, B. E. (2001). *Crisis intervention strategies* (4th ed.). Belmont, CA: Wadsworth/Thomas Learning.

Jann, M. W., Jenike, M. A., & Liberman, J. A. (1994, January 30). The new psychopharmaceuticals. *Patient Care, 28,* 47–55.

Janssen Pharmaceutica Products (2003). *Risperdal.* Retrieved November 27, 2004, from *www.janssen.com.*

Jensen, C. E. (2004). Medication for children with attention deficit disorder. *Clinical Social Work Journal, 32*(2), 197–214.

Jeppersen, U., Loft, S., Poulsen, H. E., & Brsen, K. (1996). A fluvoxamine-caffeine interaction study. *Pharmacogenetics, 6*(3), 213–222.

Johnson, K. B., Butta, J. K., Donohue, P. K., Glenn, D. J., & Holtzman, N. A. (1996). Discharging patients with prescriptions instead of medications: Sequelae in a teaching hospital. *Pediatrics, 97*(4), 481–496.

Jongsma, A. E., & Peterson, L. M. (1995). *The complete psychotherapy treatment planner.* New York: Wiley.

Kagle, J. D. (1995). *Recording. In Encyclopedia of social work* (19th ed., vol. 2, pp. 2027–2033). Washington, DC: NASW Press.

Kahn, H. G., & Svenden, C. N. Origins, functions, and potential of AdnH neural stem cells. *BioEssays, 21*(8), 625–630.

Kane, J. M. (1996). Conventional neuroleptic treatment: Current status, future role. In A. Breier (Ed.), *The new pharmacotherapy of schizophrenia* (pp. 89–104). Washington, DC: American Psychiatric Association.

Kane, R. L., Ouslander, J. G., & Abrass, I. B. (1999). *Essentials of clinical geriatrics* (4th ed.). New York: McGraw-Hill.

Kaplan, H. I., & Sadock, B. J. (1990). *Pocket handbook of clinical psychiatry.* Baltimore: Williams & Wilkins.

Kapur, S., Mieczkowski, T., & Mann, J. J. (1992). Antidepressant medications and the relative risk of suicide attempt and suicide. *Journal of the American Medical Association, 268,* 3441–3445.

Karasu, T. B., Docherty, J. P., Gelenberg, A., Kuper, D. J., Merriam, A. E., & Shadoan, R. (1993). Practice guidelines for major depressive disorder in adults. *American Journal of Psychiatry, 150*(Suppl.), 1–26.

Karper, L. P., & Krystal, J. H. (1996). Augmenting antipsychotic efficacy: New approaches. In A. Breier (Ed.), *The new pharmacotherapy of schizophrenia* (pp. 105–132). Washington, DC: American Psychiatric Association.

Kasper, S. (2003). Issues in the treatment of bipolar disorder. *European Neuropsychopharmacology, 13,* S37–S42.

Katona, C., & Livingston, G. (2003). *Drug treatment in old-age psychiatry.* New York: Martin Dunitz.

Kawas, C. H. (1999). Alzheimer's disease. In W. R. Hazzard, J. P. Blass, W. H. Etinger, J. B. Halter, & J. G. Ouslander (Eds.), *Principles of geriatric medicine and gerontology* (4th ed., pp. 1257–1269). New York: McGraw-Hill.

Keifer, D., & Pantuso, T. (2003). Panax ginseng. *American Family Physician,* 68,(8), 1539–1542.

Kent, J. M. (2000). SnaRls, NaSSas, and NaRls: New agents for the treatment of depression. *Lancet, 355,* 911–918.

Ketter, T. A., Wang, P. W., Nowakowska, C., & Marsh, W. K. (2004). New medication treatment options for bipolar disorder. *Acta Psychiatrica Scandinavica, 110*(422), 18–33.

Kirchner, J. T. (2000). Efficacy of lithium in patients with bipolar disorder. *American Family Physician, 61*(10), 3100–3103.

Kotulak, R. (1997). *Inside the brain: Revolutionary discoveries of how the mind works.* Kansas City, MO: Andrews McMeel.

Kroll, D. J. (1997). St. John's wort: An example of the problems with herbal medicine regulation in the United States. *Medical Sciences Bulletin, 240,* 1–5.

Kronenberger, W. G., & Meyer, R. G. (1996). *The child clinician's handbook.* Needham Heights, MA: Allyn & Bacon.

Kubiszyn, T. (1994). Pediatric psychopharmacology and prescription privileges: Implications and opportunities for school psychology. *School Psychology Quarterly, 9*(1), 26–40.

Kurtzweil, P. (1994). Liquid medication and dosing devices. *FDA Consumer, 28*(8), 6–9.

Labbate, L. (1999). Sex and serotonin reuptake inhibitor antidepressants. *Psychiatric Annals, 29,* 571–579.

Lam, Y. W. F. (2000). Ciprofloxacin may inhibit metabolism of olanzapine. *Psychopharmacology, 11*(2), 1.

Lambert, L. (1998). New medications aid cognition in schizophrenia. *Journal of the American Medical Association, 280,* 953.

Lambert, M. J. (1992). Psychotherapy outcome research: Implications for integrative and eclectic therapists. In J. C. Cross & M. R. Goldfried (Eds.), *Handbook of psychotherapy integration* (pp. 94–129). New York: Basic Books.

LaPuma, J. (1999). Danger of Asian patent medicines. *Alternative Medicine Alert: A Clinician's Guide to Alternative Therapies, 2*(6), 71.

Larkin, M. (1996). Health information online. *FDA Consumer, 30*(5), 21–24.

Larsen, P. D. (1999). Poly-pharmacy and elderly patients. *AORN Journal, 69*(3), 619.

Lazarus, A. A. (1997). *Brief but comprehensive psychotherapy: The multi-modal way.* New York: Springer.

Lee, K., & Carlin, P. (1997). Should you try mind–body medicine? *Health, 1,* 77–78.

Lehne, R. A., & Scott, D. (1996). Psychopharmacology. In V. B. Carson & E. N. Arnold (Eds.), *Mental health nursing: The nurse–patient journey* (pp. 523–570). Philadelphia: Saunders.

Lemonick, M. D. (1997, Sept. 29). The mood molecule. *Time, 150*(13), 74–82.

Lemonick, M. D. (1999, May 17). Beyond depression: What do these "mood drugs" really do? *Time, 153*(19), 74.

Levinthal, C. (2002). *Drugs, behavior, and Modern society.* Boston: Allyn & Bacon.

Lexapro receives FDA approval for generalized anxiety disorder. (2004, January 12). *Health and Medicine Week,* xx, 50–51.

Lois, J. (2001, April). Managing emotions, intimacy, and relationships in a volunteer search and rescue group. *Journal of Contemporary Ethnography, 30*(2), 1–28.

Longhofer, J., Floersch, J., & Jenkins, J. H. (2003). Medication effect interpretation and the social grid of management. In K. Bentley (Ed.), *Psychiatric medication issues for social workers, counselors and psychologists* (pp. 71–89). Binghamton, NY: Haworth Press.

Luby, E. D., & Singareddy, R. K. (2003). Long-term therapy with lithium in a private practice clinic: A naturalistic study. *Bipolar Disorders, 5,* 62–68.

Lumpkins, M. M. (1997). FDA health advisory. *FDA Bulletin, 27,* 2.

Lynch, T. (2003). Atomoxetine for ADHD. *American Family Physician, 68*(9), 1827–1829.

Lyons, J. (2000, February). A call for outcomes data: Psychopharmacology with children. *Outcomes and Accountability Alert, 5*(2), 1.

Magnuson, T. M., Roccaforte, W. H., Wengel, S. P., & Burke, W. J. (2000). Medication-induced dystonias in nine patients with dementia. *Journal of Neuropsychiatry, 12,* 219–225.

Mahoney, D. F. (1992a). Appropriateness of geriatric prescribing decisions made by nurse practitioners and physicians. *Health Policy in Action, 26,* 41–46.

Mahoney, D. F. (1992b). Nurse practitioners as prescribers: Past research trends and future study needs. *Health Care Issues, 17,* 44–76.

Mahoney, D. F. (1992c). A comparative analysis of nurse practitioners with and without prescription authority. *Journal of the American Academy of Nurse Practitioners, 4*(2), 71–76.

Maj, M. (2000). The impact of lithium prophylaxis on the course of bipolar disorder: A review of the research evidence. *Bipolar Disorders, 2*(2), 93–101.

Maldonado, L. A. (1987). Mexican immigrants and Mexicans: An evolving relation. *Contemporary Sociology, 16,* 682–683.

Malhotra, A. K., Pinsky, D. A., & Breier, A. (1996). Future antipsychotic agents: Clinical implications. In A. Breier (Ed.), *The new pharmacotherapy of schizophrenia* (pp. 41–56). Washington, DC: American Psychiatric Press.

Manisses Communications Group. (2002). Study: Risperdal proves more beneficial for preventing relapse. *Mental Health Weekly, 12*(2), 3–4.

Mann, J. J., & Kapur, S. (1991). The emergence of suicidal ideation and behavior during antidepressant pharmacotherapy. *Archives of General Psychiatry, 48,* 1027–1033.

Marano, E. H. (1999, March/April). Depression: Beyond serotonin. *Psychology Today, 32,* 30–36, 72–75.

Marlatt, G. A. (Ed.). (1998). *Harm reduction: Pragmatic strategies for managing high-risk behaviors.* New York: Guilford Press.

Marshall, J. R. (1994). Social phobia: From stage fright to shyness. New York: Basic Books.

Masilamani, S., & Ruppelt, C. (2003). Escitalopram (Lexapro) for depression. *American Family Physician, 68,* 2235–2236.

Matorin, S., & DeChillo, N. (1984). Psychopharmacology: Guidelines for social workers. *Social Casework, 65*(10), 579–589.

Mauri, M. C., Fiorentini, A., Cerveri, G., Volonteri, L. S., Regispani, F., Malvini, L., Boscati, L., LoBaido, R., & Invernizzi, G. (2003). Long-term efficacy and therapeutic drug monitoring of sertraline in major depression. *Human Psychopharmacology Clinical Experiences, 18,* 385–388.

Maxmen, J. S., & Ward, N. G. (1995). *Essential psychopathology and its treatment* (2nd ed.). New York: Norton.

Maxmen, J. S., & Ward, N. G. (2002). *Psychotropic drugs: Fast facts* (3rd ed.). New York: Norton.

Maxwell-Hudson, C. (1994). *Aromatherapy massage.* Boston: Houghton Mifflin.

May, W. T., & Belsky, J. (1992). Response to prescription privileges: Psychology's next call? Or the siren call: Should psychologists medicate? *American Psychologist, 47,* 427.

McAdoo, H. (1997). *Black families.* Thousand Oaks, CA: Sage.

McCabe, S. (2002). Complementary herbal and alternative drugs in clinical practice. *Perspectives in Psychiatric Care, 38*(3), 98–107.

McCall, M. D. (1998, May 12). Alternative medicine: Is it for you? *Orlando Sentinel,* p. E1.

McCullough, P. K., & Cody, S. (1993). Geriatric development. In F. S. Sierles (Ed.), *Behavioral science for medical students* (pp. 163–167). Baltimore: Williams & Wilkins.

McElroy, S. L., Strakowski, S. M., West, S. A., & Keck, P. E. (1997). Phenomenology of adolescent and adult mania in hospitalized patients with bipolar disorder. *American Journal of Psychiatry, 154*(1), 44–49.

McGrath, J. M. (1999a). Physician's perspectives on communicating prescription drug information. *Qualitative Health Research, 9,* 731–746.

McGrath, J. M. (1999b). Treatment of schizophrenia. *British Medical Journal, 319,* 1045.

McIntyre, A. (1995). *The complete floral healer.* New York: Sterling Publishing Company.

McIntyre, M. (2000). A review of the benefits, adverse events, drug interactions, and safety of St. John's wort (Hypericum perforatum): The implications with regard to the regulation of herbal medicines. *Journal of Alternative and Complementary Medicine, 6*(2), 115–124.

McLellarn, R. W., & Rosenzweig, J. (1998) Generalized anxiety disorder. In B. Thyer & J. Wodarski (Eds.), *Handbook of empirical social work practice: Mental disorders* (vol. 1, pp. 385–397). New York: Wiley.

Meadows, M. (2003). Drug research and children. *FDA Consumer, 37*(1), 13–19.

MedWatch (2004). *The FDA safety information and adverse event reporting program.* Retrieved October 2, 2004, from *www.fda.gov/medwatch/.*

Melander, H., Ahlquist-Rastad, J., Meijer, G., & Beekman, B. (2003). Evidenced-biased medicine, selective reporting from studies sponsored by pharmaceutical industry: Review of studies in new drug applications. *British Medical Journal, 326,* 1171–1173.

Mendola, K. (1997a, November). *Balance emotions with flower essences.* Retrieved October 15, 2001, from *www.healthwell.com/delicious-online/d_backs/Nov_97/hk.cfm.*

Mendola, K. (1997b, November). *Flowers for stress.* Retrieved October 15, 2001, from *www.healthwell.com/delicious-online/D_backs/Nov_97/hk.cfm.*

Mental Health Report (1999). Outpatients face higher hurdle to getting new antipsychotics. Silver Spring, MD: Business Publishers. (pp. 166–174).

Merck Research Laboratories (1992). *The Merck manual of diagnosis and therapy* (16th ed.). Rahway, NJ: Merck Research Laboratories.

Merriman, S. H. (1999). Monoamine oxidase drugs and diet. *Journal of Human Nutrition and Dietetics, 12,* 21–28.

Miller, N. S. (1997). *The principles and practice of addictive actions in psychiatry.* Philadelphia: Saunders.

Miller, R. S., Weideman, G. H., & Linn, L. (1980). Prescribing psychotropic drugs: Whose responsibility? *Social Work in Health Care, 6,* 51–61.

Misri, S., Burgmann, A., & Kostaras, D. (2000). Are SSRIs safe for pregnant and breastfeeding women? *Canadian Family Physician, 46,* 626–633.

Mitchell, P. (1999). Grapefruit juice found to cause havoc with drug uptake. *Lancet, 353*(9161), 1335–1336.

Mojtabai, R. (2002). Diagnosing depression and prescribing antidepressants by primary care physicians: The impact of practice style variations. *Mental Health Services Research, 4*(2), 109–118.

Moller, H. (2000). Are all antidepressants the same? *Journal of Clinical Psychiatry, 61*(6), 24–28.

Montagne, M. (2002). Patient drug information from mass media sources [Electronic version]. *Psychiatric Times, 16*(5), 1–6. Retrieved March 13, 2003, from *www.psychiatrictimes.com/massmedia.html.*

Moore, D. P., & Jefferson, J. W. (1997). *Handbook of medical psychiatry.* St. Louis, MO: Mosby.

Moore, T. J. (2002). Could it be that antidepressants do little more than placebos? Retrieved March 10, 2004, from *www.cognitivetherapy.com/globe_art.html.*

Morris, M. R. (1999). Antidepressants and drug interactions: Prescriber beware. *Journal of American College Health, 47*(4), 191.

Mosher, L. R. (1999). Are psychiatrists betraying their patients? *Psychology Today, 32,* 40–41.

Murphy, J. M. (1999). Preoperative considerations with herbal medicines. *AORN Journal, 69*(1), 174.

Myers, W. C., Burket, R. C., & Otto, T. A. (1993). Conduct disorder and personality disorders in hospitalized adolescents. *Journal of Clinical Psychiatry, 54,* 21–26.

Nassir, G. S., Boiman, E., & Goodwin, F. K. (2000). Insight and outcome in bipolar, unipolar, and anxiety disorders. *Comprehensive Psychiatry, 41*(3), 167–171.

Nathan, P. J. (1999). The experimental and clinical pharmacology of St. John's wort (Hypericum perforatum L). *Molecular Psychiatry, 4,* 333–338.

National Institute of Health (2004). *Herbal supplements: How they are labeled and regulated.* Office of Dietary Supplements. National Institutes of Health, Bethesda, Maryland. Retrieved July 31, 2005, from *www.ods.od.nih.gov.*

National Institute of Mental Health (2002). *Bipolar disorder.* National Institute of Mental Health, National Institutes of Health, U.S. Department of Health and Human Services, NIH Publication No. 3679. Retrieved July 24, 2005, from *www.nimh.nih.gov/publicat/bipolar.cfm.*

National Institute of Mental Health (2004). *Treatment of children with mental disorders.* National Institute of Mental Health, National Institutes of Health, U.S. Department of Health and Human Services, NIH Publication No 04-4702. Retrieved July 29, 2005, from *www.nimh.nih.gov/publicat/childqa.cfm#link3.*

Nordberg, A. (1996). Pharmacological treatment of cognitive dysfunction in dementia disorders. *Acta Neurologica Scandanavia Supplementum, 168,* 87–92.

Nordenberg, T. (1997). New drug label spells it out simply. *FDA Consumer, 32,* 29–32.

Nordenberg, T. (1998). Miracle drugs vs. super bugs: Preserving the usefulness of antibiotics. *FDA Consumer, 32*(6), 23–25.

Nordenberg, T. (1999a). Pediatric drug studies: Protecting pint-sized patients. *FDA, 33*(3), 23–28.

Nordenberg, T. (1999b). When is a medical product too risky?: An interview with FDA's top drug official. *FDA Consumer, 33*(5), 8–13.

Nordenberg, T. (2000). Pharmacy compounding: Customizing prescription drugs. *FDA Consumer, 34*(4), 11–12.

Nurnberg, H. G., Hensley, P. L., Lauriello, J., Parker, L. M., & Keith, S. J. (1999). Sildenafil for women patients with antidepressant-induced sexual dysfunction. *Psychiatric Services 50*, 1076–1078.

O'Connor, A. (2004, June 29) Wakefulness finds a powerful ally. *New York Times.* Retrieved July 31, 2005, from *www.modafinil.com/article/off-label.html.*

O'Malley, P., Trimble, N., & Browning, M. (2005). Are herbal therapies worth the risks? *Holistic Nursing Practice, 19*(1), 44–48.

Ost, L. G. (1987). Applied relaxation: Description of a coping technique and a review of controlled studies. *Behavior Research and Therapy, 25*, 397–409.

Ost, L. G., Lindahl, I. L., Sterner, U., & Jerremalm, A. (1984). Exposure in-vivo vs. applied relaxation in the treatment of blood phobia. *Behavior Research and Therapy, 22*, 205.

Ost, L. G., Salkovskis, P., & Hellstrom, K. (1991). One session therapist directed exposure vs. self-exposure in the treatment of spider phobia. *Behavior Therapy, 22*, 407–422.

Ost, L. G., Sterner, U., & Fellenius, J. (1989). Applied tension, applied relaxation in the treatment of blood phobia. *Behavior Research and Therapy, 27*, 109.

Ouslander, J. G., Osterweil, D., & Morley, J. (1998). *Medical care in the nursing home* (2nd ed.). New York: McGraw-Hill.

Parker, V., Wong, A. H., Boon, H. S., & Seeman, M. V. (2001). Adverse reactions to St. John's wort. *Canadian Journal of Psychiatry, 46*(1), 77–79.

Pary, R., & Matuschka, P. R., Lewis, S., Caso, W., & Lippmann, S. (2003). Generalized anxiety disorder. *Southern Medical Journal, 96*(6), 581–588.

Pato, M. T., Zohar-Kadouch, R., Zohar, J., & Murphy, D. L. (1988). Return of symptoms in patients with obsessive–compulsive disorder. *American Journal of Psychiatry, 145*, 1521–1525.

Pearson, L. J. (1994). Annual update on how each state stands on legislative issues affecting advanced nursing practice. *Nurse Practitioner, 19*, 11–53.

Pelham, W. E., Gnagy, E. M., Burrows-Maclean, L., Williams, A., Fabiano, G. A., Morrisey, S. M., Chronis, A. M., Forehand, G. L., Ngyun, C. A., Hoffman, M. T., Lock, T. M., Fielbelkorn, K., Coles, E. K., Panahon, C. J., Steiner, R. L., Michenbaum, D. L., Onyango, A. N., & Morse, G. D. (2001). Once-a-day Concerta methylphenidate versus three-times-daily methylphenidate in laboratory and natural settings. *Pediatrics, 107*(6), E105–108.

Perodeau, G. M., & du Fort, G. G. (2000). Psychotropic drug use and the relation between social support, life events, and mental health in the elderly. *Journal of Applied Gerontology, 19*(1), 23–41.

Perry, A., Tarrier, N., Morriss, R., McCarthy, E., & Limb, K. (1999). Randomized controlled trial of efficacy of teaching patients with bipolar disorder to identify early symptoms of relapse and obtain treatment. *British Medical Journal, 318*(7177), 149–157.

Perry, R. & Lund, B. C. (2004). Selective serotonin reuptake inhibitors and the treatment of affective illness. Retrieved November 24, 2005, from *www.vh.org/adult/provide/psychiatry/cps/13.html.*

Physicians' desk reference (1995). Montvale, NJ: Medical Economics.

Physicians' desk reference (58th ed.) (2004). Montvale, NJ: Medical Economics.

Physicians' desk reference (53rd ed.) (1999). Montvale, NJ: Medical Economics.

Physicians' desk reference (54th ed.) (2000). Montvale, NJ: Medical Economics.

Physicians' desk reference for herbal medicines (2000). Montvale, NJ: Medical Economics.

Physicians' desk reference for nonprescription drugs (18th ed.) (1997). Montvale, NJ: Medical Economics.

Physicians' desk reference for nonprescription drugs and dietary supplement (25th ed.) (2004). Montvale, NJ: Medical Economics.

Physicians' desk reference for nutritional supplements (2001). Montvale, NJ: Medical Economics.

Pieper, A., & Treisman, G. (2005). Drug treatment of depression in HIV-positive patients: Safety considerations. *Drug Safety, 28*(9), 753–762.

Plaud, J. J., & Vavrovsky, K. G. (1998). Specific and social phobias. In B. Thyer & J. Wodarski (Eds.), *Handbook of empirical social work practice: Mental disorders* (vol. 1, pp. 326–341). New York: Wiley.

Practice guidelines for the treatment of patients with bipolar disorder (2002). *American Journal of Psychiatry, 159*(4), 1–50.

Pray, W. S. (2003). *A history of nonprescription product regulation.* Binghamton, NY: Haworth Press.

Prozac (2001, March). Retrieved June 29, 2003, from *www.nami.org/helpline/prozac.htm.*

Prufer, D. (1996, April). Is your medicine safe? What pharmacists don't tell you. *Good Housekeeping, 222,* 137–138.

Public Citizens' Health Research Group (1993). *Worst pills, best pills II.* Washington, DC: Author.

Rabins, P. V. (1999). Miscellaneous psychiatric disorders. In W. R. Hazzard, J. P. Blass, W. H. Etinger, J. B. Halter, & J. G. Ouslander (Eds.), *Principles of geriatric medicine and gerontology* (4th ed., pp. 1365–1368). New York: McGraw-Hill.

Ralston, J. (2000). Beyond pill pushing: How Shoppers' Drug Mart positions itself above the pharmacy fray. *Marketing (Maclean Hunter), 105*(12), 19.

Rapee, R. M. (Ed.) (1996). *Current controversies in the anxiety disorders.* New York: Guilford Press.

Raphael, R. (2002, June 21). *A dark side to Prozac?* Retrieved June 29, 2003, from *www.contac.org/contaclibrary/medications15.htm.*

Rappaport, N., & Chubinsky, P. (2000). The meaning of psychotropic medications for children, adolescents, and their families. *Journal of American Academy of Child and Adolescent Psychiatry, 39*(9), 1198–1200.

Rauch, S. A. M., Hembree, E. A., & Foa, E. B. (2001). Acute psychosocial prevention interventions for post-traumatic stress disorder. *Advances in Mind—Body Medicine, 17*(3), 1–6.

Reaves, J. (2000). If you choose the herbal life, it is buyer beware. *Times Daily* (pages unidentified).

Regier, D. A., Narrow, W. E., Rae, D. S., Manderscheid, R. W., Locke, B. Z., & Goodwin, F. K. (1993). The de facto U.S. mental and addictive disorders service system. *Archives of General Psychiatry, 50,* 85–92.

Reid, W. H. (1997). Anxiety disorders. In W. H. Reid, G. U. Balis, & B. J. Sutton (Eds.), *The treatment of psychiatric disorders* (3rd ed., pp. 239–262). Bristol, PA: Brunner/Mazel.

Reynolds, C. F., Frank, E., Perel, J. M., & Miller, M. D. (1994). Treatment of consecutive episodes of major depression in the elderly. *American Journal of Psychiatry, 151*(12), 1740–1743.

Rhodes-Kropf, J., & Lantz, M. S. (2001). Alternative medicine: Achieving balance between herbal remedies and medical therapy on base rate. *Geriatric, 56*(8), 44–46.

Roberts, A. R. (1990). An overview of crisis theory and crisis intervention. In A. R. Roberts (Ed.), *Crisis intervention handbook: Assessment, treatment, and research* (pp. 3–16). Belmont, CA: Wadsworth.

Roberts, A. R. (1991). *Contemporary perspectives on crisis intervention and prevention.* Englewood Cliffs, NJ: Prentice Hall.

Roberts, A. R., & Dziegielewski, S. F. (1995). Foundation skills and applications of crisis intervention and cognitive therapy. In A. R. Roberts (Ed.), *Crisis intervention and time-limited cognitive treatment* (pp. 3–27). Thousand Oaks, CA: Sage.

Roberts, A. R., & Dziegielewski, S. F. (1996). Assessment typology and intervention with the survivors of stalking. *Aggression and Violent Behavior, 1*(4), 359–368.

Roberts, A. R., & Yeager, K. R. (2004). Systematic reviews of evidence-based studies and practice-based research: How to search for, develop, and use them. In A. R. Roberts & K. R. Yeager (Eds.), *Evidence-based practice manual: Research and outcome measures in the health and human services* (pp. 3–14). New York: Oxford University Press.

Rogers, D. (2002). Comparing atypical antipsychotics. *Psychiatric Times,* *19*(1), 1–11.

Roman, G. C. (2003). Vascular dementia: Distinguishing characteristics, treatment, and prevention. *Journal of the American Geriatrics Society, 51*(5s2), S296–S304.

Rosch, P. (2000). Certain foods, drugs, and supplements don't mix. *Health and Stress, 11*(11), 1–8.

Roth, A., & Fonagy, P. (1996). Anxiety disorders: I. Phobias, generalized anxiety disorder, and panic disorder with and without agoraphobia. In A. Roth & P. Fonagy (Eds.), *What works for whom? A critical review of psychotherapy research* (pp. 113–144). New York: Guilford Press.

Rounsaville, B. J., O'Malley, S., Foley, S., & Weissman, M. M. (1988). Role of manual-guided training in the conduct and efficacy of interpersonal psychotherapy for depression. *Journal of Consulting and Clinical Psychology, 56,* 681–688.

Rowland, A. S., Sandler, D. P., Umbach, D. M., Stallone, L., Bohlig, E. M., & Naftel, A. J. (2002). Prevalence of medication treatment for ADHD among elementary school children in Johnston County, North Carolina. *American Journal of Public Health, 92*(2), 231–235.

Rugino, T. A., & Copley, T. C. (2001). Effects of modafinil in children with ADHD: An open label study. *Journal of the American Academy of Child and Adolescent Psychiatry, 40*(2), 230.

Rush, J. (1993). Depression in primary care: Detection, diagnosis, and treatment. *American Family Physician, 47,* 1766–1788.

Rushton, J., Clark, S., & Reed, G. (2000). Primary care role in the management of childhood depression: A comparison of pediatricians and family physicians. *Pediatrics, 105,* 957–962.

Russo, E. (2001). *Handbook of psychotropic herbs: A scientific analysis of herbal remedies for psychiatric conditions.* Binghamton, NY: Haworth Press.

Sachs, G. S. (1996). Bipolar mood disorder: Practical strategies for acute and maintenance phase treatment. *Journal of Clinical Neuropsychiatry, 16*(2, Suppl. 1), 32–47.

Sackeim, H. A., Haskett, R. F., Mulsant, B. H., Thase, M. E., Mann, J. J., Pettinati, H. M., Greenberg, R. M., Crowe, R. R., Cooper, T. B., & Prudic, J. (2001). Continuation pharmacotherapy in the prevention of relapse following electroconvulsive therapy. *Journal of the American Medical Association, 285*(10), 1299–1307.

Sadavoy, J. (2004). *Psychotropic drugs and the elderly: Fast facts.* New York: Norton.

Safety facts (2001). Retrieved April 11, 2006, from *www.prozac.com/HowProzacCanHelp/SafetyFacts.jsp.*

Saklad, S. R. (2000). APA studies focus on side effects, efficacy of antipsychotics. *Psychopharmacology Update, 11*(1), 1.

Salazar-Martinez, E., Willett, W. C., Archerio, A., Manson, J. E., Leitzmann, M. F., Stampfer, M. J., & Hu, F. B. (2004). Coffee consumption and risk for type 2 diabetes-mellitus. *Annals of Internal Medicine, 140*(1), 1–8; 1–17.

Sanderoff, B. T. (2001). Herbal medicine: Use with caution and respect. *Generations, 24*(4), 69–74.

Schmerling, R. H. (2004). A dangerous myth: If it is over the counter, it must be safe. *Healthy Lifestyles*. Retrieved November 19, 2005, from *www.intelihealth.com*.

Schulz, S. C. (2000). New antipsychotic medications: More than old wine and new bottles. *Bulletin of the Menninger Clinic, 64*(1), 60–75.

Schwartz, D. A. (2001). Have I got an herb for you! *Chemical Innovation, 31*(9), 29–33.

Schwartz, J. B. (1994). Clinical pharmacology. In J. P. Blass, W. H. Ettinger, J. B. Halter, W. R. Hazard, & J. G. Ouslander (Eds.), *Principles of geriatric medicine and gerontology* (pp. 259–275). New York: McGraw-Hill.

Schweitzee, I. (2001). Stopping antidepressants. *Australian Prescriber, 24*(1), 13–15.

Scott, J. (2001). Cognitive therapy as an adjunct to medication in bipolar disorder. *British Journal of Psychiatry, 178* (Suppl.), 164–168.

Seaward, B. L. (1997a). Autogenic training. In Seaward, B. L. (Ed.), *Managing stress: Principles and strategies for health and wellbeing* (pp. 408–418). Sudbury, MA: Jones & Bartlett.

Seaward, B. L. (1997b). Diaphragmatic breathing. In Seaward, B. L. (Ed.), *Managing stress: Principles and strategies for health and wellbeing* (2nd ed., pp. 301–307). Sudbury, MA: Jones & Bartlett.

Segraves, R. T., & Balon, R. (2003). *Sexual pharmacology: Fast facts*. New York: Norton.

Seligson, S. V. (1998). Melding medicines. *Health*, May/June, 64–70.

Sensky, T., Turkington, D., Kingdon, D., Scott, J. L., Scott, J., Siddle, R., O'Carroll, M., & Barnes, T. R. (2000). A randomized controlled trial of cognitive behavioral therapy for persistent symptoms in schizophrenia resistant to medication. *Archives of General Psychiatry, 57*, 165–172.

Serafini, M. W. (2000a). Campaign medicine. *National Journal, 32*(2), 86.

Serafini, M. W. (2000b). No easy prescriptions on no-name drugs. *National Journal, 32*(8), 548.

Shell, R. (2001). Antidepressant prescribing patterns of nurse practitioners. *Nurse Practitioner, 26*(7), 42–47.

Shindul-Rothschild, J. A., & Rothschild, A. J. (1998). Psychotropics in primary care. In L. A. Eisenbauer & M. A. Murphy (Eds.), *Pharmacotherapeutics and advanced nursing practice* (pp. 37–51). New York: McGraw-Hill.

Sifton, D. W. (2001). *The PDR family guide to nutrition and health.* New Jersey: Medical Economics.

Simoneau, T. L., Miklowitz, D. J., Richards, J. A., Saleem, R., & George, E. L. (1999). Bipolar disorder and family communication: Effects of a psychoeducational treatment program. *Journal of Abnormal Psychology, 108*(4), 588–568.

Simonson, W. (1994). Maximizing the benefits of drug therapy for older people and minimizing the risks: Quality of life is the key. *Generations, 18*(2), 5–7.

Siris, S. G. (2000). Management of depression in schizophrenia. *Psychiatric Annals, 30*(1), 13–17.

Skinner, B. F. (1953). Science and human behavior. New York: MacMillian.

Smith, I. K. (1999). Arthritics rejoice: New drugs are reducing pain with fewer side effects for those who can afford them, anyway. *Time, 154*(23), 128.

Stack, W. A. Atherton, J. C., Hawkey, G. M., Logan R. F. A., & Hawkey, C. J. (2002). Interactions between helicobacterpylon and other risk factors for peptic ulcer bleeding. *Alimentary Pharmacology & Therapeutics, 16*(3), 497–506.

Stehlin, I. B. (1995). An FDA guide to choosing medical treatments. *FDA Consumer, 29,* 10–14.

Stein, M. T. (2004). Atomoxetine. *Journal Watch Pediatrics and Adolescent Medicine.* Retrieved January 28, 2004, from *pediatrics.jwatch.org/cgi/content/full/2004/116/1.*

Stein, M. D. (1998). Paroxetine treatment of generalized social phobia (social anxiety disorder). *Journal of the American Medical Association, 280*(8), 708–713.

Stevensen, C. J. (1996). Aromatherapy. In M. S. Micozzi (Ed.), *Fundamentals of complementary and alternative medicine* (pp. 137–148). New York: Churchill Livingstone.

Stomwall, L. K., & Robinson, E. A. (1998). When a family member has a schizophrenic disorder: Practice issues across the family life cycle. *American Journal of Orthopsychiatry, 68,* 580–589.

Stowe, Z. N., Cohen, L. S., Hostetter, A., Ritchie, J. C., Owens, M. J., & Nemeroff, C. B. (2000). Paroxetine in human breast milk and nursing infants. *American Journal of Psychiatry, 157,* 185–189.

Substance Abuse: Risks and Responsibilities (2001). *Using pharmaceutical drugs safely.* Films for the Humanities and Sciences. Available from *www.films.com.*

Surgeon General (2001). The fundamentals of mental health and mental illness. In *Mental health: A report of the Surgeon General.* Retrieved July 5, 2004, from *www.surgeongeneral.gov/library/mentalhealth/chapter2/sec1.html.*

Swendsen, J., Hammen, C., Heller, T., & Gitlin, M. (1995). Correlates of stress reactivity in patients with bipolar disorder. *American Journal of Psychiatry, 152*(5), 795–797.

Szegedy-Maszak, M. (2001). The career of a celebrity pill. *U.S. News and World Report, 131*(5), 38–39.

Teicher, M. H., Glod, C., & Cole, J. O. (1990). Emergence of intense suicidal preoccupation during fluoxetine treatment. *American Journal of Psychiatry, 147*, 207–210.

Thyer, B. A. (2004). Science and evidence-based social work practice. In H. E. Briggs & T. L. Rzepnicki (Eds.), *Using evidence in social work practice: Behavioral perspectives* (pp. 3–19). Chicago: Lyceum.

Tierney, L. M., McPhee, S. J., & Papadakis, M. A. (Eds.) (1997). *Current medical diagnosis and treatment* (36th ed.). Stamford, CT: Appleton & Lange.

Tilton, A. *Risperdal and the aggression of autism*. Retrieved March 3, 2004, from *autism.about.com/cs/medications/a/risperdal.htm.*

Tollefson, G. D., Beasley, C. M., Tran, P.-V., et al. (April 1997). Olanzapine versus haloperidol in the treatment of schizophrenia and schizoaffective and schizoreniform disorders: Results of an international collaborative trial. *American Journal of Psychiatry, 154*, 457–465.

Tollefson, G. D., Ramphey, A. H., Beasley, C. M., Enas, C. G., & Potvin, J. H. (1994). Absence of a relationship between adverse events and suicidality during pharmacotherapy for depression. *Journal of Clinical Psychopharmacology, 14*, 163–169.

Tollefson, G. D., & Sanger, T. M. (April 1997). Negative symptoms: A path analytic approach to a double-blind, placebo- and haloperidol-controlled clinical trial with olanzapine. *American Journal of Psychiatry, 154*, 466–474.

Turkington, C., & Kaplan, E. (1997). *Lithium*. Retrieved January 12, 2004, from *www.my.webmd.com/content/article/4/1680_50556.*

Ullman, D. (1993). Renegade remedies? The medical establishment is turning a blind—and biased—eye to the alternative-medicine boom. *Utne Reader, 60*, 42–44.

Valente, S. M. (2001). Treating attention-deficit/hyperactivity disorder. *Nurse Practitioner, 26*, 14–26.

Vatz, R. E., & Weinberg, L. S. (2001). Psychological help for the terrorized. *USA Today Magazine, 2130*(2678), 1–6.

Vazquez, I., & Aguera-Ortiz, L. F. (2002). Herbal products and serious side effects: A case of ginseng-induced manic episode. *ACTA Psychiatricia Scandinavica, 105*, 76–78.

Vonk, M. E., & Early, T. J. (2002). Cognitive–behavioral therapy. In A. R. Roberts & G. J. Greene (Eds.), *Social workers' desk reference* (pp. 116–120). New York: Oxford University Press.

Vuksan, V., Sievenpiper, J. L., Koo, V. Y. Y., Francis, T., Beljan-Zdravkovic, U., Zheng, X., & Vidgen, E. (2000). American ginseng (Panax quinquefolius L) reduces postprandial glycemia in nondiabetic subjects with type 2 diabetes mellitus. *Archives of Internal Medicine, 160,* 1009–1013.

Waldemar, G. (2001). New perspectives in dementia. XVII *World Congress of Neurology.*

Walker, A. F. (2000). St. John's wort: The sunshine herb. *Nutrition Bulletin, 25*(3), 189–191.

Walsh, F. (1996). Families and mental illness: What have we learned? In B. Abosh & L. Collins (Eds.), *Mental illness in the family.* Toronto: University of Toronto Press.

Walsh, N. (2001). St. John's wort raises the risk of rejection in transplant patients. *Clinical Psychiatry News, 29*(11), 21.

Walsh, T. (1998). *Child psychopharmacology.* Washington, DC: American Psychiatric Association.

Walter, K. (2000, Feb. 21). Will teenagers disappear? *Time, 55*(7), 60.

Waters, C. H. (1991). Selegiline (eldcpryl) for Parkinson's disease. *Western Journal of Medicine, 155*(1), 68–69.

Watson-Heidari, T. (2000, July/August). Generics for smart shoppers. *Humana Active Outlook,* p. 11.

Weed, L. (1969). *Medical records, medical evaluation, and patient care.* Cleveland, OH: Case Western Reserve University Press.

Weiss, R. D., Griffin, M. L., Greenfield, S. F., Najavits, L. M., Wyner, D., Soto, J. A., & Hennen, J. A. (2000). Group therapy for patients with bipolar disorder and substance dependence: Results of a pilot study. *Journal of Clinical Psychiatry, 61*(5), 361–367.

Wernicke, J., Faries, D., Girod, D., Brown, J., Gao, H., Kelsey, D., Quintana, H., Lipeta, R., Michelson, D., & Heiligenstein, J. (2003). Cardiovascular effects of atomoxetine in children, adolescents, and adults. *Drug Safety, 26*(10), 729–740.

Wetzel, M. S., Eisenberg, D. M., & Kaptchuk, T. J. (1998). Courses involving complementary and alternative medicine at U.S. medical schools. *Journal of the American Medical Association, 280*(9), 784–787.

Wilhelm, F., & Margarf, J. (1997). A cognitive–behavioral treatment package for panic disorder with agoraphobia. In W. T. Roth (Ed.), *Treating anxiety disorders* (pp. 205–244). San Francisco: Jossey-Bass.

Williams, R. D. (1997). Medications and older adults. *FDA Consumer, 31*(6), 15–18.

Wilson, J. (1992). Hooked on over-the-counter drugs. In E. Goode (Ed.), *Drugs, society, and behavior* (pp. 136–138). Guilford, CT: Dushkin.

Wimett, L., & Laustsen, G. (2003). First new ADHD treatment in 30 years. *Nurse Practitioner, 28*(12), 50–53.

Wong, A. H., Smith, M., & Boon, H. S. (1998). Herbal remedies in psychiatric practice. *Archives of General Psychiatry, 55*(11), 1033–1044.

Wood, H. (2002). In the news: Calling all kleptomaniacs. *Nature Reviews Neuroscience, 12,* 914.

Wooltorton, E. (2002). Risperidone (Risperdal): Increased rate of cerebrovascular events in dementia trials. *Canadian Medical Association Journal, 167*(11), 1269–1270.

Wooltorton, E. (2003). Paroxetine (Paxil, Seroxat): Increased risk of suicide in pediatric patients. *Canadian Medical Association Journal, 169*(5), 446.

A world of aromatherapy. Retrieved April 11, 2006, from *www.aworldofaromatherapy.com/aromotherapy-today.htm.*

Wurges, J., & Frey, R. J. (2002). Kava-kava. In K. Krapp & J. L. Longe (Eds.), *The Gale encyclopedia of alternative medicine* (pp. 1–5). Farmington Hills, MI: Gale Group.

Young, A. H., Karine, A. N., Macritchie, A. N., & Calabreses, J. R. (2000). Treatment of bipolar affective disorder. *British Medical Journal, 321*(7272), 1302–1303.

Zal, H. M. (2000). Herbal medicine and the treatment of anxiety. *Psychiatric Times, 17*(3), 1–9.

Zellmer, W. A. (1993). Medication error versus medication misadventure: What's in a name? *American Journal of Hospital Pharmacy, 50,* 315–317.

Zepf, B. (2003). Risperidone for aggressive behaviors in autistic children. *American Family Physician, 67*(3), 18–28.

Zink, T., & Chaffin, J. (1998). Herbal health products: What family physicians need to know. *American Family Physician, 58*(5), 1133–1140.

Index